Firearms Law
Of
North Carolina

First Edition

Thomas Faulk, Jr.

Attorney

Post Office Box 49433

Charlotte, North Carolina 28277

www.ncfirearmslaw.com

Published by Clermont Book Publishing Company
Charlotte, North Carolina

Cataloging Information

Copyright © 2006 by Thomas Faulk, Jr.

Published by Clermont Book Publishing Company
P.O. Box 49433, Charlotte, NC 28277

ISBN 0-9776081-0-7

Printed in the United States of America.

Copyright Protection

Disclaimer

Book Purchases

Copies of this book may be purchased directly from the publisher. Use the order form at the end of this book. An order form may also be found at the publisher's website at www.ncfirearmslaw.com.

Copies of this book may be purchased at selected firearms dealers, gun shops, gun shows, and gun clubs. Bulk sales of this book are available at reduced prices. Specially printed editions of this book are available with exclusive sponsor advertising or corporate personalization.

Lectures and Training Sessions

The author gives lectures and training sessions to interested groups.

Expert Witness Services

The author offers services as an expert witness on firearms and firearms law litigation.

Consulting Services

The author offers consulting services on firearms law. Gun shops, gun clubs, political action groups, and shooting ranges would be typical parties seeking consulting services.

Legal Representation on Firearms Law

The author offers legal representation on matters concerning firearms law. The author does not represent criminal defendants or practice criminal defense law. The author may assist criminal defense attorneys in matters related to firearms law.

Suggest a Topic For The Next Edition

Suggestions of topics to be included into the next of this book are welcome.

Contact The Publisher

Contact the publisher to discuss any matters described above.

Firearms Law of North Carolina
www.ncfirearmslaw.com

About the Author

Thomas Faulk, Jr., is a business law attorney in Charlotte, North Carolina.

Mr. Faulk was admitted to practice law in Florida in 1992 and North Carolina in 1998. Mr. Faulk graduated from the University of North Carolina at Chapel Hill in 1983, earned an MBA from the College of William and Mary in 1985, and earned his law degree at Florida State University in 1992.

Mr. Faulk practices general business law, commercial and corporate law, real estate law, and condominium and homeowners association law. Mr. Faulk serves many business clients in Charlotte.

Mr. Faulk was born and raised in Charlotte, N.C. He served in the U.S. Army Artillery from 1977 to 1981, and in the North Carolina Army National Guard from 1981 to 1983.

Mr. Faulk is a member of the National Rifle Association and the Charlotte Rifle and Pistol Club in Charlotte, North Carolina, and holds a North Carolina Concealed Handgun Carry License.

Firearms Law of North Carolina
www.ncfirearmslaw.com

Acknowledgements and Appreciation

Many thanks to my family who understood the many hours of writing and editing.

I also express my appreciation to Ed, an excellent mentor and gentleman, who offered many wise thoughts, observations, common sense ideas, and words of encouragement about this book.

Table of Contents

Subject   Page

Scope of This Book………………………………………….. 13
Prohibited Places to Carry Concealed Firearms……………………. 14
Firearms Safety Rules………………………………………….. 15
How to Improve Your Chances in Court After a Shooting……………. 16
Parents, Children, and Firearms – Rules to Live By………………… 17
Places to Legally Shoot Firearms…………………………………. 18
People Who Need This Book Today………………………………..19
Effective Date and Future Editions of This Book……………………20
Definitions…………………………………………………………21

Selected Technical Descriptions and Discussions……………………. 29

   Barrel Rifling………………………………………..29
   Assault Rifles………………………………………..30
   Battle Rifles………………………………………… 39
   Carbine Rifles……………………………………….40
   Bolt-Action Rifles…………………………………...43
   Machine Guns………………………………………..43
   Submachine Guns…………………………………… 44
   Lever-Action Rifles…………………………………. 45
   Pistols………………………………………………. 47
   Revolvers…………………………………………… 47
   Semiautomatic Pistols………………………………. 49
   Handguns for Self Defense – The Best and the Worst………..51
   Muzzleloaders and Breechloaders……………………….53
   Rate of Fire…………………………………………..53

Cartridges and Bullets…………………………………………....55

   Cartridge Identification………………………………...55
   Bullet Types, Design, and Size…………………………..56
   Shell Casings………………………………………… 62
   Primers……………………………………………… 63
   Magic Bullets………………………………………...64
   Cartridges for Self Defense…………………………… 64
   Handloaded Cartridges………………………………... 66
   Proper Storage of Ammunition………………………... 67
   Gunpowder and Propellant……………………………. 68

What is Law?... 71
Sources of Law.. 71
North Carolina Firearms Law in General..................................... 75
Top Ten Topics Summarized... 77

North Carolina Constitution...85

North Carolina Statutes..91
    Chapter 1 (Civil Procedure)..95
        Negligent Supervision of a Minor Child.................95
    Chapter 7B (Juvenile Code)...96
    Chapter 14 (Criminal Law)..97
        Assault on a Government Officer.........................97
        First Degree Rape With a Firearm...................... 97
        Felonious Assault With a Firearm.......................98
        Assault on a Handicapped Person With a Firearm......99
        Assault With a Firearm................................. 100
        Assault by Pointing a Gun...............................101
        Discharging a Firearm Into Occupied Property......... 102
        Assault on a Government or Police Officer............. 103
        Teflon Bullets Prohibited............................... 104
        Assault on Correctional Facility Employee............. 105
        Felonious Restraint.....................................106
        Using Firearms Against A Home Invader..............107
        The Castle Doctrine....................................113
        Theft of a Firearm..................................... 114
        Robbery With a Firearm................................114
        Removal of Serial Numbers on Firearms...............117
        Carrying Concealed Firearms...........................118
        Firearms on School Grounds...........................122
        Firearms at Assemblies of People...................... 124
        Firearms Where Alcohol is Sold and Consumed....... 124
        Firearms at Courthouses................................ 124
        Prohibition on Handguns for Minor Children........... 125
        Firearms at Parades.................................... 126
        Firearms at Funeral Processions.......................126
        Firearms at Picket Lines...............................126
        Firearms at Health Care Facility Demonstrations...... 126
        Riots and Civil Disorders............................... 127
        Transporting Firearms During an Emergency..........127
        Weapons of Mass Death and Destruction.............. 128

Unlawful Firearms Training............................134
Selling or Giving Firearms to Minor Children..........134
Storage of Firearms to Protect Minor Children.........136
Warnings on Sale of Firearms to Protect Children..... 137
Allowing Children to Use Firearms..................... 138
Sheriff's Permits to Purchase Handguns................139
Machine Guns and Like Weapons......................... 144
Purchase of Rifles and Shotguns Out of State..........145
Statewide Uniformity of Firearms Laws.................146
Sport Shooting Range Protection Act................... 148
Possession of Firearm by Felon Prohibited.............150
Possession of Firearm by Insane Person Prohibited....151
Concealed Handgun Permit Act..........................151
Chapter 15 (Criminal Procedure)...................................165
Chapter 15A (Criminal Procedure)................................167
Detention by Citizens ("Citizen's Arrest").............. 168
Increased Sentencing if Firearm Used in a Crime......172
Chapter 19 (Offenses Against Public Morals)....................174
Nuisance.. 174
Chapter 50B (Domestic Violence).................................. 176
Chapter 74C (Private Security Guards)............................179
Chapter 74E (Company Police Act)............................... 182
Chapter 74G (Campus Police Act)................................. 184
Chapter 99B (Products Liability)...................................187
Chapter 113 (Wildlife Commission)............................... 191
Reporting of Firearms at Schools................................ 198
Chapter 122C (Mental Health and Firearms)..................... 199
Chapter 127A (The State Militia)...................................202

Uncodified Local Laws, Also Known as Session Laws.................... 211
The North Carolina Administrative Code.................................. 213
Common Law..215
City and County Ordinances...233
Torts.. 235
Negligence... 235
Intentional Torts...239
Lack of North Carolina Statutes...241
Urban Myths About Using Firearms in Self-Defense..................... 255
Gun Club Liability.. 259

Index...263
Book Order Form..269

11

Scope of This Book

This book is about firearms which use burning propellant (i.e., gunpowder or smokeless powder) to propel a solid projectile (i.e., a bullet). This book does not discuss laws on BB guns, air pistols, CO_2 guns, spring guns, or tasers. This book is about "small arms" and does not discuss large bore cannon, howitzers, etc.

This book focuses on North Carolina statutes and caselaw concerning firearms. The relevant text of every known North Carolina firearms statute is presented, along with applicable court cases to illustrate and explain the statute. The statutes are paraphrased into plain English.

A comments section is included for almost every statute. Issues, history, or observations about most statutes are discussed. Commentary tends to bring statute text alive, and to better relate the statute to the average reader of this book.

This book goes beyond the statutes and caselaw. The common law, the law of torts, and State Constitutional law regarding firearms are also discussed in detail.

Many other States and jurisdictions have all types of firearms laws. This book discusses many laws which North Carolina *does not have*, to better educate readers of this book about laws which *do not apply* in North Carolina. This book also discusses various urban legends about firearms and carrying concealed firearms, and their basis in law (if any).

This book explains many technical terms and concepts. It is important to know technical terms to understand firearms in general, and firearms law in particular. This book also thoroughly describes firearm types, cartridges, and bullets.

Several subjects have been centralized for quick reference, such as:

- How To Improve Your Chances in Court After a Shooting
- Parents, Children, and Firearms – Rules to Live By
- Prohibited Places to Carry Concealed Firearms
- Places to Legally Shoot Firearms
- Firearms Safety Rules

This book is thorough, detailed, and complete with examples and actual court cases.

This book is the best single resource a gun owner can have on North Carolina firearms law.

Prohibited Places to Carry Concealed Firearms

This is a summary of places and times where concealed firearms <u>may not be carried</u> in North Carolina. Review the text of this book for detail on each prohibition listed.

Schools, school grounds or campus, school bus. NCGS 14-269.2; 18 USC 922.
Assemblies of people where a fee was charged for admission. NCGS 14-269.3
Places where alcoholic beverages are sold and consumed. NCGS 14-269.3.
Courthouses. NCGS 14-269.4.
The State Capitol. NCGS 14-269.4.
The Governor's official homes. NCGS 14-269.4.
Parades. NCGS 14-277.2.
Funeral processions. NCGS 14-277.2.
Picket lines. NCGS 14-277.2.
Demonstrations at private health care facilities. NCGS 14-277.2.
Any public place owned by a governmental unit. NCGS 14-277.2.
Anywhere except one's own premises where a state of emergency exists.
    NCGS 14-288.7.
Anywhere except one's own premises at or near where a riot is occurring.
    NCGS 14-288.7.
State legislative buildings and grounds. NCGS 120-32.1.
Any place prohibited by federal law. NCGS 14-415.11.
Law enforcement facilities. NCGS 14-415.11.
Correctional facilities (jails, prisons). NCGS 14-415.11.
Buildings housing only State or federal offices. NCGS 14-415.11.
State or federal government offices. NCGS 14-415.11.
Financial institutions (banks, etc.). NCGS 14-415.11.
Premises where a notice is posted prohibiting concealed weapons.
    NCGS 14-415.11.
Anywhere a firearms carrier is consuming alcohol. NCGS 14-415.11.
Anywhere a firearms carrier has alcohol remaining in his blood. NCGS 14-415.11.
Anywhere a firearms carrier has a controlled substance in his blood.
    NCGS 14-415.11.
Anywhere a firearms carrier does not have his permit on him. NCGS 14-415.11.
Anywhere a firearms carrier does not have identification on him. NCGS 14-415.11.
Anytime someone is barred by a court order from carrying firearms.
    NCGS 14-269.8.
Anyone carrying a concealed firearm when that person has a concealed carry permit
    from a State *without* reciprocity with North Carolina. NCGS 14-415.24.
Anytime the concealed firearm is a rifle or shotgun. NCGS 14-269(a.1).

Firearms Law of North Carolina
www.ncfirearmslaw.com

Firearms Safety Rules

1. Always treat a firearm as if it were loaded.

2. Always point a firearm in a safe direction.

3. Keep your finger off the trigger until ready to fire.

4. Unload and safe a firearm before handing the firearm to another person.

5. Check to see if a firearm is on safe when picking up or receiving the firearm.

6. Use correct ammunition.

7. Unload a firearm before placing it into storage.

8. Eject any cartridge in the chamber when unloading a semiautomatic firearm.

9. Read the instruction manual appropriate for the firearm.

10. Keep the firearm on "safe" until ready to fire.

11. Be sure what lies beyond your target before you fire.

12. If you have a hang-fire, squib-fire, or misfire, keep the muzzle downrange.

13. Wear eye and ear protection when shooting.

14. Train and practice on your specific firearm.

15. Do not shoot firearms when affected by alcohol or drugs.

16. Properly clean firearms so that they will operate properly.

17. Avoid ricochets by never shooting at flat surfaces like water or concrete.

18. Keep firearms unloaded until ready for use.

19. Safely store firearms away from children.

20. Never rely solely on the mechanical safety of a firearm.

How To Improve Your Chances in Court After a Shooting

The actions listed below may improve your chances in court after a shooting to avoid or minimize your liability.

1. Purchase and possess your firearm legally.

2. Have your concealed carry permit on you when carrying concealed firearms.

3. Use hollow-point, not full metal jacket, ammunition.

4. Use common ammunition, not exotic ammunition with fierce-sounding names.

5. Use new, unmodified, store-bought ammunition.

6. Avoid magnum, +p, +p+, or other over-pressure ammunition.

7. Give a warning shout if appropriate ("Halt or I will shoot!").

8. Fire a warning shot if appropriate.

9. Fire only enough times to stop the imminent threat.

10. Call "911" before shooting if possible, to get the danger on the record.

11. Call the police immediately after shooting.

12. Take classes to show your proficiency and safety training with firearms.

13. Do not be in an illegal place with your firearm (school grounds, a bank, etc.).

14. Do not shoot someone if escape or avoidance are reasonable choices.

15. Hire a defense lawyer immediately if you shoot someone.

16. Do not modify the trigger or trigger pull pressure on your firearm.

17. Have a very good explanation if you shoot someone in the back.

18. Avoid carrying "cocked and locked" pistols.

19. Keep all safety devices intact on your firearm.

20. Make deliberate and intentional shots; no spray-firing.

21. After the shooting, ask witnesses to corroborate your actions to the police.

Firearms Law of North Carolina
www.ncfirearmslaw.com

Parents, Children, and Firearms – Rules to Live By

Parents with firearms and children in the home have a special responsibility to safeguard their children's lives from the dangers of firearms. Options for consideration by parents to safeguard children are listed below.

1. Children shooting firearms must have direct and immediate adult supervision.

2. Children who use firearms must have firearms safety training.

3. Trigger locks for stored firearms.

4. Gun safes for stored firearms.

5. Ammunition stored in a location separate from firearms.

6. Store firearms unloaded except when kept for home defense.

7. Store firearms disassembled.

8. Educate children to immediately report firearms they see at school or elsewhere.

9. Educate children to immediately leave if other children are playing with firearms.

10. Parents should learn the law on safe storage of firearms.

11. Parents should learn the law on children using firearms.

12. Properly store firearm cleaning supplies, which are usually toxic and flammable.

13. Dispose of unwanted firearms, which pose an unnecessary risk in the home.

14. Ask parents in homes where your children visit about their firearm storage rules.

15. Educate children that firearms are not toys, and are not ever to be played with.

16. Own a firearm with a manual safety.

17. Educate children never to touch any firearm they find.

18. Use more stringent rules if your child suffers from depression, moodiness, etc.

Places to Legally Shoot Firearms

There are many types of people who desire a place to legally shoot firearms. Many newcomers to the sports of firearms, marksmanship, or hunting, or beginning firearms training as a part of self-defense planning, have no real idea as to where they can legally shoot. This article provides some guidance.

1. Gun clubs that have a shooting range.

2. Gun clubs which sponsor group tours to firing ranges.

3. Commercial shooting ranges are usually locally available.

4. Cowboy Action Shooting clubs usually arrange for firing range access.

5. Local police or Sheriff ranges which may be open to the public.

6. Gun clinics or schools. These are businesses offering firearms training.

7. Hunt preserves or reservations may offer range access.

8. Privately owned land with owner's permission (review local ordinances).

9. North Carolina public hunting lands (North Carolina Wildlife Resources Commission).

10. Federal public hunting lands (U.S. Fish and Wildlife Service; National Park Service).

11. Ask at your local gun shop.

12. Ask at the firearms section of your sporting goods store.

Firearms Law of North Carolina
www.ncfirearmslaw.com

People Who Need This Book Today

Carrying or having a firearm ready to possibly kill or maim another human being is a serious matter of massive proportions. It is absolutely essential that everyone who carries the power of life and death in their hands know the law of firearms. This book is the absolute best resource a gun owner can have on North Carolina firearms law. The people who need this book today are listed following.

1. Concealed firearms carriers; concealed firearms permit holders

2. Gun shop owners

3. Law enforcement officers

4. Gun clubs and members

5. Private sellers of firearms

6. Firearm owners; anyone who keeps a firearm for self-defense

7. Firearm purchasers

8. Firearm owners with children living in the home

9. District Attorneys and prosecutors

10. Criminal defense attorneys; Public Defender attorneys

11. Hunters

12. Shooting ranges

13. State legislators

14. Individuals and special interest groups involved in the politics of firearms

15. Attorneys who defend civil firearms claims

16. Law libraries; public libraries

17. School officials

18. Pawn shops which stock firearms

19. Armed-guard private security companies

Effective Date and Future Editions of This Book

The text of the statutes cited in this book includes all Session Laws passed through the Regular Session of the North Carolina Legislature which closed September 2, 2005. There was a one-day special session on October 12, 2005, but no new laws were enacted.

Cases cited in this book are those published and released to the public by May 15, 2005, which are generally the most recent published cases available as of December 1, 2005.

The Second Edition of this book is scheduled for availability in Spring 2008, which will incorporate changes in the law made during the Long Session ending in late 2007.

This book, like computer technology, was out of date even as it was being printed. Statutes may be changed, enacted, or repealed virtually anytime during a year, depending upon when the State Legislature is in session. Effective notice to the public about changes to statutes is inconsistent at best. New laws, which are called "session laws," are reasonably available to knowledgeable researchers, but the average citizen usually only learns of a new law through the happenstance of public media such as television newscast, newspaper, or radio news.

New cases may be issued any time which limit, modify, expand, nullify, or interpret any statute. Effective notice to the public is virtually nonexistent about the effect on statutes of rulings in court cases.

Changes in firearms laws will be collected and discussed in future editions of this book. Persons with high relative sensitivity to firearms law changes (gun shop owners, concealed firearms permit holders, gun clubs, law enforcement officers, criminal prosecutors, etc.) should review the publisher's website annually for availability of a new edition of this book.

Persons with low relative sensitivity to firearms law changes (citizens who keep a firearm at home or business for self-defense, etc.) should review the publisher's website every three years for availability of a new edition of this book.

Owning a firearm with the resolve to use it in self defense, which means the intention of killing or maiming another human being, is a serious matter of maximum degree. Firearms owners should demonstrate the responsibility that comes with being the owner of a firearm by keeping current on firearms law.

Definitions

Definitions of a word in the world of firearms often vary. The definition of a particular word can vary depending upon whether the word is used in the literal sense, under State or federal statutes, as in common or military usage, as slang, or in furtherance of political agendas or marketing efforts.

Antique Firearm. An antique firearm is any firearm manufactured in or before 1898; any firearm using a matchlock, flintlock, percussion cap, or similar type of ignition system; or any firearm using ammunition manufactured in or before 1898.

Assault Rifle. An assault rifle is generally held to be a short, compact rifle, firing a round of intermediate power between submachine gun and rifle cartridges, and which rifle has selective fire capability. See the specific section in the text of this book on Assault Weapons for greater detail. Also see "battle rifle."

Assault Weapon. The definition of assault weapon is similar to "assault rifle" except it is broader, including such items as semiautomatic shotguns, etc. See the specific section in the text of this book on Assault Weapons for greater detail.

Automatic Weapon. An automatic weapon will fire multiple rounds with one press of the trigger. Most types of automatic weapons will continue to fire so long as the trigger is being pressed until the ammunition is exhausted. Legal ownership of automatic weapons by civilians is very restricted and therefore rare. Many people erroneously refer to semiautomatic weapons as an "automatic" or an "auto." See "semiautomatic weapon."

Barrel.   The barrel of a firearm is a cylindrical tube, usually 3-6 inches long on a pistol, and 16-25 inches long on a rifle. A bullet ready to be fired is placed into the rear of the barrel. When fired, the bullet travels down the inside of the barrel, emerging at the end of the barrel, which is called the muzzle. The open inside of the barrel is called the "bore." The process of aiming the firearm involves pointed the barrel at the target.

Battle Rifle. Battle rifles generally are full-size military rifles (or replicas or civilian versions of such rifles). See the section in the text of this book on Battle Rifles for greater detail. Also see "assault rifle."

Bayonet.   A bayonet is a specialized knife attached to the front of a military rifle. A bayonet is attached to a rifle by affixing the bayonet to the "bayonet lug" which is a fixed part of the rifle.

Bolt.   Some firearm designs use a bolt, which is usually a metal cylindrical part. The bolt is located just to the rear of a cartridge when the cartridge is in the firing chamber ready to fire, and locks the cartridge in place for firing. The bolt will slide back and forth to allow spent casings to be ejected and new cartridges to be maneuvered into the chamber.

Bore.   The open inside of the barrel is the "bore." The bullet, when the firearm is fired, travels down the bore. The bullet exits the end of the bore at the muzzle.

Bullet. A bullet is the projectile portion of a round of ammunition. A bullet is typically cone-shaped and streamlined to some degree. Bullets typically have a core of lead and an outer sheath of copper. Bullets are most often described by their diameter, either in millimeters (such as 9mm or 7.62mm) or in a fraction of an inch expressed in decimal form (such as .357 or .45).

Burst Fire. Burst fire is a form of automatic firing capability. With burst fire, one pull of the trigger will cause the firearm, usually a rifle, to fire a certain limited number of rounds, usually three rounds. This is in contrast to semiautomatic firearms, which will fire only one round per trigger pull, and full automatic firearms, which will continue to fire rounds so long as the trigger remains pulled. The purpose of burst fire is to allow some of the volume of automatic fire, but to eliminate the waste of ammunition by, in the heat of battle, simply holding the trigger down and emptying a full magazine all at once. It is believed that burst fire prompts a soldier to adjust aim for each three-shot group, resulting in more effective use of ammunition.

Cartridge. A cartridge is one complete unit of fire, comprised of a bullet, shell casing, load of gunpowder, and primer. A cartridge may also be called a "round." A round is often referred to improperly as a bullet (a bullet is only one component of a round).

Case. See "shell casing."

Case Hardening.   Case hardening is a metallurgical process where certain steel parts of a firearm are treated by a process called "case hardening." The process involves packing the steel parts into a certain carbon-rich material called "case hardening compound" and then heating the steel parts and hardening compound in a certain manner. The steel parts absorb carbon during the process into perhaps the top millimeter of the surface of the parts. Addition of carbon into the steel makes the steel very hard, and improves its wear resistance to other moving parts with which it comes into contact. Case hardening allows the interior of the steel parts to retain the tough but relatively soft strength of steel, but gives the exterior surfaces a harder wear-resistant finish. Case hardening gives steel a colorful rainbow hued tint, a feature highly appreciated by some fans of revolvers of the American West.

Casing. See "shell casing."

Clip.   A clip is a flat strip of metal used to hold a group of cartridges together by their base, to keep the cartridges oriented properly for loading the cartridges into a magazine, in preparation for firing. A clip can also be used as a storage device for cartridges, keeping cartridges ready for loading into a magazine. Magazines are referred to in slang as a "clip," which is incorrect.

A "stripper clip," also called a "charger," is used to load the cartridges directly into a built-in magazine in the firearm, or into a magazine for later insertion of the magazine into a firearm.

An "en bloc clip" is a clip where the clip and its cartridges are all loaded into the firearm together. The empty clip usually ejected from the firearm after the last cartridge is fired.

Compensator.   A compensator is a part affixed to the muzzle of a firearm which uses the rushing gasses exiting the muzzle upon firing to reduce muzzle climb upon firing, which decreases the time necessary to bring the firearm back into alignment with the target for following shots. See "muzzle brake."

Dealer. According to NCGS 14-409.39(1), a dealer in firearms is any person licensed as a dealer under 18 USC 921 or NCGS 105-80.

Derringer. A derringer is a pistol of the smallest design feasible for a given caliber. Derringers usually minimize features to decrease size and increase simplicity. Derringers are inaccurate except at very short ranges. Derringers usually hold only 1-4 rounds. Derringers as a rule are carried concealed. Derringers are usually carried in a pocket (hence the name "pocket pistol") or in a purse. Derringers are named for a misspelling of Henry Deringer, a maker of small pistols in the 1800's.

Double-Tap.   A double-tap is a slang term meaning two shots fired rapidly from a semiautomatic pistol at the same target. This is mainly a police and military technique used by trained shooters.

Energy.   Energy is a measure, in pounds, of how hard a bullet would hit a target at a given distance from the firing point. This is a computed figure, taking into account bullet velocity and bullet weight.

Extractor.   The extractor is a metal part which removes spent shell casings from the firearm after firing and ejects them to the side.

Firearm. A firearm is a handgun, shotgun, or rifle while expels a projectile by action of an explosion.

Firing Pin.   The firing pin is a metal part in many firearm designs. The firing pin, often shaped like a sophisticated nail, is as a rule in line with and behind the cartridge when the cartridge is resting in the firing chamber. Upon pulling the trigger, the sharp end of the firing pin strikes the primer at the base of the cartridge, firing the cartridge.

Flash Suppressor. A flash suppressor is a metal assembly affixed onto the muzzle of a firearm (usually only rifles). The purpose of a flash suppressor is to shield the eyes of the firearm operator from the bright flash of flame when firing at night. The goal is to minimize affecting the night vision of the firearm operator by the flash of firing his own firearm. Flash suppressors offer minimal, if any, benefits at suppressing the flash of firing from persons located in front of the firearm fired.

Folding Stock. A folding stock is a stock, usually on a rifle or carbine, usually constructed of metal wire, which can be folded alongside the body of the rifle. Folding the stock shortens the length of the rifle, increasing ease of concealability and ability to carry. The rifle can often be fired with the stock folded closed or opened.

Grain.   A grain is a unit of measurement of weight. There are 7000 grains per pound. Bullets and the gunpowder charge inside of a cartridge are measured in grains. Manufacturers typically provide a variety of bullet weights for a particular caliber bullet. Different bullet weights of the same caliber usually have different ballistic characteristics.

Gun.   See "firearm." This word is often used as a synonym or slang term for "firearm." The proper military definition of "gun" means a long-barreled artillery weapon which fires a projectile at high velocity on a flat trajectory. The modern word "gun" comes from the word "gonne" or "hand gonne," originating in the 1400's from old English or French. Most firearms hobbyists, sportsmen, and professionals prefer to use more precise terms, such as pistol, revolver, derringer, rifle, etc., instead of the crude word "gun."

Hammer.   The hammer is the small part of some firearm designs which is drawn back when the firearm is cocked, and when the trigger is pulled, the hammer springs or flies forward, striking the primer in the cartridge, thus firing the weapon. The

24

hammer may strike the primer directly, or it may strike some other part (i.e., the firing pin) which, in turn, strikes the primer.

Hammer Bite.   The long metal slide on the top of a semiautomatic handgun slides rapidly to the rear when the firearm is fired. The rearward movement of the slide also pushes the hammer down into the cocked position on many firearm models. This movement of the slide and the hammer can cut the hand of the person firing the weapon, usually in the web of the hand between the thumb and forefinger. This is called "hammer bite." Firearms prone to this condition usually have a "hammer spur" designed onto the back of the firearm to physically keep the firer's hand down and out of the way of the slide.

Handgun. A handgun is a pistol, revolver, or other gun that has a short stock, usually small in size, which is normally fired with one hand.

Long Gun.   A long gun is a generic term for rifles, carbines, and shotguns. Long guns are not pistols, revolvers, or handguns. Long guns are also called "shoulder arms." Long guns are intended to be fired with the stock of the firearm pressed into and supported by the shoulder of the firer. Long guns are intended to be fired with two hands.

Machine Gun.   A machine gun is a firearm which shoots, is designed to shoot, or can be readily restored to shoot, automatically more than one shot, without manual reloading, by a single function of the trigger. The term also includes the frame or receiver of such firearm, or any combination of parts designed to convert a firearm into a machine gun.

Magazine. A magazine is a box-like container designed to hold cartridges. The magazine is inserted and locked into the firearm, and the magazine feeds the cartridges into the firearm as needed, until empty. Magazines can be ejected when emptied, and a full magazine inserted into the firearm. Magazines generally hold from 5 to 15 cartridges, although some magazines hold 30 to 50 rounds. Politically correct speech refers to magazines which hold more than 10 rounds as "high capacity" magazines. Some firearms possess fixed internal magazines and will not accept detachable magazines.

Misfires.   A cartridge that will not fire properly is called a misfire. There are sub-categories of misfires. A "squib fire" is where the round fired, but very weakly, possibly leaving a bullet stuck in the bore. A "hang fire" is a delayed fire where the round does fire, but only after a delay. This is dangerous if the shooter has redirected the barrel in any direction except for downrange.

25

Muzzle Brake.   A muzzle brake is a part affixed to the muzzle of a firearm which uses the rushing gasses exiting the muzzle upon firing to reduce recoil upon firing. See "compensator."

Pistol.   The word "pistol" is currently synonymous with "handgun." In older usage, this word meant a handgun other than a revolver.

Primer. The primer is installed in the base of a cartridge. The primer, when sharply struck on its base by the firing pin of a firearm, will explode inside of the shell casing, thus igniting the gunpowder in the shell casing.

Rate of Fire. This phrase refers to how many bullets per minute a firearm can fire. A detailed discussion appears below.

Receiver.   The receiver on a firearm is the housing which contains the operating parts of the firearm. The barrel and the stock are attached to the receiver. The receiver is the heart of the firearm. Revolvers are designed differently, and have no receiver, strictly speaking.

Recoil.   Recoil is the rearward pressure or movement of a firearm upon firing. A slang term for recoil is "kick," as in "The firearm kicks hard when fired." Excessive recoil is bad. Recoil force is measured in pounds. Various factors affect recoil, such as firearm weight, bullet weight, and gunpowder loading. The amount of recoil can be mathematically computed for a given combination of factors for comparison purposes. The "felt recoil" is a more subjective assessment of recoil as actually felt or experienced by the shooter. Certain features of the firearm, such as special handgrips or the material of which the firearm is constructed, can reduce the amount of felt recoil.

Rifle.   A rifle is a firearm with spiral grooves machined into the inner surfaces of the bore intended to impart a spin to a bullet when fired, which firearm is designed to be fired from the shoulder.

Round.   A round is the same thing as a cartridge.

Safety Mechanism.   The safety mechanism, or simply the "safety," is part of some firearms which when activated will block the firearm from firing, even if the trigger is pulled and a round is in the chamber. "External safeties," usually a button or switch located on the outside of the firearm, can be manually operated.

Semiautomatic Weapon. A semiautomatic firearm will fire one round with each press of the trigger. Thereafter, the trigger must be released, and then pressed again,

26

to fire a second round. The rate of fire of the firearm depends upon how quickly the firearm operator can repeatedly pull the trigger. "Full automatic" means that new rounds continue to be loaded into the chamber and fired so long as the trigger is depressed. "Semiautomatic" means that only the first part of the cycle (loading the next round into the chamber ready to be fired) is performed, and the firearm operator must manually press the trigger for each bullet to be fired.

Shell. The word "shell" and "cartridge" are used synonymously. A shell is an older term not often used. The word "shell" refers to an entire cartridge, while "shell casing" refers only to the cylindrical brass component of a cartridge.

Sling. A sling is a flexible strap of leather or other material attached to a rifle used in carrying the rifle slung over the shoulder of the carrier.

Shell Casing. A shell casing is cylindrical cup-shaped metal container which holds gunpowder, has a primer fixed into the bottom, and is sealed with a bullet. Shell casings are typically made of brass, and are yellowish in color.

Stock. The stock of a rifle is the back part of the rifle, opposite from the muzzle end. The stock is generally all that part of the rifle to the rear of the receiver and bolt assembly. A rifle stock is generally the largest part of the rifle, and fits against the shoulder of the rifle operator when firing. Stocks are most commonly made of wood, and military rifle stocks are often made of a plastic or fiberglass substance. Shapes of rifle stocks vary greatly. Some rifle stocks, such as the American M-16, have both a traditional shoulder-fitting stock, and a "pistol grip" protruding from the bottom of the stock. A pistol grip on a rifle stock aids in firing the firearm on automatic fire, and also aids in firing the firearm when holding the rifle in positions other than the traditional shoulder-mounted manner. The stock of a handgun, usually called the "butt," is much smaller than a rifle stock, and is that portion of the pistol which is grasped by the hand when firing. In semiautomatic pistols, the magazine typically fits inside the hollow stock. The stock of a handgun is also called a "pistol grip."

Submachine gun. The statutory definition of a submachine gun is a firearm which shoots, is designed to shoot, or can be readily restored to shoot, automatically more than one shot, without manual reloading, by a single function of the trigger. NCGS 14-409(a). The military definition of a submachine gun is similar to the statutory definition, but adding that it is firearm of rifle design, usually short and compact, which fires pistol-size cartridges. The classic example is the Thompson submachine gun.

Suppressor. See "flash suppressor."

27

Trigger.   The trigger is the part of a firearm which, when pulled, fires the cartridge. The trigger is usually curved to fit the forefinger of the person firing the firearm.

Wadcutter.   Wadcutters are cylindrical bullets with flat ends, a very non-aerodynamic shape. Wadcutters are intended for use in target shooting, where this bullet shape punches a clean hole in the target paper, making scoring easier and more accurate. Wadcutters are normally used in revolvers because they do not feed well from magazines due to their shape.

Selected Technical Descriptions and Discussions

A discussion and description of selected subjects appear following. A good grounding in these subjects is needed to best understand firearms laws. For example, there has been a tremendous amount of misinformation, disinformation, and confusion in recent years regarding assault rifles. Possessing a good grounding in technical facts is an excellent first step at understanding the subject and the relevant law.

Further, the discussions below will demonstrate that the terms for various rifles, guns, and pistols generally have very technical definitions, at least in the historical and military sense. Many speakers, political groups, and the media have blurred and confused the distinctions. This has been intentional and unintentional.

Barrel Rifling

The inner surface of firearm barrels was manufactured smooth for centuries after firearms were invented. That is the origin of the phrase "smoothbore rifle." There were no grooves or channels cut into the metal surfaces of the bore.

It was discovered that if the bullet could be made to spin upon firing, that the bullet would be gyroscopically stabilized in flight. A stabilized bullet is more accurate than a bullet fired from a smoothbore firearm. Greater accuracy also means greater effective range.

The solution was to cut or machine grooves into the bore. Grooves were cut into a slow spiral within the bore. The bullet, fitting down into the grooves as it moved down the bore, would begin spinning. The bullet would continue spinning as it emerged from the muzzle of the barrel and on through its flight to the target.

The original barrel surfaces remaining after the grooves are cut into the barrel are called "lands." The interior of a firearm barrel is thus primarily composed of lands and grooves. The edges of typical lands are sharp where the adjoining groove has been machined away. There is an alternate process called polygonal or hexagonal rifling, where the edges of the lands are machined away at an angle. This alternative process may produce higher bullet velocities, longer barrel life, and better accuracy. Very few manufacturers routinely offer this alternative rifling process.

The "twist rate" or rate of spin refers to whether the spiral grooves within the bore are a tight or a gentle spiral. A tight twist rate will cause the bullet to spin more quickly than a gentle twist rate. The twist rate of a particular barrel is usually expressed as a ratio, such as 1:7. A 1:7 ratio means that a bullet will make one rotation for every 7 inches that it travels down the barrel. A 1:12 twist rate is more gentle than a 1:7 twist, because it takes 12 inches for the bullet to make one complete rotation. A tighter twist rate, such as a 1:7, will cause the bullet to rotate more quickly in flight than a slow twist rate of 1:12.

There is the technique of "gain twist rifling" where the twist rate starts out slow near the firing chamber, but gradually increases to a maximum twist rate near the muzzle. There are said to be advantages to gain twist rifling, but gain twist rifling is rarely used today.

Generally, the heavier the bullet, the faster the twist rate needed to stabilize the bullet. Lighter bullets may not need a faster twist, and may even disintegrate with the greater stresses of more radical twist. The American M-16 family of rifles is a good study of this concept. The older 55-grain 5.56mm bullet worked best in a 1:12 barrel. The newer 62-grain bullet works best in a 1:7 barrel. Many commercial manufacturers of this firearm provide a 1:9 barrel, which will stabilize both the 55-grain and 62-grain bullets reasonably well.

Faster twist generally leads to better stabilization, but once the bullet is sufficiently stabilized, increasing the twist rate accomplishes little. Increased twist rates also lead to faster bore wear.

Most firearms owners never heard of rifling twist, have no idea of the twist rate of their firearm, and have no idea whether their twist rate is optimal for the weight of bullet they use. Most owners simply buy "standard" bullets of the correct caliber, and start shooting. Considering twist rate can lead to improved safety, accuracy, and barrel wear.

The lands and grooves leave certain unique marks on the bullet during its passage down the bore. These unique marks allow law enforcement forensic specialists to check "ballistics" and sometimes match bullets fired from a particular firearm.

Virtually all modern rifles and pistols have rifling. Shotguns do not have rifling. The term "rifle" for a long gun derives from a time when non-rifled long guns (such as muskets) existed, and the term was useful in distinguishing a firearm with a rifled barrel from a firearm which did not have a rifled barrel.

Assault Rifles

Assault weapons and assault rifles have recently been exhaustively discussed and hotly debated, especially after the Columbine High School incident, the

Washington, D.C., sniper attacks, and with the expiration of the federal Assault Weapons Ban in September 2004. It is likely that there will be continued attempts to legislate assault weapons at the federal level and in many States. Assault weapons are at the center of the right to bear arms debate in America today.

Therefore, a detailed discussion on assault weapons is provided here to provide detailed information on this hot topic.

Definitions Vary

An "assault weapon" is a broad class of different weapons, of which "assault rifles" are by far the most common, well known, and regulated. This discussion centers on assault rifles.

There are many laws giving different definitions for "assault rifle" or "assault weapon." Many people and political groups offer additional definitions.

The military has long had its technical definition for assault rifles, defined here as the historical definition. The historical definition is based upon technical characteristics of the cartridge and the firearm. The historical definition is devoid of emotion, ideology, or politics.

Some speakers broaden the definition of assault rifle. This tendency is associated with those supporting greater gun control. Firearms marketers are known to use an expanded definition for assault rifle, apparently to profit from the cachet to some purchasers of the assault rifle.

Generally, the military definition of assault rifle is relatively narrow, and the definition used by gun-control advocates is relatively broad.

The definition of assault weapon or assault rifle is thus variable. A reader or listener should confirm the definition being used to ensure clarity.

General Definition

The military and historical definition of assault rifle is generally held to be a short, compact rifle, firing a cartridge of intermediate power between pistol and full-size rifle cartridges, and which rifle has selective fire capability. "Selective fire" means that the firearm operator can select from semiautomatic and full automatic fire (or burst fire).

Assault rifles have an actual effective range of approximately 200 yards, with

31

published effective ranges of up to 300 yards. Assault rifles are designed to provide massed anti-personnel fire at short to medium ranges.

Assault rifles usually accept magazines of varying capacity. Magazines of 20 rounds and 30 rounds are common. This magazine capacity exceeds the 5-7 round capacity of many hunting rifles.

History

Virtually all military rifles at the start of World War II in 1939 were full-size rifles known today as "battle rifles." The American version was the M-1903 Springfield rifle, a bolt-action rifle introduced in 1903, and adapted to fire the .30-06 cartridge when it was introduced in 1906. The replacement for the Springfield was the M-1 Garand, also firing the .30-06 cartridge, introduced in 1936, but not widely distributed by the time of America's entry into World War II. There was no such class of firearms at that time known as assault rifles, although submachine guns did exist.

Full-size battle rifles were capable of firing aimed rounds further than the average infantryman could accurately identify and engage an enemy. Studies showed that most infantry fighting took place at 100-200 yards or less, and that the typical soldier was unable to accurately aim at a human target at over 400 yards. Battle rifles are capable of accurate fire up to 800 yards. Therefore, so the reasoning went, the battle rifle was too big and heavy, and its capabilities were generally not usable by the average infantryman.

The philosophy of the assault rifle was that if the rifle and cartridge were smaller, *usable* effectiveness would not be affected, but, with a lighter firearm and ammunition, each soldier could carry more ammunition. Further, with a less powerful cartridge, assault rifles could be designed for automatic fire. Full-size cartridges were too powerful for automatic fire in a rifle design, resulting in difficulty controlling and aiming the rifle when firing.

Assault rifles brought about a tactical change as well. Soldiers would use automatic assault rifles to throw a heavy rate of unaimed or partially aimed fire towards the enemy instead of depending upon slow aimed fire. This tactical philosophy harmonized with the emerging concepts of the blitzkrieg ("lightning war"), assault troops, shock troops, and fast mobile troops who needed to maintain a high rate of fire while on the move. Standard machine guns were too heavy and cumbersome for such use. Lightened machine guns firing standard cartridges were hard to control. Submachine guns were unsuitable for assault troops, having too little range and power due to their pistol-sized cartridges.

The assault rifle concept is credited to the Germans in World War II, with the introduction in 1942 of the Maschinen Karabiner 42 ("machine carbine") of 7.92mm caliber. A later version was known as the Maschinen Pistole 43. A "machine pistol" is another name for submachine gun, and so is intentionally misleading with this firearm, which was actually a machine *carbine*. The machine pistol nomenclature was intended to deceive Adolf Hitler, who at first disapproved production of the MK42. This firearm was finalized as the Maschinen Pistole 44. The MP44 was renamed the SturmGewehr 44 in December 1944. "SturmGewehr" is "storm rifle" or "assault rifle" in German. The StG-44 was the first true assault rifle. It is legend that Adolf Hitler himself named this firearm an "assault rifle" to maximize the propaganda value of this new firearm. The intention was to add fuel to the belief and expectations of Germans and Allies that Germany had or would soon reveal decisive war-winning secret weapons. The StG-44 was used heavily on the Eastern Front against the Russians, and was successful wherever introduced. The StG-44 was intended to become the predominate rifle in the German army.

The Russians examined the German StG-44 and introduced their first assault rifle, the Kalashnikov AK-47 in 7.62mm in 1947. There is a great similarity between the StG-44 and the AK-47. The very successful AK-series firearms are possibly the most widely distributed rifles in history. The StG-44 and AK-47 adopted the philosophy of a large caliber bullet with a smaller shell casing and gunpowder charge, resulting in a relatively large slow bullet.

The Russians superseded the AK-47 with the Kalashnikov AK-74 in 1974. The AK-74, very similar in appearance to the AK-47, is chambered instead for a smaller 5.45mm cartridge, thus adopting the American philosophy of a small caliber bullet with a larger shell casing and gunpowder charge, resulting in a relatively small fast bullet.

The United States produced its version of the assault rifle, the Armalite AR-15, taken into the military as the M-16, in the early 1960's. The M-16 adopted the philosophy of a small caliber bullet with a larger shell casing and gunpowder charge, resulting in a relatively small fast bullet. The M-16 is widely distributed, and has been the standard rifle of the United States since 1964. The M-16 and its variants are discussed in detail below.

The United States began development of the next generation assault rifle in the 1990's, which was known as the XM-29. The XM-29 project was cancelled in 2004. An offshoot of the XM-29 is the XM-8 rifle, which would be named the M-8 after introduction into the military. The XM-8 is a futuristic firearm firing the same 5.56mm cartridge as the M-16. The XM-8 is 20% lighter than a comparable M-16, an advantage to infantrymen. The XM-8 was scheduled for full production in 2005, was placed on hold in July 2005, and was canceled in late 2005.

Assault Rifle and Full-Size Cartridges Compared

An assault rifle bullet is more likely to only injure or wound an enemy soldier compared to a standard size rifle cartridge bullet. The standard assault rifle cartridge in the United States is 5.56mm, and the standard full size cartridge is .308 (7.62mm).

The 5.56mm assault rifle round is generally also known as the .223 Remington cartridge. These two cartridges are similar, but not exactly the same. The military designation for the modern 5.56mm round is the M855. The M855 round has a 62-grain bullet, a muzzle velocity of 3,100 feet per second, and has 897 foot-pounds of energy at 200 yards. One popular civilian loading of the .223 Remington round with a 62 grain bullet has a muzzle velocity of 3,100fps and 825 ft-lbs of energy at 200 yards. A popular civilian loading of the 5.56mm round with a 55 grain bullet has a muzzle velocity of 3,270fps and 797 ft-lbs of energy at 200 yards.

The 7.62mm full size round is generally also known as the .308 Winchester cartridge. The military designation for the 7.62mm full metal jacket round is the M59. The M59 round is a 150-grain bullet, with a muzzle velocity of 2,800 feet per second, and with 1,705 foot-pounds of energy at 200 yards.

The .30-30 cartridge is the classic deer cartridge, with no military heritage. The .30-30 bullet is the same diameter as the 7.62mm round (.308 inches). The .30-30 is, among modern hunting rounds, classified as a very moderate round in power, range, recoil, and energy delivered to a target. A 150-grain .30-30 cartridge has a muzzle velocity of 2,390 feet per second with 858 foot-pounds of energy at 200 yards.

The .30-06 cartridge is the modern preeminent deer cartridge, and is also of .308 caliber. The .30-06 has a rich military heritage, serving in the Springfield bolt-action rifle and the M-1 Garand. A common 150-grain .30-06 cartridge has 1,827 ft.-lbs. of energy at 200 yards, more than the 7.62mm round.

The full-size 7.62mm bullet has approximately two times the energy of the 5.56mm assault rifle bullet at 200 yards. The 7.62mm bullet has a 38% greater diameter than the 5.56mm bullet, likely to cause relatively greater blood loss. The .30-06 deer cartridge is even more powerful. The 5.56mm bullet is even out-classed by the "moderate" .30-30 round, which has 133% more energy than the 5.56mm round at 200 yards.

34

Therefore, assault rifles do not fire "high powered" rounds, as some literature, political debates, and impassioned anti-gun rhetoric imply or state. Assault rifles have attributes other than sheer power of individual bullets which make them more appropriate for their intended task compared to full-size rifles.

Automatic vs. Semiautomatic Fire Capability

A rifle must be able to fire in a full automatic or burst fire mode to qualify as an assault rifle under the historical and military definition. Civilian semiautomatic rifles are not assault rifles under that definition.

The defunct federal Assault Weapons Ban contained a definition for assault rifles broader than the historical and military definition. The Assault Weapons Ban included semiautomatics within the definition, so long as the firearm possessed certain cosmetic features.

Additional Data

Assault rifles are generally designed to be more durable and able to withstand adverse operating conditions than traditional sporting or hunting rifles. Assault rifles typically have a simple design compared to hunting rifles, which contributes to durability.

Virtually all assault rifles are owned by the military or government agencies. Federal law severely restricts ownership of automatic firearms by civilians.

Some people and political groups erroneously refer to semiautomatic rifles which are similar in appearance to automatic military weapons as assault rifles. The two classic modern assault rifles are the American M-16 and the Soviet AK-47 series. All assault firearms under the military or historical definition fire full automatic. The phrase "semiautomatic assault rifle" is an oxymoron.

An assault rifle is not a "battle rifle." A battle rifle is a full size, full power rifle. An assault rifle is certainly intended for used in military battles. See the separate definition for battle rifle for additional description.

Assault rifles are not used in hunting, because they are not generally possessed by civilians and because the cartridges they fire are too light for most game larger than varmints. Civilian-style semiautomatic versions of assault rifles are rarely used for hunting large and medium-sized game due to their relatively low-powered cartridges and shorter effective ranges.

The 5.56mm military round is generally known to civilians as the .223 Remington "varmint" round. This round is very popular for use against varmints (squirrels, raccoons, opossums, coyotes, foxes, etc.). The cartridge is used for this purpose because the bullet is large enough for these smaller animals, the flat trajectory means greater accuracy potential, and the low recoil means quick and accurate follow-up shots.

The M-16 Assault Rifle and Its Civilian Counterparts

The M-14, essentially an upgrade of the M-1 Garand, replaced the M-1 in 1957. However, the large 7.62mm cartridge in the M-14 was too powerful to allow effective aiming with a standard rifle design when fired on full automatic. The large cartridges were also relatively heavy, limiting the quantity of ammunition a soldier could carry. The large and bulky M-14 was generally unsuitable for jungle or urban warfare.

Eugene Stoner and a small company named Armalite developed an assault rifle known as the AR-15. The AR-15 was adopted by the U.S. Air Force as the M-16 in 1964, partly to remedy the shortcomings of the M-14.

The M-16 was fielded in Vietnam in answer to the shortcomings of the M-14. The M-16 was lighter and shorter than the M-14, and so more maneuverable than the M-14. The M-16 is much more controllable when fired on full automatic than the M-14. A soldier can carry many more rounds of the lighter 5.56mm ammunition for the M-16 than of the 7.62mm rounds for the M-14. The M-16 earned a reputation in early Vietnam use for jamming, reportedly partially due to the rifle being issued to troops without proper cleaning equipment. Also, the composition of the gunpowder used in the military cartridges was changed, to better avoid jams caused by fouling. A "forward assist" lever was added to the M-16, and the M-16A1 variant was thus created.

The U.S. Army adopted the M-16A1 in 1967. Millions of these rifles were produced. The M-16 and M-16A1 are indelibly associated with the United States in the Vietnam War. The M-16, manufactured of all-black parts, developed an aura of the sinister "black rifle." The M-16, for good or bad depending upon your point of view, became famous or infamous for the projection of America's power abroad, much as the AK-47 became the symbol for Communist military power.

The M-16A2, an improved version of the rifle, was introduced in the 1980's. The M-16A2 featured better adjustable sights, a heavier barrel, and modified rifling grooves in the barrel. The M-16A4 has since been widely issued, a primary feature

36

being that it is designed to accept an extremely wide range of accessories and aftermarket devices.

There are many variants of the M-16 that were or are in military use. The M-16 and its variants remains the primary American military rifle as of 2005.

Many firearm manufacturers make civilian versions of the M-16 in numerous styles. Any civilian version of the military's M-16 is often referred to generically as an AR-15, Armalite's original designation for this rifle type. AR-15's are very widely used in shooting sports.

A major advantage of the AR-15 is that the rifle has a modular design, such that all manner of accessories and options can be added to the AR-15 or interchanged with existing rifle components. Modular design, coupled with a vast availability of accessories and options, makes the AR-15 an extremely popular rifle design in the United States.

The AR-15 is also the primary example of an assault rifle on the list of every politician or activist desiring to ban assault rifles. The AR-15 was one of the assault rifles specifically banned under the defunct federal Assault Weapons Ban. Many AR-15 versions have most or all of the cosmetic features found so objectionable under the Assault Weapons Ban, such as bayonet lugs, flash suppressors, and pistol grip stocks. The AR-15 is rarely used in committing crimes, because it is a rifle (criminals prefer handguns), because AR-15's are relatively expensive, because the AR-15 tends to attract unwanted attention to the criminal compared to more mundane firearms, and because criminals untrained in the unique operation and functioning of an AR-15 are more likely to choose a more traditional firearm instead.

Ammunition For the M-16 Family of Rifles

The vast majority of M-16-type rifles are chambered for 5.56mm cartridges, generally also known as the .223 Remington. The military 5.56mm round is the same external size as the civilian .223 round, but has differences. The military version of this cartridge is usually characterized as the "5.56mm NATO" round. The civilian version is usually characterized as the ".223 cartridge" or more correctly as the ".223 Remington."

One difference is that the brass shell casings for military cartridges are usually more robust. The military cartridge is usually loaded with a more powerful gunpowder charge, which produces higher pressures in the rifle and faster bullet velocity.

Ammunition generally comes in a civilian loading, a United States military specifications ("mil-spec") loading, or in a NATO loading. Mil-spec ammunition is loaded in accordance with United States military requirements. NATO loadings are loaded in accordance with NATO military specifications. Civilian loadings are loaded to the loading criteria set by the commercial manufacturer of the cartridge. Military loadings are generally more powerful than civilian loadings.

The original standard full metal jacket cartridge for the M-16/AR-15 featured a bullet weighing 55 grains, designated as the M193 cartridge in the United States. The European designation for this cartridge is 5.56x45mm. An upgraded cartridge, designated the M855 in the United States, with a 62 grain bullet, was adopted by the United States in 1980.

M855 cartridges usually have their bullet tips painted green to distinguish them from M193 rounds. M855 rounds have a steel penetrator core inside the bullet to allow its use against lightly armored targets. The older M193 rounds have no such steel core. The M855 cartridge uses a bullet of Belgian design known as the SS109.

Bullets in the M855 cartridge require a barrel rifling twist rate of 1:10 or faster, or accuracy can be dangerously degraded. Many modern military M-16's use a 1:7 twist for the M855 cartridge. The older M193 cartridges can be fired with barrel rifling twist rates of 1:12 or faster.

Many AR-15's are currently manufactured with 1:10, 1:9, and 1:8 twists, an average twist which will stabilize either the M855 or M193 cartridges reasonably well.

AR-15's surged in popularity among competitive marksmen and in the shooting sports in the 1990's. This resulted in the introduction of a wide variety of bullet types and weights, and cartridge loadings. Wise AR-15 owners should carefully determine the bullet types, weights, and loadings acceptable for their particular rifles.

Firing Chamber Differences in the M-16 Family of Rifles

There is also a critical difference in the design of the firing chambers of the M-16 family of rifles. Some rifles have a 5.56 NATO chamber, also known as a "military chamber." Some rifles have a .223 Remington chamber, also known as a "civilian chamber," or a "SAAMI chamber." A few manufacturers use a rare third type of design called a "Wylde" chamber, which is in between a 5.56mm and .223 chamber in size.

The primary difference in firing chambers is in the "leade" (also known as the "freebore length"), which is the portion of the barrel between the firing chamber and the start of the rifling of the barrel. The freebore area, also known as the "throat," is the portion of the rifling which has been removed to provide an open space for the bullet to rest when the cartridge is loaded into the chamber, ready for firing. The leade in a 5.56 NATO chamber is *longer* than in a .223 chamber, and the freebore *diameter* is larger in a 5.56 NATO chamber than in a .223 chamber.

The .223 chamber is slightly more accurate and can produce higher bullet velocities. The 5.56 NATO chamber is slightly better at cycling and feeding ammunition from magazines.

The issue is that a shorter leade generally increases chamber pressure during firing, and use of a higher-pressure 5.56 NATO cartridge in a rifle with a .223 chamber may combine to produce excessive pressure during firing such that the rifle bursts from over-pressure. This is a real danger, because both 5.56 NATO and .223 Remington ammunition is commonly available, as are M-16-type rifles in the 5.56 NATO and .223 chamber designs. Rifles should be inspected to determine the chamber design. Many rifle manufacturers engrave AR-15 barrels with the chamber design type, but the method and accuracy of such markings varies between manufacturers.

Rifles with the 5.56 NATO chamber can safely fire both military and civilian ammunition. Rifles with .223 chambers should fire only .223 Remington ammunition not loaded to military specifications.

As stated above, wise AR-15 owners should carefully determine the bullet types, weights, and loadings acceptable for their particular rifles.

Battle Rifles

A "battle rifle" is not a legal term, but was apparently created by firearms enthusiasts and/or rifle marketers to distinguish them from assault rifles. The phrase also invokes the heritage of their use in "morally acceptable" wars such as World War I and World War II, as distinguished from the use of assault rifles in "morally troubled" wars such as Vietnam, or by terrorists.

Battle rifles generally are full-size military rifles (or replicas or civilian versions of such rifles). Examples are the M-1 Garand, M-14, and M-1A.

Battle rifles fire full-size rounds, such as a 30-06 or .308 (7.62mm) round.

The effective range of a battle rifle may be double that of an assault rifle.

Most battle rifles are semiautomatic. Some M-14 versions allowed full automatic fire, but were ineffective because the typical rifle design is unsuitable for firing full-size cartridges on automatic. The smaller 5.56mm round fired by the M-16 is a more effective choice of ammunition for full automatic use in a rifle compared to the 7.62mm round.

The most recent battle rifle in the American inventory is the M-14. The M-14 fires a cartridge with a 7.62mm bullet which is essentially the civilian .308 Winchester cartridge. This round is officially known by its European or NATO designation of 7.62x51mm, denoting a bullet with a width of 7.62mm placed into a shell casing 51mm long. The United States military designation for the 150.5-grain full metal jacket version of this round is the M59, and M80 for the 146-grain version. Muzzle velocity for both rounds is 2750 feet per second, and a muzzle energy of 2527 foot-pounds for the M59 and 2452 ft-lbs for the M80. The military version of this cartridge is not exactly the same as the civilian version, as the military version generally has a stronger brass casing. Differences (and alleged differences) between the military and civilian versions of this cartridge are endlessly debated. A common civilian loading of this cartridge has a 147 grain bullet, with a muzzle velocity of 2800 feet per second, with a muzzle energy of 2562 ft-lbs.

The 7.62mm NATO round is not the same as the 7.62mm Russian round. The Russian round, more properly known as the 7.62x39mm cartridge, is perhaps the most popular assault rifle cartridge in history. One popular loading of the 7.62x39mm round loads a 123 grain bullet, with a muzzle velocity of 2355 feet per second, with a muzzle energy of 1515 foot-pounds. The 7.62x39mm Russian round, being slightly weaker than even the moderate .30-30 hunting rifle cartridge (150 grain bullet, 2390 fps at the muzzle, 1902 ft-lbs at the muzzle), is certainly not a battle rifle cartridge.

Battle rifles are rarely issued to line military units today, and then only to specialized soldiers such as snipers. There has been a demand by the U.S. Army in Afghanistan and Iraq for issuance of a few M-14 rifles to each infantry squad, to provide the capability for aimed fire at distances greater than what the M-16 can deliver.

Carbine Rifles

Carbines were originally made as shorter versions of standard rifles. Many rifle "systems" had a standard sized infantry model, and a shorter and lighter carbine version. Typically, both models had a number of interchangeable parts, and fired the same ammunition. Carbines were originally developed for cavalry soldiers, who needed a shorter and lighter rifle than a standard infantry rifle for use on horseback.

Carbines were distinguishable from submachine guns by the type of cartridge used. Submachine guns used pistol cartridges, and carbines used rifle cartridges.

The advent of the assault rifle essentially represented a blending or merging of the submachine gun and the carbine, with the typical assault rifle using a cartridge more powerful than a pistol cartridge, but less powerful than a standard rifle cartridge.

The definition of the term "carbine" has in recent years become more generalized to mean any rifle of a size between a pistol and the now-standard rifle of most militaries, the assault rifle.

The M-1 Carbine

The most famous American carbine is the classic M-1 Carbine. This rifle was first issued in 1942, and used in World War II, Korea, and Vietnam. Over six million M-1 Carbines were produced in World War II. More M-1 Carbines were produced than any other American military firearm until surpassed in approximately the year 2004 by the M-16.

The M-1 Carbine is a semiautomatic rifle weighing 6.5 pounds, firing a .30 caliber round with a 110-grain bullet. A full automatic version was issued, dubbed the M-2. The M-1 Carbine is unique because it was not designed as a smaller and lighter version of a standard sized rifle. The M-1 Carbine was, oddly enough, intended to be the replacement for the standard military *pistol* of the era, the Colt M-1911A1 in .45 caliber. The M-1 Carbine was not a smaller version of the standard-sized military rifle of World War II, the M-1 Garand, with which it shares few if any parts.

The .30 caliber cartridge used in the M-1 Carbine was uniquely designed for the carbine. The .30 Carbine cartridge was not shared with any full-sized rifle. The round has a muzzle velocity of 1,990 feet per second. The M-1 Carbine round has 373 foot-pounds of energy at 200 yards, which is only 58% of the 5.56mm round and 22% of the 7.62mm round.

The .30 caliber M-1 Carbine round has 600 foot-pounds of energy at 100 yards. Popular civilian loadings of certain common pistol cartridges have an energy deposit at 100 yards as follows: 115-grain 9mm Luger round at 242 ft.-lbs; a 125-grain .357 Magnum round at 330 ft.-lbs.; and a 165-grain .40 caliber round at 340 ft.-lbs. The 5.56mm rifle round, at 100 yards, has 1,025 ft.-lbs. The M-1 carbine

41

round is therefore very much in between the power of an assault rifle cartridge and a pistol cartridge.

Comparing the M-1 Carbine to the firearm it was intended to replace, the Colt .45 pistol, a .45 ACP round of 230 grains has 300 ft.-lbs. of energy at 100 yards, compared to the 600 ft.-lbs. of the M-1 Carbine at that range. The M-1 Carbine has exactly twice the energy as the .45 ACP. The Colt round is more than twice as heavy as the carbine round, but the carbine round travels over twice as fast as the Colt. The standard M-1 Carbine magazine holds 15 rounds, over twice the 7 rounds of the military-era Colt .45 pistol. The M-1 Carbine also accepts widely available 30-round magazines, not an option with the Colt .45 pistol. The M-1 Carbine is more accurate for most shooters than the Colt .45. Despite these comparisons favoring the M-1 Carbine, the M-1 Carbine never replaced the Colt, and the carbine was phased out of active military service in the early 1960's with the introduction of the M-16. The Colt remained in service until the introduction of the Beretta 9mm in the late 1980's.

The M-1 Carbine was used widely in World War II. The carbine was intended for officers, artillerymen, support and rear echelon troops, etc. The carbine was not intended for use by infantrymen. The carbine, being extraordinarily handy, ergonomic, and light, quickly found its way in substantial numbers to the front lines. The carbine compared unfavorably to the full-size M-1 Garand for front line combat on the open plains of Europe, for which the carbine was not designed. The M-1 Carbine was criticized in Korea for freezing up in extreme cold, which malady also affected other light firearms. The carbine served well in the jungles of the Pacific and Vietnam, where freezing weather was nonexistent and where shooting distances were often within range of pistol cartridges.

Military surplus M-1 Carbines are widely available today, as is ammunition for the firearm. These carbines are always popular because they are simple, ergonomic, accurate, light, and certainly a piece of American history. Certain models of the M-1 Carbine are in great demand by collectors, such as those carbines manufactured by IBM (the computer manufacturer) and by Rock-Ola (a jukebox manufacturer).

M-4 Carbine

The carbine currently in service with the U.S. military is the M-4, a shortened version of the standard M-16. The M-4 is more of a true carbine than the M-1 Carbine, since it is a shortened and lightened version of the M-16, and fires the same 5.56mm assault rifle cartridge.

Bolt-Action Rifles

A bolt-action rifle is a rifle where the loading of cartridges into the firing chamber, and ejection of spent shell casings after firing, is accomplished by the manual working of the bolt by the rifle operator. The bolt has a handle directly affixed. The operator works the handle to rotate the bolt out of the firing position and pull the bolt to the rear. Pulling the bolt to the rear ejects the spent shell casing and exposes the breech. A new cartridge is manually inserted or moved into place automatically by the magazine. The operator manually pushes the bolt closed, and then locks the bolt closed by rotating the bolt. The rifle is then ready for the next shot.

Replacing spent shell casings with fresh cartridges with bolt-action rifles is much slower than with a semiautomatic rifle, and is even slower than a lever action rifle. However, the parts to a bolt-action rifle are extremely stout, resulting in a rifle design able to withstand high-powered cartridges better than any other design. Bolt-action design is also superior in potential accuracy.

The bolt-action rifle was invented by Nicholas Dreyse in 1840. Mauser introduced the first bolt-action design featuring the metallic cartridge in 1871. James P. Lee introduced the box magazine in 1879, first incorporated into a bolt-action rifle with the Remington-Lee rifle of 1884. With this development, the essential elements of modern bolt-action rifle design were present.

The bolt-action rifle became the standard military rifle design in most countries in the late 1800's, and a standard hunting rifle along with the lever-action. The U.S. Army adopted the Krag-Jorgensen bolt-action rifle in 1892, which rifle performed poorly in the Spanish-American War. The rifle was soon replaced with the legendary Model 1903 Springfield. The Springfield served the U.S. Army long after the introduction in 1936 of the semiautomatic M-1 Garand. Bolt-action rifles are extremely rarely used today in the military, and then typically only for some sniper duties.

Machine Guns

Machine guns are firearms capable of firing typically on full automatic and rarely on semiautomatic. A poor definition for machine gun is any automatic firearm, which can include rifles and carbines.

The military usage of "machine gun" is any "crew served" or squad support automatic firearm. Crew served firearms are typically fully automatic, and are much larger and heavier than assault rifles. Machine guns typically have provisions for volume ammunition feed, such as 100-round belts of ammunition. Machine guns are also designed for continuous fire by linking ammunition belts together. These crew served firearms typically are fired while placed on a firing mount, tripod, or bipod resting on the ground, rather than as a shoulder-fired firearm. Machine guns are typically used to lay down a "cone of fire" into a generalized target area.

Generally, then, machine guns are distinguished from automatic rifles in that machine guns are heavier, larger, are designed for continuous fire, are usually crew served, are usually not fired from the shoulder, and have provisions for continuous ammunition feed.

The most famous American machine gun is the M2-HB .50 caliber heavy machine gun. The .50 caliber has an effective range of 1,830 meters, and weighs 84 pounds. Its cyclic rate of fire is 550 rounds per minute. The .50 caliber round is a half-inch in diameter. Ammunition is fed into the side of the firearm by a belt of rounds linked together.

The American M60 machine gun was a Cold War and Vietnam War medium machine gun introduced in 1957. The M60 fires 7.62mm rounds which can also be fired in the M-14 rifle. The M60 weighs 23.2 pounds. The M60 was widely issued throughout the U.S. Army, especially during Vietnam and in Europe during the Cold War because the Army had no light machine gun at that time. The M60 was replaced by the M240B medium machine gun in the 1980's.

The Army's light machine gun, the Browning Automatic Rifle, was phased out in the 1950's, leaving the military without a light machine gun. The M60 medium machine gun was widely issued to serve in this role, which hampered foot mobility of infantry units. The M-14 and the M60E3 were introduced to serve as light machine guns, with no success. The M249 Squad Automatic Weapon ("SAW"), introduced in 1982, however, has become a successful light machine gun currently in widespread use in the U.S. Army. The SAW fires the 5.56mm M-16 round, and can be operated and transported by one soldier. The SAW fires linked ammunition from belts or magazines, and can also accept standard M-16 magazines. The SAW is intended to offer a "base of fire" for an infantry squad. The SAW is light enough (15 pounds) to be fired from the shoulder.

Submachine Guns

Submachine guns are short compact rifles capable of automatic fire, and may or may not fire semiautomatically. They are chambered for pistol cartridges, usually .45 or 9mm rounds. This characteristic of firing pistol cartridges is what distinguishes submachine guns from carbines and assault rifles. Submachine guns are usually lightweight firearms for short-range firing. Submachine guns usually accept large quantity magazines, such as 50 and 100-round drums for the Thompson.

The most famous submachine gun in the United States is the Thompson submachine gun, designed by General John T. Thompson. The Thompson was made infamous by the gangsters of the 1920's, but was widely used in World War II by various countries. The Thompson fired a standard .45 caliber pistol cartridge. The Thompson, nicknamed the "trench broom," was originally designed for use in trench warfare, where long-range accuracy mattered less than volume of fire and ammunition capacity. The first Thompsons were en route to the war zone in 1918 when World War I ended. The Thompson was officially replaced in the American military during World War II by the M3 "grease gun," also of .45 caliber.

The Germans widely issued the MP38/MP40 submachine gun in World War II. The MP40 was also known as the Schmeisser, after a prominent German firearm designer. The MP40 was not designed by Schmeisser, but was designed by Heinrich Follmer. Schmeisser designed the MP28, which was an early inspiration for the MP40. The MP40 fired a 9mm round. Submachine guns are also called "machine pistols," as in the German "maschinen pistole," or "MP."

The most popular modern submachine guns are the Heckler and Koch MP5 (9mm) and the Israeli Uzi (9mm).

The use of submachine guns declined with the advent of assault rifles, especially with the carbine versions of assault rifles.

Lever-Action Rifles

Repeating pistols existed in the Civil War. However, most rifles were single-shot rifles. Rifle design did not lend itself to use of a revolving chamber design as with revolver pistols. A single-shot rifle is a rifle which holds only one cartridge at a time, and the rifle must be manually reloaded between shots. It is cumbersome and time consuming to be fumbling with and loading bullets one at a time between shots in the heat of battle. The Spencer repeating carbine existed for Union cavalry troops, but by and large, most line infantrymen used single-shot rifles.

A very successful design was the Henry system, devised by Benjamin T. Henry originally in 1850. Henry's design featured a finger-loop underneath the rifle and a tubular magazine underneath the barrel. The firearm operator would hold and fire the rifle with his fingers through the finger-loop. The operator would push the loop downward after firing, which moved a lever connected to the interior of the rifle, which ejected the spent shell casing. The magazine spring then pushed a fresh cartridge into position. The operator then pulled the lever back into the closed position, which moved the fresh cartridge into the firing chamber. This lever-action sequence could be performed quickly, often in a second or less. This reloading sequence was vastly quicker than reloading single-shot rifles, which may take 15-20 seconds. The Henry rifle, produced by Winchester, saw limited use in the Civil War. The original Henry design was modified into its modern form with the introduction of the Winchester 1866 model, which featured a side-mounted loading flap compared to the earlier method of loading by disconnecting a cap from the front end of the tubular magazine. Ammunition loading with the Winchester 1866 was safer, quicker, and more suited to combat conditions. The rifle was redesigned and offered as the Winchester 1873 model. The Winchester 1866 and 1873 models, usually considered together, are known as "The Rifle Which Won the West." This rifle is strongly associated with the Wild West, cowboys, and Western mythology. John Browning redesigned the Henry system, and Winchester produced the Browning-designed modern lever-action rifle as the Winchester 94 in 1894. The Winchester 94, a nearly perfect design, has been in continuous production since, except for during World War II, when Winchester produced military firearms.

A lever-action rifle is a "repeater" or a "repeating rifle." This distinguishes the rifle from a single-shot rifle. A repeater is not a semiautomatic rifle, since spent shell casings must be manually ejected and fresh cartridges manually inserted into the breech by moving the lever.

Magazine capacity of a lever-action rifle varies with the caliber in which the rifle is chambered. Full-length magazines can hold 7 rounds of .30-30 caliber ammunition, or 12 rounds of .357 magnum ammunition. Carbine models hold fewer cartridges.

The lever-action, for all its advantages over single-shot rifles, and despite its heavy use in the American West, was never heavily used by the American military. The standard American infantry rifle as late as 1892 was still a single-shot rifle. The lever-action rifle had two major flaws in military use. First, it is difficult to operate the lever in a prone firing position. The second reason is more complicated. The bullets are stored in a tubular magazine underneath the barrel, with the tip of each bullet resting directly upon the primer of the bullet ahead of it. That was not a problem when bullets were designed with blunt tips, which are unlikely to ignite primers. However, pointed bullets are likely to ignite the primer of the bullet located in front of it in the magazine during recoil of a cartridge being fired. Therefore, when the military adopted pointed bullet design in the late 1800's, the lever-action design became even less suitable as a military design. However, blunt-tipped bullets are admirably suited for hunting game in wooded areas. Lever-action rifles have been sold by the millions for hunting, especially deer.

46

Pistols

Virtually all modern handguns are one of two types of designs, either semiautomatic pistols or revolvers. Revolvers are an older design, most recognizable in the United States in the cowboy Westerns set in the 1800's. Demands for higher rate of fire, quicker reloading capability, and increased magazine capacity led to the development of the semiautomatic pistol in the very late 1800's. Both designs remain widely available. Research and development is almost exclusively devoted to semiautomatic pistols.

Most definitions make "pistol" synonymous with "handgun." Some define "pistol" to describe only those handguns with a single cartridge chamber, such as semiautomatic or single-shot handguns, with multi-chambered firearms (such as a revolver) not included within the definition of pistol.

Revolvers

Revolvers are a type of pistol or handgun. Revolvers are recognizable by a large rotating cylinder mounted longitudinally in the frame just above the pistol grip. Chambers in the cylinder hold the cartridges. The cylinder rotates as needed to bring a fresh unfired cartridge into position ready for firing. Revolvers do not have detachable magazines. The cylinder is, in essence, a fixed magazine. Most revolvers have a 5 or 6 shot capacity. Revolvers generally have only 33% to 50% of the magazine capacity of common magazine-fed handguns.

Various methods exist to empty the cylinder chambers of spent casings, and to reload the chambers with fresh cartridges, depending upon design of the particular revolver. Reloading a revolver is almost always slower than with a magazine-fed handgun. Gate-loaded revolvers are especially slow to load and unload, but some revolver designs allow loading and unloading almost as quickly as a semiautomatic pistol.

Cylinder chambers will generally accommodate only one bullet caliber. However, some cylinders will accept different bullet types. For example, many .357 cylinders will also accept .38 Special rounds. Further, some revolvers will accept cylinders of different calibers. For instance, one model revolver is sold with one cylinder firing .357 Magnum and .38 Special cartridges, and a separate cylinder firing 9mm cartridges. Thus, by switching cylinders, one firearm can fire three types of cartridges. Of course, the actual caliber of the various bullets must be the same, or nearly so, since the same barrel is used for bullets fired with either cylinder. The 9mm bullet is, for example, .355" in diameter, while the .357 and .38 Special bullets are both .357" in diameter.

47

Revolvers are of a more simple design than most semiautomatic handguns, so are theoretically more reliable and durable. Revolver design is especially suitable to fire large caliber or powerful cartridges compared to the typical semiautomatic.

Revolvers may be single-action or double-action. With a single-action design, the hammer must be manually cocked, and then the trigger pulled, to fire the firearm. With a double-action, pulling the trigger will first cock the hammer, then release the hammer, firing the weapon. Single-action design allows greater accuracy, since the relatively light pressure required to pull a single-action trigger is less disturbing to aiming compared to the higher pressure and longer trigger-pull travel of a double-action. Double-action firearms, however, can usually be fired quicker than single-action designs. Some revolvers can be fired in either single-action or double-action mode.

Bullets are stored in the cylinder "chambers" ready for firing. The chambers are cylindrical holes bored completely through the cylinder. The chambers are sized just barely large enough to accept the cartridges with a tight fit. The rim at the base of the cartridges prevents cartridges from falling completely through the cylinder. The bullet, upon firing, travels through the remaining length of the cylinder. The cylinder narrows towards the end of the cylinder, called the "throat." The throat area begins to channel the bullet more precisely into alignment with the bore of the barrel, and holds the bullet until the burning gunpowder can build up enough pressure to properly launch the bullet. The bullet then exits the cylinder and leaps across the gap between the cylinder face and the back of the barrel. The back of the barrel, called the "forcing cone," is cone-shaped to better catch the bullet, and channel the bullet into the bore, where the rifling starts. If the cylinder is not exactly in line with the forcing cone, the revolver is "out of time" and should be adjusted. The bullet then engages the rifling, passes down the bore, and exits the bore at the muzzle.

History of the Revolver

The first revolvers appeared in the early 1800's. Samuel Colt, founder of the famous firearms manufacturer bearing his name, produced his first revolver in 1836. Most revolvers in the first half of the 1800's were of the percussion design, which involved slow and cumbersome loading and unloading of the separate cartridge components. Revolvers were widely used by the time of the Civil War in the 1860's. Revolver design, particularly that incorporating full metallic self-contained cartridges, stagnated until the expiration of a certain patent in 1869 which had given the firearms manufacturer Smith and Wesson a near monopoly on revolver sales. Colt introduced the Single Action Army revolver (also called the "Peacemaker") in

1873, shortly after the expiration of the Smith and Wesson patent in 1869. The Single Action Army became an icon, an indelible feature of the settling of the American West in the last decades of the 1800's. The Single Action Army featured full metallic centerfire cartridges loaded by use of a "loading gate." A loading gate is a hinged flap which, when opened, allows cartridges to be loaded into the rear of the revolving cylinder, and likewise allows empty shell casings to be manually ejected from the cylinder. The Single Action Army design remains popular even today, over 130 years after its introduction and despite numerous advancements in firearms design. Popularity of the Single Action Army design is based partly on nostalgia, and partly because the design is simple, robust, and dependable.

A modern revolver based on the classic Single Action Army design is the Ruger New Model Blackhawk, a single action, gate loading, six shot, solid frame, heavy caliber revolver of Ruger's typically stout design. Ruger is the largest American firearms manufacturer.

Advancements in revolver design after the Single Action Army was introduced in 1873 typically focused upon cylinder design, in an attempt to speed up the loading and unloading process. Various improvements were hinged barrels, swing-out cylinders, and mechanical plungers or devices designed to eject all spent casings at once.

Revolver design had reached a plateau in the very early 1900's. Revolvers began to be replaced in the military role in World War I (1914-1918), due to the higher magazine capacity and quicker reloading times of semiautomatics. Semiautomatics have become near-universal in the police market for the same reasons.

Revolvers remain popular with home defenders and criminals because of the simplicity, durability, and ease of use of revolvers for the poorly-trained user. Revolvers also remain a very common firearm because many millions were manufactured. Revolvers, with minimal maintenance, may last decades, if not centuries. Revolvers continue to be manufactured to serve the considerable market for the sports of cowboy action shooting and for Single Action Army competition.

Semiautomatic Pistols

The force of exploding gunpowder in a cartridge fired in a revolver is devoted to the single purpose of propelling the bullet from the pistol. Loading of a fresh cartridge in preparation for firing the next round, and ejecting fired shell casings from the revolver after firing, are done manually.

Semiautomatic pistols are designed such that part of the force of firing a cartridge is used to eject the spent shell casing from the pistol after firing. Part of the force of the exploding gasses of firing pushes the slide on the firearm to the rear of the firearm, ejecting the spent shell casing out of a side port. A recoil spring then pushes the slide forward back into position, along the way picking up a fresh cartridge from the top of the magazine, and inserts the fresh cartridge into the firing chamber, ready to be fired. All this movement, unloading, and loading is accomplished automatically in a fraction of a second.

"Semiautomatic" means that, with one pull of the trigger, the pistol will fire one round, eject the one spent casing, and load one fresh cartridge. Another pull of the trigger is required to fire the next round. Holding the trigger down after the shot will accomplish nothing; the firearm will not fire. This is distinguished from "automatic," where the firearm will continue to cycle (firing round after round, ejecting cartridges, and loading fresh cartridges) for as long as the trigger is pressed down. It is extremely rare to find a firearm manufacturer offering a true automatic pistol; virtually all such firearms are of semiautomatic design.

Virtually all semiautomatic pistols are designed with cartridges stored inside of a magazine. Magazines are usually a rectangular box-like container. Magazines are inserted and locked into the bottom of the pistol, usually inside of the butt. The magazines feed the cartridges into the pistol as needed.

Semiautomatic pistols have several advantages over revolvers. Semiautomatic pistols, because they automatically eject spent casings and load the next round, are capable of firing more quickly than a revolver. Most semiautomatics can hold more ammunition than revolvers, often twice as much or more. Most semiautomatics can be reloaded with a fresh supply of cartridges more quickly than a revolver. Semiautomatic pistols tend to be flatter in design than revolvers, giving an advantage in concealed carry. These are important advantages, especially to a soldier or police officer.

Semiautomatic pistols have some disadvantages compared to revolvers. Semiautomatics tend to be more complicated to operate, disassemble, and clean than revolvers. Semiautomatics are arguably less dependable than revolvers, because semiautomatics contain more smaller parts than revolvers. Revolvers are less sensitive to variations in ammunition, because no part of the propelling charge is used to cycle the firearm to eject shell casings or load new cartridges. Semiautomatics are sometimes affected by "limp wristing," where if the shooter does not hold the pistol firmly, the pistol may not cycle properly and so may fail to load the next cartridge. Ammunition loading in revolvers, being entirely manual, is entirely unaffected by limp-wristing. The slide on a semiautomatic must be

Firearms Law of North Carolina
www.ncfirearmslaw.com

manually cycled to eject a misfired cartridge, where with a revolver, all that is needed is to pull the trigger again (double action) or cock the hammer and pull the trigger again (single action). Revolvers are generally more able to withstand firing truly heavy caliber cartridges than semiautomatics.

The most famous semiautomatic pistol in the United States is undoubtedly the Colt M1911A1 firing the .45 ACP cartridge, issued with 7-round magazines as standard. The M1911A1 was adopted by the U.S. Army in 1911 as the M1911, and was widely used in World War I. The pistol was revised and adopted in 1926 as the M1911A1, a classic firearms design. The M1911A1 was widely issued and served the United States well in World War II, Korea, Vietnam, and any number of lesser conflicts. The M1911A1 was replaced in a controversial move by the U.S. Army in 1985 by the M9 pistol, better known as the Beretta 9mm Model 92FS. This replacement of the M1911A1 by the Beretta remains controversial even today, 20 years later.

The Beretta Model 92FS, known to the U.S. Army as the Model M9, has been the standard service pistol of the U.S. Army since 1985. The Model 92FS is chambered for the 9mm Luger round, with standard magazine capacity of 15 rounds. The U.S. Army designation for the 9mm full metal jacket cartridge is M882. Predecessors of the Model 92FS had teething problems, but the Model 92FS as accepted into the military performed very well in the First Gulf War in the early 1990's. The primary complaint about the Model 92FS is not the firearm itself, but the supposed ineffectiveness of its 9mm ammunition, usually compared unfavorably to the .45 ACP cartridge by proponents of the Colt pistol it replaced. Military personnel are required to use full metal jacket ammunition under Geneva Convention rules, and standard 9mm ball ammunition is often believed to have less knock-down power than standard .45 ACP ball ammunition. Civilians loading the Model 92FS with hollow-point 9mm +p ammunition have a highly effective cartridge rivaling lesser loadings of the .357 Magnum, in a firearm with less felt recoil than a Colt .45, and with over twice the ammunition capacity. The Model 92FS is notable because its adoption by the U.S. military in 1985, followed by widespread adoption of the 9mm Glock 17 by police departments, greatly spurred civilian interest and purchases, and is widely credited with bringing the 9mm cartridge into mainstream America. The main drawback of the Model 92FS to civilian concealed firearm carriers is its size and weight. It is a full size firearm weighing 34.3 ounces empty, considered heavy for a concealed handgun.

Handguns for Self Defense – The Best and the Worst

The average person owning a handgun for self defense is not a firearms hobbyist with extensive knowledge of any aspect of firearms, and usually has no plans to acquire such knowledge. This section offers to that audience general criteria on selecting a handgun for self defense.

The Worst Choice For a Self Defense Handgun

Handguns which display one or more of the following characteristics are very probably not a good choice for a self defense handgun for the average person. These characteristics are in no particular order.

1. A handgun named after an elite military unit or hostage rescue team.
2. A handgun whose main selling point is elaborate engraving and gold accents.
3. Anything with "tactical," "combat," or "elite" in the name or advertisements.
4. A handgun finished in chrome buffed to a mirror finish.
5. A handgun of uncertain origin and odd caliber brought back by Granddad as a World War I souvenir.
6. A handgun which is the current fad of hoodlums and gangsters on television.
7. A four-pound hunk of steel monster.
8. A .50 caliber anything.
9. A civilian version of a military automatic machine pistol.
10. Anything with the letter "X" in the name, like "Max," "Xtreme," or "Exotic."
11. Any product of Wherezitkistan or some other obscure place.
12. A handgun festooned with a laser aiming device, a flashlight, adjustable night sights, and extended magazine.
13. The most expensive handgun you can buy.

The Best Choice For a Self Defense Handgun

The best choice of a handgun for the average person also will have certain characteristics, listed below in no particular order.

1. Made in America, Germany, or Austria.
2. Chambered in a common moderate caliber, such as 9mm, .40, or .45ACP.
3. Manufactured by a major manufacturer, not an off-brand.
4. Fits the hand of its owner very well.
5. Light enough in weight so that the owner will carry the firearm when needed.
6. A handgun emphasizing dependability, durability, and functional quality.
7. A handgun where glitz, glamour, and bells and whistles are minimized.
8. Exterior finish preferably in flat black, or non-shiny brushed stainless steel.
9. A good seller in the manufacturer's line of handguns; not a specialty firearm.
10. A standard or compact version of the handgun model; not a target version.
11. One for which exact-fit accessories are available (holsters, magazines, etc.).
12. A standard barrel muzzle; no compensators, muzzle brakes, etc.

52

Muzzleloaders and Breechloaders

Most firearms from the invention of firearms until the mid-1800's were muzzleloaders. With muzzleloaders, a charge of gunpowder is loaded into the muzzle end of the gun barrel, and then rammed with a ramrod down to the closed rear of the barrel. A loose bullet is then inserted into the muzzle, and rammed down to the gunpowder. With a few other preparatory steps, the firearm is ready to fire. This is a time consuming and cumbersome process, especially so in the rain or the dark. Someone practiced in the use of muzzleloaders might be able to fire three rounds per minute.

Muzzleloaders were replaced by breechloaders starting in the mid-1800's. Cartridges are loaded into the rear of the barrel of a breechloader in preparation for firing. The breech is then closed behind the rear of the cartridge, sealing the cartridge into the rear of the barrel, ready for firing. The breech is often closed in rifles by the bolt, a mechanical part designed for that purpose. With many semiautomatic pistol designs, the mass of the slide serves the same purpose.

Breechloading design is superior to muzzleloading design for various technical reasons. Virtually all modern firearms are breechloaders. Muzzleloaders still exist, primarily seen in Civil War reenactments. There is a small amount of competition use of muzzleloaders, as there is for hunting. Muzzleloaders are generally rare, and most people will never see one. Muzzleloaders may be of a "long gun" or pistol design, but most muzzleloaders today are long guns. Muzzleloaders were historically smoothbore, that is, without a rifled bore, but can be rifled.

A muzzleloader is treated like any other firearm for most legal purposes. The two primary legal differences are that muzzleloaders are generally considered as antiques, and some laws expressly exclude muzzleloaders from their coverage. Also, there are special hunting rules issued for muzzleloaders.

Rate of Fire

The rate of fire of a firearm refers to how many bullets per minute that firearm can fire. There are four different common definitions of this term.

The "cyclic" rate of fire is the number of rounds that a fully automatic firearm can fire per minute, assuming no jams, no reloading, etc. As an example, the cyclic rate of fire for an M-16 rifle is 800 rounds per minute. The cyclic rate of fire is often theoretical, since few firearms have magazines large enough to hold enough cartridges for one minute's worth of firing. Also, few firearms can fire continuously for one minute without first destroying the barrel from overheating.

The "automatic" rate of fire is the number of rounds that a fully automatic firearm can fire per minute but allowing time for changing magazines and resuming firing. As an example, the automatic rate of fire of an M-16A2 rifle with the triple-burst feature is 90 rounds per minute.

The "semiautomatic" rate of fire is the maximum number of rounds per minute that a firearm can fire in the semiautomatic mode. The semiautomatic rate of fire for an M-16 rifle is 45 rounds per minute.

The "sustained" rate of fire is the number of rounds that a firearm can fire per minute where the rate of fire does not overheat the barrel. The sustained rate of fire for an M-16 rifle is 12-15 rounds per minute.

Cartridges and Bullets

In General

A cartridge is one complete unit of fire, comprised of a bullet, shell casing, load of gunpowder, and primer. A cartridge may also be called a "round."

Cartridge Identification

There are many different methods used to identify cartridges. Cartridges were historically identified in the United States as the bore diameter and the weight of the gunpowder. An example is the famous .30-30 cartridge, signifying a .30-caliber bullet with a shell casing holding 30 grains of gunpowder.

This identification system is sometimes modified to show the bullet weight. For example, the .30-30-150 would identify a 30-30 round with a 150gr bullet.

Some cartridges are named for their diameter and the company that invented them. An example is the .308 Winchester. The .30-30 round was originally named the .30-30 Winchester.

Cartridges have also been identified by their bore diameter and the year of introduction. An example is the .30-06 rifle cartridge, which is a .30 caliber cartridge introduced in the year 1906.

Cartridges have been identified by some characteristic of the round. An example is the .30-30 Winchester Centerfire, identifying it as a centerfire cartridge. Cartridges with the word "Magnum" in their name signify a relatively powerful cartridge. Cartridges with the word "Express" in their name may signify high velocity rounds. The proportion of accurate technical description to marketing hype in these types of labels varies.

Cartridges are sometimes identified by the brand of firearm for which they were originally designed. An example is the .45 ACP. The "ACP" stands for "Automatic Colt Pistol." This is an attempt to gain a marketing advantage by the firearms manufacturer. Generally, other firearms manufacturers will design a firearm chambered for the cartridge, with the name reduced to initials, or dropped altogether, to negate the marketing disadvantage.

The European method of describing a cartridge is to identify the width of the bullet in millimeters and the length of the shell casing in millimeters, separated by the letter "x." An example is the common "9x19" nomenclature for the 9mm pistol round, denoting a bullet 9mm in width, inserted into a shell casing 19 millimeters long. The .380 ACP round (as known in the United States), is known in Europe as the 9x17 round, which is a 9mm bullet used in a shell casing 17 millimeters long. This 9x17 round is also known as the 9mm Kurz ("Kurz" is German for "short"), because the .380ACP/9x17 round is simply a 9mm bullet placed into a shorter casing than the "standard" casing for a 9mm cartridge of 19 millimeters. The .357SIG would be known in Europe as the 9x22mm cartridge, which is a 9mm bullet used in a casing 22 millimeters long.

Some cartridges and casings are known by multiple names. The 9mm pistol round described above is known as the 9x19, the 9mm Parabellum, and the 9mm Luger. The 9mm round was developed by Georg Luger, and is widely marketed a hundred years later as the 9mm Luger. The 9mm was developed for military use, and is commonly known by the nomenclature of "parabellum," which means "for war" in Latin.

Modern cartridges, that is, cartridges introduced since approximately 1866, are called "metallic cartridges." Metallic cartridges are self-contained fixed-component items, with exterior surfaces made entirely of metal. Prior to metallic cartridges, cartridges might be composed of a small gunpowder charge contained in a paper tube, with perhaps a separate loose bullet, and separate percussion caps, all of which had to be loaded into the firearm separately. The process of loading non-metallic cartridges was time consuming and difficult at night or when in combat.

Bullet Types, Design, and Size

There is a huge variety of bullet types, designs, and sizes. Bullet design greatly affects bullet performance, characteristics, and effectiveness. Laws often refer to certain bullet characteristics, and laws can affect uses and sales of certain bullets. Therefore, a basic knowledge of bullets is helpful to understanding the law on firearms.

Bullet Size

The primary characteristic of a bullet is its size. Bullet size is generally measured by its width (diameter) at its widest point. The length of the bullet or the shell casing are irrelevant to measurement of the bullet diameter.

Bullet size is expressed in millimeters, or in fractions of an inch expressed in decimals. An example of a bullet expressed in millimeters is the common 9mm bullet. An example of a bullet expressed in fractions of an inch is the common .45

56

bullet. Generally, bullets developed in Europe are identified in millimeters, and bullets from the United States are identified in inches.

Bullet size may only be approximate. The stated bullet size may be set at an arbitrary number for marketing reasons. For example, the common .380 ACP bullet is actually a .355" bullet, but the .38 Special is a .357" bullet. The .357 Magnum is a .357" bullet, but the .357 SIG is a .355" bullet.

Bullet width was historically measured in the United States using the "bore diameter." The bore diameter is the distance between the lands in the barrel. In a rifled barrel, grooves are machined into the metal barrel. The lands are the barrel surface before the grooves were cut into the barrel. The bore diameter may also be called the "nominal caliber."

Bullets must actually be wider than the bore diameter, since the bullet needs to be wide enough to fit down into the rifling grooves. For example, a .50 caliber bullet is named for the bore diameter of the gun it is used in, which has a nominal bore size of .50". However, the .50 caliber bullet is .510" in actual diameter. Likewise, the .30-30 bullet, fired from a rifle with a nominal caliber of .30", is actually .308" wide.

It became common in the 1950's to identify bullets by their "groove diameter." The groove diameter is the diameter of the barrel, measured between the bottoms of opposite grooves comprising the rifling of the barrel. The groove diameter will by definition always be larger than the bore diameter of a barrel. The groove diameter is the actual diameter of the bullet.

European bullets are generally identified by their nominal bore diameter (not groove diameter), in millimeters. The European practice is to also identify the length of the shell casing in millimeters, separated by the letter "x". An example is the "9x19" nomenclature for the 9mm pistol round, denoting a bullet 9mm in width, inserted into a shell casing 19 millimeters long. The NATO standard machine gun round, essentially the .308 Winchester cartridge, is officially known by its European designation of 7.62x51mm.

Bullet Weight

A common characteristic used to describe bullets is the weight of each bullet (not the entire cartridge). The unit of measurement is the "grain." There are 7,000 grains to the pound. Manufacturers almost always offer bullets of different weights for a given caliber. For example, 9mm bullets are manufactured in 115gr, 124gr, 135gr, 147gr, and other weights.

Weight differences affect bullet trajectory, velocity, energy upon impact, and effective range. A firearm will usually fire any weight bullet of the correct size cartridge. A revolver will almost always fire any weight bullet of the proper caliber, but individual semiautomatic pistols may get finicky with certain bullet weights, especially those bullets at the high or low end of the available range of bullets. While a casual shooter will not likely notice a difference between bullet weights, the astute shooter will select the proper bullet weight for best results for the task intended.

Bullet Jackets

Bullets are composed of a solid metal core, usually lead. Most bullets are "jacketed" at least partially with a harder metal, usually an alloy of 90-95% copper and 5-10% zinc. Jacketing means that the bullet exterior is sheathed or coated in a hard metal.

A copper jacket on the sidewall of the bullet allows the bullet to hold the rifling of the bore better than soft lead. Coating the bullet in copper eliminates fouling of the bore with lead residue, a problem called "leading" which decreases accuracy of the firearm.

Jacketing the tip of the bullet improves the ability of the bullet to penetrate upon impact, because copper holds its shape better than lead. Jacketing the bullet tip also allows the bullet to be designed in a more aerodynamic shape, since hard copper will hold a pointed shape more readily than soft lead. Leaving the soft lead of the bullet interior exposed, however, which is a "softpoint," allows the bullet to expand upon impact, which is common for hunting bullets.

Bullets sheathed in copper only along their sidewalls are called "partially jacketed." Bullets totally sheathed with copper are called "full metal jacket," "total metal jacket," or "ball" ammunition. The base of the bullet is rarely jacketed, even with a "full" or "total" metal jacket. The base of the bullet is the bottom, the end opposite of the tip.

Premium hunting bullets may have sophisticated jacket design and internal construction between the jacket and the lead core. These bullets are variously designed to mushroom open, split open in prongs like a flower petal, etc. Some hunting bullets have a hard metal or plastic tip embedded into the bullet nose which tip is separate from the sidewall jacket. The hard tip acts as a wedge upon bullet impact to increase expansion of the bullet.

Firearms Law of North Carolina
www.ncfirearmslaw.com

Some bullets have a groove cut into the jacket encircling the bullet midway between the bullet tip and the rear of the bullet. This groove is called the cannelure. The top of the casing is crimped into the cannelure when the bullet is manufactured. Crimping the casing into the cannelure helps hold the bullet in place, preventing movement of the bullet in the casing during handling and loading into the breech. Crimping into the cannelure also improves sealing of the cartridge propellant. The cannelure is a weak point in the bullet jacket, and some bullets, notably the American 5.56mm round, will fragment at the cannelure if impacting at high velocity.

Specialty Bullets

Specialty bullets exist. Examples are tracer bullets (bullets which leave a trail of burning particles to allow the shooter to see the bullet path); teflon bullets (see separate description); exploding bullets (bullets which explode upon impact); frangible bullets (bullets which break up into several smaller parts upon impact); and armor-piercing bullets (specially hardened bullets designed to pierce armor). Most specialty bullets are illegal for sale to civilians, unobtainable commercially, expensive, and rare.

Armor Piercing Bullets

Armor piercing bullets are bullets specially designed to have a greater ability to penetrate armor than regular bullets. A typical bullet has a lead core enclosed with a copper jacket. The lead interior is a relatively soft metal. The copper jacket is moderately hard, but not so hard as to damage or unduly wear on the barrel when the firearm is fired.

Armor piercing bullets are of various designs and materials. A common design is to have the same copper jacket with lead interior, but to manufacture a steel core or "penetrator" into the center of the bullet. If the bullet impacts an armored target, the steel penetrator will have a better chance to pierce the target than would a standard lead and copper bullet. A common example of this design of armor piercing bullet is the American M855 "green tip" round for the M-16 family of rifles.

The most publicized armor piercing rounds were KTW bullets. The name "KTW" was styled after the inventors of the round, Kopsch, Turcos, and Ward. KTW bullets are designed to penetrate hard targets such as doors and windshields of motor vehicles better than standard bullets. KTW ammunition is also more able to penetrate body armor worn by police officers. This increased ability to penetrate body armor earned KTW bullets adverse publicity as a "cop killer bullet." Armor-piercing KTW ammunition is not available to the general public, and is legally

59

available only to the military and law enforcement agencies. Federal law expressly provides that committing a crime using KTW bullets results in harsher penalties.

One version of KTW bullets developed in the early 1980's were bullets made of brass. The hard brass caused excessive wear on pistol barrels. Heavy wear was reduced by coating the bullets in teflon. Teflon has an extremely high ability to reduce friction and stickiness between moving parts. KTW and teflon bullets became synonymous, incorrectly so, since not all KTW bullets were teflon coated, and various non-KTW bullets are teflon coated.

Bullet Shape

Bullets shape ranges from a very blunt, almost flat frontal surface design, to a very pointed streamlined design. The pointed, streamlined bullets are often called bullets of "spitzer" design. There are advantages and disadvantages of both designs.

Very generally, blunt bullet designs are of older design, while spitzer bullets are of more modern design. Development of spitzer bullets generally came with the development of more powerful, higher velocity cartridges where aerodynamics became more important.

Pistol bullets are generally of the blunt design. Pistol cartridges are not high velocity or long range cartridges, so aerodynamics are less important.

Blunt bullets seem less affected than spitzer bullets when fired through leafy underbrush or forest growth. Many hunting cartridges are therefore designed with blunt bullets.

Lever-action rifles, extremely common in the United States, require cartridges with blunt bullets, since the cartridges lie nose-to-tail in the magazine. If the bullets were spitzers, the recoil shock of firing a round could cause the tip of one bullet to act as a firing pin, and fire the bullet ahead of it in the magazine.

Hollow Point Bullets

Hollow point bullets are bullets where a cavity was molded into the nose of the bullet at manufacture, hence the name "hollow point." This cavity is plainly evident upon visual inspection of the bullet tip. The cavity causes the bullet to expand upon impact, causing a much wider wound channel in the target than was the bullet's original diameter. A full metal jacketed bullet would not expand at all. A slang term for a hollow point bullet is a "dum dum bullet," so named because they were developed by the British at the Dum-Dum Arsenal in India in the 1890's.

60

Hollow points are heavily the bullet of choice for self-defense rounds. Hollow points are often used by hunters. Hollow pointed are illegal for military use under the Geneva Conventions.

Hollow point cartridges are more expensive than comparable full metal jacket rounds. For example, 9mm hollow point cartridges may cost four to five times as much as comparable full metal jacketed 9mm cartridges.

Bullet Energy

The bullet energy or "projectile energy" is the kinetic energy of a bullet, usually referred to simply as "energy," is a computed number, expressed in foot-pounds, or simply "pounds." The amount of energy that a bullet delivers to the target is the "terminal energy." The terminal energy of a particular bullet depends upon the weight of the bullet and the velocity at which it impacts the target. The caliber of a bullet is immaterial in calculating energy.

Energy is a measure of the amount of "work" a bullet can deliver. The energy of a fired bullet is constantly decreasing as the bullet slows down in its flight to the target. The energy is highest as the bullet leaves the muzzle upon firing, and immediately begins decreasing.

Most cartridge manufacturers publish energy levels of various factory cartridges at selected distances from the muzzle for comparison and analysis purposes. Readers should take the published energy quotations only as a general guide for comparison purposes, especially those from different manufacturers. Figures cited by manufacturers may also become outdated after that manufacturer changes the gunpowder formula. Actual performance of a bullet will likely vary significantly when fired in firearms different from that used by the manufacturer to compile their velocity/energy tables.

Bullet energy is often used as one means to compare bullet effectiveness. There are many factors to consider when selecting an appropriate bullet or cartridge for a specific intended use, but the calculated energy of a bullet is one common factor.

Sectional Density of a Bullet

The sectional density of a bullet is a number computed by dividing a bullet's weight by its diameter, and then squaring that result. Translated, heavy slender bullets will have higher sectional densities, and lighter fatter bullets will have lower sectional densities. Bullet shape and internal construction of the bullet do not affect sectional density.

The higher the sectional density, the better the bullet will penetrate a target, other things held equal. An appropriate sectional density for medium game animals might be .235, and .280 for large game animals.

Generally, the sectional density of a particular bullet is obtained from the manufacturer or in a cartridge reloader's manual. This is a relative obscure characterization, and is typically not printed on cartridge boxes.

Ballistic Coefficient of a Bullet

The ballistic coefficient of a bullet is a measurement, expressed in a decimal form, of the ability of a bullet to maintain its velocity during flight. It is a measurement of the streamlining of a particular bullet shape. The ballistic coefficient, stated differently, is a measurement of air drag on a bullet in flight.

All other things held equal, bullets with a high ballistic coefficient will fly faster, have a flatter trajectory, and will hit the target harder, than bullets with a lower ballistic coefficient.

Ballistic coefficients become more important with longer range shooting.

Generally, the ballistic coefficient of a particular bullet is obtained from the manufacturer or in a cartridge reloader's manual. This is a relative obscure characterization, and is typically not printed on cartridge boxes.

Shell Casings

A shell casing is cylindrical cup-shaped metal container which holds gunpowder, has a primer fixed into the bottom, and is sealed at the top with a bullet. Shell casings are typically made of yellowish brass metal. Shell casings are often referred to as simply "brass," as in "Pick up your brass after firing." Some casings are made of nickel, or are nickel plated. Other casings, usually of lesser quality, are made of steel or aluminum.

Shell casings remain in a revolver after firing, and casings are ejected automatically after firing from a semiautomatic or automatic firearm. Spent casings are frequently discarded as trash, although reloading used brass is a thriving hobby.

There are different shell casing shapes. Straight casings are very cylindrical, where bottleneck casings are tapered or streamlined (wider at the bottom, narrower at the top).

It is believed by some that a firearm will make unique identifying marks upon a shell casing upon firing, thus creating a fingerprint of sorts. It is this theory which underlies programs in a very few States to compile a database of fired shell casings identified with particular firearms. The theory is that spent shell casings recovered at the scene of a crime could be compared with the database, and the firearm (and its owner) identified. There is no known instance as of 2005 where such a database resulted in identifying even one firearm used in a crime.

Every mainstream modern cartridge uses a metallic shell casing. Experiments are underway as of 2005 with "caseless" ammunition. Caseless ammunition involves various types of alternative technology to propel bullets from firearms. Investigation also exists regarding manufacture of a shell casing which burns up and disappears upon firing. These technologies have not been perfected, much less entered production, as of 2005.

Primers

The primer is installed in the base of a cartridge. The primer, when sharply struck on its base by the firing pin or striker of a firearm, will explode inside of the shell casing, igniting the gunpowder in the shell casing. A primer is thus a small explosive. Each cartridge has one primer. Primers are expended upon firing the cartridge, and must be replaced if the shell casing is to be reloaded.

There are two types of primers, the Boxer and Berdan types. These types are named after their inventors. Boxer primers are used in the United States, with Berdan used in Europe. An advantage of cartridges using Boxer primers is that they can be reloaded.

Primers generally come in two sizes, large and small. Primers also differ based on the type of firearm in which the cartridge will be used (i.e., pistol, rifle, rifle magnum, etc.).

Ammunition is sometimes described as "corrosive" or "non-corrosive." This particularly refers to the materials contained in the primer, such as potassium chlorate or metallic oxides. Corrosive ammunition will corrode and damage the inner barrel surfaces and other metal parts with which the corrosive material comes into contact. Corrosive ammunition is acceptable if the firearm is cleaned out in a certain way immediately after firing. Most people are well advised to avoid corrosive ammunition altogether. Most corrosive ammunition is manufactured outside of the United States. Most ammunition manufactured inside of the United States is non-corrosive. Some foreign ammunition is advertised as non-corrosive when, by United States standards, it is corrosive. Corrosive primers tend to be more reliable and resistant to harsh conditions, and may have a longer shelf life than non-corrosive primers. Primers sold for civilian use in the United States are almost entirely non-corrosive. Lead-free primers were introduced in the late 1990's, and seem to be a popular choice to reduce exposure of lead to the environment.

"Magic Bullets"

Advertising by cartridge manufacturers and gunwriters will often tout the latest "magic bullet." The capabilities of these magical bullets usually reach mythical proportions. These rounds are either the fastest, hardest-hitting, deadliest, most incapacitating, or most technologically advanced bullets available. A hit by one of these magic bullets anywhere on a target's body will always drop the target in his tracks. Magic bullets often have a ferocious or fierce tradename. Magic bullets are usually supported by a lavish marketing campaign. Magic bullets are often sold in upscale packages, with each bullet carefully nestled in excessive packing material. Magic bullets are usually marketed as self defense rounds, playing on a consumer's willingness to pay inflated prices to get the very best when his or her life is at stake.

Magic bullets should generally be avoided by the average person. There are many proven, widely available, and reasonably priced defensive rounds on the market.

There is another consideration concerning magic bullets. Prosecutors at a criminal trial, or Plaintiff's attorneys for the shooting victim, may attempt to "assassinate the character" of the person shooting in self defense. One way they might attempt character assassination is to assert that the shooter's use of such ferocious and fierce ammunition confirms that the shooter was not merely acting in self defense, but was an out of control maniacal gun nut gleefully hunting down the unfortunate armed burglar who broke into his home late one night.

Cartridges For Self Defense

Much ink has been spilled in firearms magazines discussing the best cartridges. This topic is a never-ending argument between fans of competing cartridges. The purpose of this section of this book is to give some practical advice to the average firearm owner who is not interested in exotic concepts or trivial differences between cartridges. This text assumes that the self defense firearm will be a handgun.

The best bullet for self defense is almost always, if not always, a hollow point. Do not use full metal jacketed bullets for self defense. This is a rarely disputed cardinal rule. The only time a full metal jacketed round is advisable is if a particular semiautomatic pistol will feed properly only with full metal jacketed ammunition. Some fans of the .45ACP round assert that the bullet is already wide enough to serve as a defensive round without the expansion characteristics of hollow point rounds.

The best selection is almost always a "jacketed hollow point" (i.e., "JHP") cartridge. There are other types of hollow points in existence, but JHP cartridges are likely all the average self defense firearm owner will need to use.

Use commercially manufactured ammunition, not handloaded ammunition. Use American-made ammunition for best quality and consistency. Stay away from exotic "magic bullet" ammunition discussed in the section above.

Choose an average weight bullet, not at the high or low end of available weights for the caliber of your firearm. Average weight is 115gr or 124gr for 9mm bullets, 155gr or 165gr in .40 caliber, and 185gr or 230gr in .45ACP caliber.

The average person would be advised to use standard pressure ammunition, and stay away from magnum, "+p" or "+p+" ammunition. This is over-pressure ammunition with a greater gunpowder charge propelling the bullet to a higher velocity. Many advocates recommend such hot ammunition in self defense loads, especially the .357 Magnum. However, for the typical untrained firearm owner who rarely practices with his or her firearm, who is likely to use the firearm in the dark defending a home containing other family members, it is best not to use such hot ammunition. Such a bullet can easily pass through several walls, even if it first passed through the home intruder, thereby endangering other family members. Over-pressure cartridges are best left to experienced and trained shooters. One exception is the .38 Special +p cartridge, which is not excessively over-powered because the standard .38 Special is relatively weak.

Choose a common caliber of ammunition, such as 9mm, .40, or .45ACP. Ammunition for these calibers is widely available. Make certain that you choose ammunition which your firearm was manufactured to shoot!

Choose a cartridge of or between .38 Special and .45 caliber in size. Calibers of .380ACP and lower are too weak, and anything larger than .45 is overkill. The major calibers in this range are .38 Special, .40, .45ACP, and 9mm. The .40 caliber round is more correctly known as the .40 Smith and Wesson, or the .40S&W. The

.38 Special is a round for revolvers, where the other three cartridges are primarily found in semiautomatics.

Test-fire your self defense firearm with your ammunition of choice to ensure that ammunition will feed properly with your particular firearm. Some semiautomatic pistols show a preference for some ammunition brands over others.

Practice with the ammunition of your choice, so that you become familiar with how it performs. Specifically, you must get familiar with the level of recoil it produces, the light level of its flash, and its sound, upon firing it from your firearm. It is important to determine the typical point of impact on the target of your choice of ammunition as fired from your particular firearm. It is not uncommon for some brands of cartridges to consistently hit high, low, left, or right of the point of aim, while other brands perform differently. Practice builds critical firearms skills, and is a way to use older ammunition being replaced with fresh ammunition.

Knowing that this will ignite the usual debate, a cartridge of 9mm caliber, with jacketed hollow point bullet design, in 115gr or 124gr bullet weight, of American manufacture, and of standard pressure design, is the recommended self defense cartridge for handguns to be used by the average firearm owner. Ammunition for 9mm is widely available anywhere ammunition is sold and the cost per cartridge is extremely low. This caliber is very accurate with a flat trajectory. There are dozens if not hundreds of models of firearms made which chamber this caliber. The ammunition is relatively light, a factor when carrying a concealed firearm. Recoil from firing the 9mm is relatively light compared to the .40 and .45ACP rounds. The typical 9mm handgun magazine will hold more cartridges than .40 or .45ACP handguns, a factor for very many concealed firearms carriers who do not carry spare magazines for reloads. The smaller dimensions and lower pressure generated by 9mm rounds upon firing are such that the typical 9mm firearm weighs less than a .45ACP handgun, a factor for someone carrying the firearm all day.

Handloaded Cartridges

Cartridges generally come in two types: those manufactured by a factory or commercial manufacturer, and those assembled privately by someone possessing their own equipment to assemble cartridges.

Factory ammunition can either be manufactured entirely from new components, or with all new components except for using previously-fired brass. Factory ammunition is usually always manufactured for sale to the military or retail sale to the public.

Individual persons possessing their own reloading equipment can assemble their own ammunition. This is called "handloading" or "reloading." Reloading is the hobby of acquiring components (bags of bullets, boxes of primers, jugs of gunpowder, etc.) and assembling custom made cartridges. Reloaders do this for various reasons, such as cost savings, to obtain loadings not commercially available, or simply for the intrinsic enjoyment of a hobby. Rarely do reloaders assemble cartridges for commercial sale. The quality of the reloading, and the proper matching of the components, varies widely according to the skill, attentiveness, and equipment quality of the handloader.

The average person is strongly advised to use only factory ammunition.

Proper Storage of Ammunition

There are certain rules which will make the storage of ammunition in the home or workplace safer, and will increase shelf-life of the ammunition. These rules are especially relevant to those with children in the home, for those with a significant supply of ammunition, or for those considering long term storage of ammunition. The rules are listed below in no particular order.

Store ammunition in a secure location. Store ammunition away from children. Store the ammunition in a hidden or locked location, to be safe from thieves.

Store ammunition away from firearms, unless the firearms and ammunition are in a locked gun safe. It is safer to store firearms and ammunition separately, because children who gain access to stored firearms will still need to find ammunition somewhere else.

Store ammunition in a cool place. Data suggests that 60 degrees is very good, and anything less than 72 degrees is acceptable, for long term storage. There seems to be a lack of hard data reasonably available on this subject, presumably because no one has conducted a test where ammunition was thoroughly evaluated, stored under exacting conditions for 30 years, and then re-tested.

Store ammunition in a dry place. A dry place means a place where ammunition is not exposed to standing or running water, but it also means low humidity. Excessive humidity can shorten the shelf life of ammunition. "Sealed" ammunition, such as much military spec ammunition, withstands high humidity better than non-sealed ammunition.

Store ammunition in a dark place. Sunlight, especially, breaks down ammunition.

Store ammunition away from flammables, such as pilot lights, home heaters, paint storage rooms, etc.

Use storage containers for long term storage. Opaque airtight plastic containers or surplus metal military ammunition boxes are good choices. These storage containers are durable, stackable, and keep out light and humidity.

Use desiccant pouches for long term storage. Desiccant pouches contain a substance which absorbs and holds humidity. The pouches can be placed into an airtight ammunition storage box for long term storage.

Mark your boxes of ammunition with the date of purchase, to enable rotation of ammunition. Use the oldest ammunition first. Rotation of ammunition keeps ammunition supplies as fresh as possible.

Prevent rapid temperature swings in the ammunition storage area. Rapid temperature swings seem to accelerate deterioration of gunpowder.

Purchase "sealed" ammunition if ammunition supplies will be stored for an extended period of time. Sealed ammunition has been sealed at the primer area and where the bullet is inserted into the shell casing. Sealing ammunition primarily protects gunpowder from being contaminated by moisture and water intrusion into the shell casing.

Hard data is again scarce, but properly stored modern ammunition is said to have a shelf life of "indefinite" or "in excess of thirty years." Few people expect to test the accuracy of that conclusion except perhaps the military or survivalists. However, proper storage and rotation of ammunition should maximize ammunition performance while increasing safety around the storage area.

Gunpowder and Propellant

Gunpowder was invented by the Chinese in about 800 A.D. Gunpowder, a mixture of sulfur, charcoal, and potassium or sodium nitrate, was used in all firearms and cannon for centuries, until smokeless powder was invented in 1886. Gunpowder is still used today in antique firearms. Gunpowder is also called "black powder."

The burning of black powder upon discharging a firearm produces a large amount of thick smoke. A large smoke cloud is a major disadvantage in a military situation because it reveals the firing position and obscures vision for following shots. Another disadvantage is that black powder is highly corrosive to metal firearm parts. Another disadvantage is that burning black powder leaves a great amount of

68

soot and residue inside the firearm after firing, not conducive to smooth functioning of semiautomatic or automatic firearms.

The first type of smokeless powder was introduced in 1886, followed by other competing types. Smokeless powder has no black powder as a component. Burning smokeless powder produces mainly gases, resulting in little or no gun smoke or corrosive sooty residue. Smokeless powder is more powerful than an equivalent weight of black powder, allowing increased bullet velocities, range, and accuracy.

Many varieties of smokeless powder are available. All modern firearm ammunition uses smokeless powder except for a very small number of hobbyist firearms manufactured to use black powder or its substitutes.

Many people refer to modern smokeless powder as "gunpowder." Some firearms enthusiasts refer to smokeless powder as "propellant."

Most readers of this book will never see any gunpowder because cartridges are sold as sealed units. Most readers will never inquire about or learn what type of powder is loaded into cartridges they use. The only factor relevant or accessible to most firearms owners concerning gunpowder charge will be the various *bullet velocities* of cartridges available for their caliber firearm. Altering the quantity or manufacturing design of the gunpowder usually affects bullet velocity and accuracy, recoil force, and cartridge price.

What is Law?

Law on any particular subject is established from various sources, described below. There is no one place where the law on firearms, or most other subjects, can be found.

Firearms law is heavily regulated at the State and federal level, with many statutes and court cases. Federal firearms law is generally concerned with rights to possess and sell firearms. State firearms law is more concerned with rules of carrying, concealment, and use of firearms.

Sources of Law

Federal Constitution.   The United States Constitution is a type of federal law. The federal constitution generally overrides all other conflicting law; it is the "law of the land." The federal constitutional provision most relevant to firearms is the Second Amendment to the Bill of Rights, which grants the right to keep and bear arms.

Federal Statutes.   Federal statutes are one type of federal law. Federal statutes are printed laws enacted by the United States Congress. Federal statutes are called the "United States Code," or "USC." Federal statutes generally override conflicting State statutes. Statutes are also called "black letter law" because the statutes are organized and printed into statute books.

Federal Caselaw.   Federal caselaw is the written record of actual federal court cases. Caselaw is important. Caselaw interprets federal statutes so that their meaning can become clearer. Many cases seem to "make new law." Cases bridge the gap between statutes. Some cases limit the effect or reach of statutes. Courts may, by caselaw, invalidate part or all of a statute by finding it unconstitutional. Proper interpretation of a statute includes review of cases involving that statute.

State Constitution.   North Carolina has a State constitution.   The State constitution generally overrides State statutes. Federal law and the United States constitution generally override conflicting provisions of the State constitution.

State Statutes.   State statutes are one type of State law. State statutes are printed laws enacted by the State legislature. North Carolina's state statutes are called the "North Carolina General Statutes," or "NCGS." Federal statutes will generally override conflicting State statutes. Statutes are also called "black letter law" because the statutes are organized and printed into statute books. State statutes are also called "statutory law." There is a small body of North Carolina law called "local laws" which are statutes enacted by the legislature which have not been codified into the North Carolina General Statutes. This is discussed more in detail below.

State Caselaw.   State caselaw is the written record of actual State court cases. Caselaw is important. Caselaw interprets State statutes so that their meaning can become clearer. Cases bridge the gap between statutes of similar topics. Some cases limit the effect or reach of statutes. Courts may, by caselaw, invalidate part or all of a statute by finding the statute unconstitutional. Some cases impose procedural rules as to how a statute can be applied. Some cases overrule or modify rulings made in prior cases. Proper interpretation of a statute should always include review of all cases involving that statute. Some cases seem so distant from existing statutes that they seem to "make new law," which caselaw is sometimes called "judge-made law."

Common Law.   Common law is the common custom or practice of society over a long period of time, which customs and practices matured into enforceable law. English common law generally extended to other societies through the English colonies, including the United States. Common law provides an immense body of law on numerous subjects. Many common law principles have been expressly adopted as State statutes called "codified" common law. Common law, if not contradicted by State statute, etc., remains valid law. Statutes override conflicting common law. NCGS 4-1.

County Ordinances.   County ordinances are laws enacted at county level. County ordinances are generally valid only in the county where they were enacted.

City Ordinances.   City ordinances are laws enacted at the city or town level. City ordinances are generally valid only in the city where enacted.

Attorney General Opinions.   Certain law enforcement officers and elected officials may ask the North Carolina Attorney General to issue a legal opinion on a specified question of law. Many Attorney General opinions are published. Some opinions involve application of firearms law. These opinions may not have the force of law, but they probably will guide actions taken by government officials in relevant situations, and may carry persuasive value before a court.

Penalties For Violating the Law

There are two general types of laws: criminal and civil laws. These two types of laws are discussed below.

Criminal Laws

Criminal penalties generally involve possible confinement in jail or prison. Some criminal laws involve payment of a money fine. Many firearms laws provide criminal penalties for violating the law. Most criminal statutes specify the seriousness of the criminal penalty, expressed as some level of misdemeanor or felony. Misdemeanors are less serious than felonies. Some criminal acts have a civil law version, such as assault. Prosecution for violation of criminal laws is performed by the government, such as by the District Attorney's Office. The victim of the crime, if there was one, is only a witness in the prosecution. The decision about whether to prosecute the case is generally up to the District Attorney's office, not the victim of the crime. Trials and court activity for criminal law violations are brought in criminal court, following criminal procedural rules.

Misdemeanors.   Misdemeanors are defined as less serious crimes which do not rise to being a felony, and which are punishable by a term of imprisonment of one year or less.

Felonies.   Felonies are usually defined as serious crimes punishable by a maximum term of imprisonment in excess of one year. Also see NCGS 14-1.

Civil Laws

Civil laws generally involve penalties resulting in payment of money damages to the victim of the wrong. Civil cases are brought in civil court using rules of civil procedure. The victim is the person bringing the case and managing its progress, not the State or the District Attorney's office. Penalties do not involve jail time. There are no specific dollar amounts or limits set by each statute for violation of that statute, like criminal statutes. The damage award is usually based on a dollar estimate of the damages suffered by the victim. Judgment for a monetary award, if paid, is paid to the victim. The victim must generally hire an attorney to conduct the case because a government-paid District Attorney is not involved to prosecute the case.

Double Jeopardy

A person who violates a firearms law may suffer two types of penalties for the same act. The act may violate a criminal law, and the State may prosecute the violator under that particular law, seeking fines or imprisonment authorized by that statute.

The act may violate both State and federal criminal law, and the perpetrator may be prosecuted under both laws without being placed in double jeopardy.

73

The violation may give rise to civil damages, and the victim may sue the violator in civil court for a judgment for money damages against the violator. This is not "double jeopardy" under State or federal law.

Priorities Among Conflicting Laws

Higher laws generally override lower laws. For example, federal laws generally override conflicting State laws. The sources of law described above are listed in order of their precedence or priority.

This book is about North Carolina firearms law. Readers must be aware that federal law may impose additional restrictions upon the purchase, ownership, carry, transport, or possession of a firearm or ammunition. Federal law may preempt State law in some areas. Federal law may rarely contradict State law. Federal law may change on a schedule different from when State laws are updated. A firearm owner, to fully understand the totality of laws affecting firearms in North Carolina, in addition to studying this book on North Carolina firearms law, must study a similar text on federal firearms law.

Some law-making government bodies (say, a State legislature), may "preempt" an area of law to itself. Preemption means that the government body is reserving to itself the right to make laws on that particular subject, such that a subordinate government body (say, a County) would not be permitted to make ordinances on that subject. There are many examples of preemption in firearms law, as governments struggle to create some uniformity and acceptability in a hotly contested legal field.

North Carolina Firearms Law in General

North Carolina is generally a pro-firearm rights State. This is demonstrated by the fact that North Carolina has the following:

- a constitutional right to keep and bear arms
- an interpretation of the right to bear arms as an individual personal right
- a concealed handgun permit law
- a "shall issue" concealed handgun permit procedure
- an energetic stance on reciprocity of concealed handgun permits
- special protections for shooting ranges
- a law requiring State-wide uniformity of firearms laws
- a law prohibiting singling out gun shows for burdensome restrictions
- much rural acreage, where firearms are more useful and tolerated
- a rich military heritage, where firearms are more of a part of society
- an active hunting population, Wildlife Commission, and hunting areas
- a relatively conservative and Bible-Belt political outlook typical of
      the southern United States, which is usually pro-firearm rights.

North Carolina's position as a pro-firearm rights State is also demonstrated by the lack of the following in North Carolina:

- a ban on so-called assault weapons
- bans on "high capacity" magazines
- experimentation with novel laws to restrict firearms
- firearms registration
- firearm owner's identification cards
- large urban areas (where calls for gun restrictions seem most prevalent).

North Carolina's firearms laws are rarely political campaign issues and generate little publicity. There is no activity to make drastic changes in State firearms law. This contrasts with other States and cities where firearms laws are hotly debated, usually motivated by groups trying to increase prohibitions on firearms.

North Carolina courts and citizens as a general rule accept the right to keep and bear firearms, and to primarily hold the *individual* who used a firearm in committing a crime *personally accountable* for their misdeeds. This is in contrast to some other States which do not trust their citizens to possess firearms, or which would rather hold firearm or ammunition *manufacturers* responsible for the acts of criminals. That difference in approaches to resolve the problem of criminals using firearms to commit crime is a hot topic in firearms law nationally.

75

Firearms Law of North Carolina
www.ncfirearmslaw.com

Top Ten Topics Summarized

Most, if not all, of the various statutes on a given topic are scattered in separate places among unrelated statutes. Statutes on the same topic, even when grouped together, can be difficult to understand as a cohesive concept because they are fragmented into consecutive parts.

Some topics are known to be the source of greatest inquiry and interest by firearms owners, concealed weapons carriers, firearms purchasers, and parents with firearms and children in the home.

Some readers want to limit or start their understanding of a given topic with a general overview or summary of the topic.

Therefore, with these issues in mind, the top ten topics regarding firearms and North Carolina state law are summarized below.

The topic summaries below are necessarily general in scope. It is very much recommended, after the general overview is understood, that a reader review the detailed information presented in the following relevant chapters in this book.

Purchasing a Firearm

North Carolina law requires that a prospective purchaser of a handgun obtain a permit from the local Sheriff before obtaining the handgun. There is no such State requirement to obtain a permit before purchasing a rifle or shotgun. There will still be a background search when a rifle or shotgun is purchased, but the requirement for that is based in federal law, not State law. The requirement of obtaining a permit before purchasing a handgun is waived for holders of concealed handgun permits. The rationale of this waiver is that, since concealed handgun permit holders have already been thoroughly investigated in connection with approving their concealed handgun permit application, little would be gained by conducting the more cursory investigation for a pistol purchase permit. The Sheriff will conduct a background search on the applicant for a pistol purchase permit before issuing an approval or rejection.

Statutes: 14-402 (Sale of certain weapons without permit forbidden)
14-403 (Gun purchase permit issued by Sheriff; form of permit)
14-404 (Issuance or refusal of permit; appeal; etc.)

Storage of Firearms

North Carolina does not have a general law which requires any sort of storage of firearms, safe storage or otherwise. There is no general requirement that firearms be locked up when in storage. There is no requirement that ammunition be stored separately from firearms. The lack of a State law on these subjects does not preclude the use of common sense and an appreciation for security of valuable and dangerous items by firearms owners.

There is a statute requiring parents to safeguard firearms stored in the home where minor children reside. Various statutes give governments the right to impose storage requirements during emergencies. A firearm owner may have liability for improper storage under the tort of negligent storage, but none of the cases confirming the existence of this tort are from North Carolina.

Statutes: 14-315.1 (Storage of firearms to protect minors)

Transporting Firearms

Firearms cannot be transported concealed, unless the person transporting the firearms carries a concealed weapons permit, and that only applies to handguns. Exceptions exist for police, soldiers, etc.

Concealed handgun permit holders may transport concealed handguns under the concealed handgun permit law.

Transporting firearms is restricted in areas of emergency, riots, and civil disorder, as discussed below.

There are places where firearms cannot generally be legally transported, such as school grounds, banks, courtrooms, etc.

Firearms can generally be transported in an open and obvious manner in places not off-limits. Carrying firearms in the open avoids the concealed firearm restrictions, important to someone who does not possess a concealed carry license.

However, carrying firearms in an open and obvious manner creates the possibility that the firearms carrier will be accused of brandishing a firearm, or that the public will be unduly alarmed, or that a passing police officer will detain and investigate the firearms carrier.

Statutes: There is no express State statute on where a firearm *can* be carried, only very many statutes on where a firearm *cannot* be carried.

Children and Firearms

There are various State laws on firearms and children. Parents may be liable for injuries or damage their children cause with a firearm at school. Firearms are generally prohibited on school grounds. It is a misdemeanor for a minor to possess or carry a firearm, except when supervised by an adult, or in certain other situations. It is a felony to sell or give a firearm to a minor, except under certain circumstances. Generally speaking, it is illegal for a parent to leave a firearm in the home unsecured where a minor child obtains the firearm and causes injury, brandishes the firearm, or commits a crime. A certain warning about leaving unsecured firearms accessible to children in the home must be given to the purchaser of any firearm, and must be posted by retail sellers of firearms. It is illegal for any parent to allow a child under age 12 to have possession of or use a firearm, except when being supervised by that parent.

Statutes: 1-538.3 (Negligent supervision of a minor for injuries/damages at school)
14-269.2 (Firearms on campus or school grounds)
14-269.7 (Prohibitions on handguns for minors)
14-315 (Selling or giving weapons to minors)
14-315.1 (Storage of firearms to protect minors)
14-315.2 (Warning upon sale or transfer of firearm to protect minors)
14-316 (Permitting young children to use dangerous firearms)

Concealed Carry of Firearms

Carrying concealed firearms in North Carolina is generally prohibited, and is otherwise heavily restricted. Anyone intending to carry a concealed firearm is well advised to read the relevant text of this book several times.

The general rule is that carrying concealed firearms is prohibited except for police, military personnel, holders of concealed firearms permits who are carrying a handgun, and persons while on their own premises.

There are numerous places where concealed handgun permits are not valid to authorize the carry of concealed handguns. Examples are banks, courthouses, and schools.

There are certain times when concealed firearms cannot be carried, even if the carrier is otherwise entitled to carry a concealed firearm. Examples are when the carrier is drinking alcoholic beverages or taking illegal drugs, when such alcohol or drugs remain in his or her system, or when the carrier does not have his or her concealed weapons permit and personal identification in their possession.

Applicants may apply for a concealed weapons permit from the local Sheriff. There is an application, background search, fingerprints, and approval/rejection process. North Carolina is a "shall issue" State, meaning that the Sheriff's discretion is limited and the Sheriff must issue a permit if the applicant qualifies. Permits expire in five years from date of issuance, unless revoked or suspended earlier.

North Carolina has entered into reciprocity agreements with a number of other States, such that concealed weapons permits from those States are honored in North Carolina, and vice versa.

Concealed weapons permits in North Carolina are more correctly termed as "concealed *handgun* permits." The permit does not allow the concealed carry of any weapons or firearms other than handguns.

Article 54B of Chapter 14 of the North Carolina statutes is where most of the concealed weapon permit statutes are collected, specifically NCGS 14-415.10 through 14-415.24. NCGS 14-269 is also a significant relevant statute, being the general prohibition against carrying concealed firearms.

Statutes: 14-269 (Carrying concealed weapons)
      14-415.10 (Definitions)
      14-415.11 (Permit to carry concealed handgun)
      14-415.12 (Criteria to qualify for a concealed handgun permit)
      14-415.13 (Application)
      14-415.15 (Issuance or denial of a permit)
      14-415.16 (Renewal of a permit)
      14-415.18 (Revocation of permit)
      14-415.24 (Reciprocity of permit with other States)

Use of a Firearm in Self-Defense in and About the Home

Prior to 1994, there was one rule for defending against an intruder already in the home, and a different rule for defending against an intruder trying to get inside the home. That two-rule scenario changed in 1994 with the enacting of NCGS 14-51.1, which created one rule covering both situations. This statute, summarized, states:

> An occupant of a residence may use any degree of force, including deadly force, that the occupant reasonably believes is

necessary against an intruder to prevent forcible entry into the home or residence, or to terminate the intruder's entry, if the occupant reasonably believes that the intruder: 1) may kill or inflict serious bodily harm to the occupant or others in the home, or 2) intends to commit a felony in the home. An occupant in the residence has no duty to retreat from an intruder.

Statutes: 14-51.1 (Use of deadly force against an intruder)

Use of a Firearm in Self-Defense In a Place Outside of the Home

NCGS 14-51.1 is a statute expressly governing home invasions, and use of a firearm to defend oneself from an attack in and about the home. There is no comparable statute expressly covering situations involving self-defense in places other than the home.

There is, however, the common law which addresses the subject. Various subjects governed by the common law are discussed following the sections on the State statutes.

A statement by the courts on the general right of self defense is as follows:

> "The right to act in self-defense rests upon necessity, real or apparent, and a person may use such force as is necessary or apparently necessary to save himself from death or great bodily harm in the lawful exercise of his right of self-defense. A person may exercise such force if he believes it to be necessary and has reasonable grounds for such belief. The reasonableness of his belief is to be determined by the jury from the facts and circumstances as they appeared to the accused at the time. However, the right of self-defense is only available to a person who is without fault, and if a person voluntarily, that is aggressively and willingly, enters into a fight, he cannot invoke the doctrine of self-defense unless he first abandons the fight, withdraws from it and gives notice to his adversary that he has done so."

The courts converted this general statement into a list of elements, as:

> "It is well settled that perfect self-defense which excuses a killing altogether arises where, at the time of the killing:

(1) it appeared to defendant and he believed it to be necessary to kill the deceased in order to save himself from death or great bodily harm; and

(2) defendant's belief was reasonable in that the circumstances as they appeared to him at the time were sufficient to create such a belief in the mind of a person of ordinary firmness; and

(3) defendant was not the aggressor in bringing on the affray, i.e., he did not aggressively and willingly enter into the fight without legal excuse or provocation; and

(4) defendant did not use excessive force, i.e., did not use more force than was necessary or reasonably appeared to him to be necessary under the circumstances to protect himself from death or great bodily harm."

The "perfect" defense stated above excuses the killing altogether if all four elements are satisfied. A perfect defense would result in the dropping of criminal charges, a finding of "not guilty" on criminal charges, or a finding of "no liability" in a civil lawsuit.

If some, but not all, of the elements exist, then the person using the firearm in self defense has an "imperfect" defense. An imperfect defense may not cause all criminal charges to be dropped and may not result in a finding of "not guilty" on those criminal charges, but the imperfect defense may result in a *lessening* of the charges made against the person using a firearm in self defense. The effect of an imperfect defense in a civil case depends upon the claims brought against the person using a firearm in self defense.

The common law on this subject is discussed in more detail in the section on the common law.

The comments on self defense in NCGS 14-32 are also relevant. A Defendant may defend himself by assaulting a person with intent to kill only if such force was necessary or reasonably appeared to him to be necessary under the circumstances to protect himself from death or great bodily harm. Likewise, the Defendant may be absolved from liability for the assault with intent to kill only if he acted in self-defense when he was in actual or apparent danger of suffering death or great bodily harm. To repel a felonious assault, a Defendant may employ deadly force in his defense, but only if it reasonably appears necessary to protect himself against death or great bodily harm. See NCGS 14-32 for more detail.

Civil Disorders, Riots, Emergencies

There are a dozen statutes referring to the power of government to impose restrictions or prohibitions on the use, possession, sale, transport, and storage of firearms during emergencies, riot, or civil disorder. Some of these statutes are not current restrictions in that they authorize the government to impose restrictions of some type if and when an emergency occurs. Otherwise, it is illegal for anyone to transport a firearm off of their premises during a riot or other emergency.

Statutes: 14-288.1 (Definitions for Article 36A, Riots and Civil Disorders)
14-288.7 (Transporting firearms during emergency; possession)
14-288.9 (Assault on emergency personnel)
14-288.10 (Frisk of persons during violent disorders)
14-288.11 (Warrants to inspect vehicles in riot areas or
during emergencies)
14-288.12 (Powers of cities to enact ordinances to deal with emergencies)
14-288.13 (Powers of counties to enact ordinances to deal
with emergencies)
14-288.14 (Power of county to extend restrictions imposed by a city)
14-288.15 (Authority of Governor to exercise control in an emergency)
14-288.16 (Effective time of emergency proclamations, ordinances, etc.)
14-288.17 (City and county ordinances may be immediately effective)
147-33.2 (Emergency war powers of the Governor)

Weapons of Mass Death and Destruction

It is generally illegal to own, possess, sell, transport, store, or manufacture weapons of mass death and destruction. Firearms which are weapons of mass death and destruction are sawed-off shotguns, rifles with a barrel less than sixteen inches long, large-bore firearms, and fully automatic firearms. There are exceptions, and certain authorized persons may own, possess, sell, etc., such firearms. Such firearms are heavily regulated by federal law.

Statutes: 14-288.8 (Possession, sale, etc., of weapons of mass death and destruction)
14-409 (Machine guns)

Firearms Law of North Carolina
www.ncfirearmslaw.com

Assault Rifles

North Carolina statutes do not define "assault weapon" or "assault rifle," as do some other jurisdictions or the defunct federal Assault Weapons Ban statute. North Carolina does not therefore ban or restrict such firearms. North Carolina heavily restricts fully automatic firearms, the primary feature of an assault weapon. North Carolina does not restrict features that some other jurisdictions define to be a feature of assault rifles, such as bayonet lugs, pistol grips, flash suppressors, or magazine capacity.

Statutes: None specific.

North Carolina Constitution

Old Constitutional Law

Article 17 of the North Carolina Constitution enacted in 1776 contained a right to bear arms, reading as follows:

> "That the people have a right to bear arms, for the defense of the State; and as standing armies, in time of peace, are dangerous to liberty, they ought not to be kept up; and that the military should be kept under strict subordination to, and governed by, the civil power."

The North Carolina Supreme Court in State v. Huntly, 25 N.C. 418 (NC 1843), interpreted the State constitutional provision as giving the right to individuals to bear arms. The Huntly case concerned someone who was accused of carrying firearms to the terror of the public. The court held that:

> "It is to be remembered that the carrying of a gun per se constitutes no offense. For any lawful purpose—either of business or amusement—the citizen is at perfect liberty to carry his gun. It is the wicked purpose—and the mischievous result—which essentially constitute the crime."

Huntly was the only major case to interpret the original State constitutional right to bear arms. Huntly was clear that North Carolina's Constitution granted to individuals the right to keep and bear firearms.

Modern Constitutional Law

North Carolina made significant changes in the State Constitution in 1868, just after the Civil War. Section 30 of Article I of the North Carolina Constitution became the State constitutional provision on the right to bear arms. Section 30 is modeled on the Second Amendment to the United States Constitution. Section 30 states:

> "A well regulated militia being necessary to the security of a free State, the right of the people to keep and bear arms shall not be infringed; and, as standing armies in times of peace are dangerous to liberty, they shall not be maintained, and the military shall be kept under strict subordination to, and governed by, the civil power. Nothing herein shall justify the practice of carrying

85

concealed weapons, or prevent the General Assembly from enacting penal statutes against that practice."

The first sentence of Section 30 was adopted by North Carolina in 1868. The second sentence concerning concealed weapons was adopted in 1875. Section 30 has not changed since 1875.

Section 30 of the State Constitution does not expressly make the right to keep and bear arms a right of *individual* citizens. The State constitutional provision, like the federal Second Amendment upon which it is based, appears on its face to grant the right to the people *collectively* to keep arms, for the purposes of a *militia*. Many academic discussions, hot political debates, and impassioned social pleas have centered on whether the federal Second Amendment grants the right to bear arms to citizens *individually*, or to the people *collectively*.

There is little practical difference between the old and new State constitutional provisions. The North Carolina Supreme Court held that: "Insofar as they affect an individual's right to carry arms, we perceive no difference in the constitutional provision of 1776 and our present constitution." State v. Dawson, 159 S.E.2d 1 (NC 1968)

There are only a few key cases dealing directly with Section 30 of the State Constitution.

State v. Speller, 86 NC 697 (NC 1882), was a case which upheld the right of the State to enact concealed firearms restrictions. The case implied that a citizen's right to bear arms is not an unqualified right, but can be in some ways restricted by laws.

State v. Kerner, 107 S.E. 222 (NC 1921), is a key case. The Supreme Court extolled the "sacred right" of citizens to arm themselves. The court invalidated a county ordinance prohibiting the carrying of a firearm by an owner off the owner's premises, openly or concealed, without a permit obtained in advance from the local court. While the court affirmed the right of the legislature to enact *reasonable* laws regulating firearms, the ordinance at issue was *unreasonably broad* and so amounted to a prohibition. An important part of the Kerner decision was that the court recognized that *individual citizens* have the right to bear arms under Section 30 of the State constitution. The court construed "arms" to mean rifles, shotguns, and pistols.

The Kerner case stated that, while armies have developed modern artillery, airplanes, submarines, etc., that:

Firearms Law of North Carolina
www.ncfirearmslaw.com

"the ordinary private citizen, whose right to carry arms cannot be infringed upon, is not likely to purchase [artillery, airplanes, or submarines.] To him, the rifle, the musket, the shotgun, and the pistol are about the only arms which he could be expected to "bear," and his right to do this is that which is guaranteed by the Constitution. To deprive him of bearing any of these arms is to infringe upon the right guaranteed to him by the Constitution."

State v. Dawson, 159 S.E.2d 1 (NC 1968), was a case where a man was charged with violating the common law rule against going in public armed with firearms to the terror of the people. The Dawson court recognized that State courts have interpreted the State Constitution as guaranteeing the right for individual citizens to keep and bear arms. The court stated that such right was not absolute, but can be subject to regulation. Dawson provides good commentary on the State constitutional right to keep and bear arms.

The North Carolina Supreme Court in Dawson addressed the issue of the right of individual citizens under the State constitution to bear arms, stating that:

"while the purpose of the constitutional guaranty of the right to bear arms was to secure a well regulated militia and not an individual's right to have a weapon in order to exercise his common-law right of self-defense, this latter right was assumed. In any event, the guaranty made the militiaman's arms available to him for that purpose. North Carolina decisions have interpreted our Constitution as guaranteeing the right to bear arms to the people in a collective sense--similar to the concept of a militia-- and also to individuals."

State v. Fennell, 382 S.E.2d 231 (NC App 1989), is a North Carolina Court of Appeals case, and involved the carrying of a sawed-off shotgun, alleged to be a violation of North Carolina's "weapon of mass death and destruction" statute. The court stated that the North Carolina constitutional provision "has been interpreted to guarantee a broader right to individuals to keep and bear arms" than the federal Second Amendment.

The Fennell court also stated that governmental restrictions on the right to keep and bear arms "must be reasonable and not prohibitive, and must bear a fair relation to the preservation of the public peace and safety."

It has been asserted that the government may only regulate the "time, place, and manner" of carrying firearms, and could not outright ban a type of firearm. North

Carolina courts have held, however, that courts may regulate more than just the time, place, and manner in which a firearm is borne, owned, or carried. Fennell. North Carolina courts hold that certain sub-classes of firearms can be banned, such as pistols of certain small size (Kerner), or sawed-off shotguns (Fennell). "To exclude all pistols, however, is not a regulation, but a prohibition, of arms, which come under the designation of "arms" which the people are entitled to bear." Kerner and Fennell.

Fennell should be read with care, as it has been modified by subsequent court holdings, but not as to the general discussion cited above.

Commentary: Basis For the Right to Bear Arms

The basis for the federal (and, by extension, the State) constitutional right to bear arms was to provide the populace with an effective means of protecting their lives, liberty, and freedom from assault, whether the aggressor is a foreign power or their own government. Americans at the time of the Revolutionary War felt greatly oppressed by the British, our government at the time. Firearms in the hands of citizens was seen by the Founding Fathers of the United States as the means to prevent the yoke of oppression.

Therefore, the "arms" envisioned by the drafters of the constitutional right to bear arms certainly included arms adequate for combat against soldiers and other human oppressors.

Gun-control activists often condemn a certain firearm type as not being a hunting or sporting firearm, implying that if the firearm is not suitable for hunting, then it is not protected by the constitution. Some gun-control activists imply or state citizens have no valid or reasonable purpose to own a firearm not designed for hunting or sports.

The State constitutional right to bear arms says nothing about the right being oriented or limited to protecting the rights of hunters or target shooters. The constitutional provision was certainly not based on preserving hunter's rights. Limiting the criteria of "acceptable" firearms to those firearms suitable for hunting and sporting purposes misses the intent of the constitutional right to bear arms.

Conclusion

North Carolina constitutional law is clear and consistent that individual citizens have a limited right to keep and bear arms, but that this right is not absolute, and may be reasonably restricted in maintaining a balance between the right of

88

individual citizens to bear arms and the collective need to police dangerous firearms. This is important to North Carolinians since the federal Second Amendment has arguably been held by the United States Supreme Court *not* to grant a right to individual citizens to keep and bear arms. The North Carolina constitutional right is based in the right of citizens, both individually and collectively, to have a means to protect their life, liberty, and freedom, and is not limited to hunting and sporting purposes.

There is no one chapter or section of the North Carolina statutes where firearms law is centralized. Many statutes are scattered among many chapters. A reader will often have to review the law from various sections to get a full picture of State firearms law for any particular situation. Therefore, the following data is organized in order of statute number, lowest to highest.

Statutes may be cited below verbatim or may be paraphrased. Many statutes listed below are paraphrased because the actual text of many statutes is dense, hard to read, excessively wordy, or written in stilted legalese. If a reader determines that a statute is relevant to a particular situation, and the situation is important to the reader, the reader may consider obtaining the actual text of the statute for precise study.

Statutes are cited with the prefix "NCGS" which stands for North Carolina General Statutes. The general format is listing by chapter and then section, separated by a hyphen. For example, NCGS 1-538 is North Carolina General Statutes Chapter 1, Section 538.

Statutes are primarily enacted, modified, or repealed by the State legislature. The legislature meets in a Regular Session (or, the "Long Session") every odd-numbered year, usually from January to August. The legislature meets in a "Short Session" every even-numbered year, usually from May to August. The Short Session usually focuses on budget adjustments. Special sessions (called "Extra Sessions") may be held any time. NCGS 120-11.1; Art. 2, State Constitution. Firearms statutes may be enacted, modified, or repealed at any of these sessions. The Senate and the House of Representatives traditionally open and close their sessions on the same date, but that is not required.

Proposed laws are called "bills." Bills must be passed by both the Senate and the House of Representatives. Bills which are passed by both houses are called "ratified bills." Ratified bills are presented to the Governor.

If the Governor signs, or takes no action upon, the ratified bill within 10 days, the bill becomes law. If the Legislature has adjourned, the time period is 30 days. The Governor may instead veto the bill, whereupon the bill goes back to the Legislature. The Legislature can override the Governor's veto, and make the bill become law despite the veto, if a certain supermajority of legislators vote to make the bill a law.

Once the ratified bill becomes law, it is no longer a "bill." The new law is called a "session law," and is assigned a session law number for temporary identification purposes.

Most session laws are "public laws," which apply generally throughout North Carolina. Session laws which are public laws are inserted into the State Statutes in the proper place, and are assigned a statute number, which is the permanent identification. This assignment of a statute number is called "codification" or as being "codified."

Session laws which apply to only one county, or to a small number of counties, are called "local laws," and generally are not codified with a statute number. The session law number is the permanent identification number for most local laws. Local laws, not being codified, are relatively difficult to locate. Uncodified session laws are also unlikely to be well interpreted by published court cases. Some local laws may be codified with a statute number.

Caselaw

Selected caselaw involving the statutes appears immediately following each statute cited below, if cases are available. Various courts may issue case rulings, but the most common courts are the North Carolina Court of Appeals and the North Carolina Supreme Court. Cases cited are only "published" cases, which generally do not include trial court cases (District Courts or Superior Courts in the State courts system). All North Carolina published cases are therefore either the Court of Appeals or the Supreme Court. There are additional cases in these courts which are not published. Unpublished cases certainly exist, are generally unavailable to the public, and do not carry any controlling or persuasive authority to the public at large.

Cases are cited in common citation format, the case name first, the citation, the court, and the year of the case. For example, State v. Jones, 458 S.E.2d 876 (N.C. App 2004), cert.den., 463 S.E.2d 357 (NC 2005), is the case of State v. Jones, a case located at volume 458 of the Southeast Second Edition of published cases, on page 876, which case was decided by the North Carolina Court of Appeals in the year 2004. The "cert.den." means that there is an entry at volume 463 of the Southeast Second Edition, page 357, showing that the appeal to the North Carolina Supreme Court was denied in the year 2005. The citation is used to locate the case in caselaw book volumes. Many citations are cited below for legal points stated or court rulings given so that a reader can easily have a precise starting point to conduct detailed research on the point of law stated.

The Southeast Second Edition of reported cases is a series of hundreds of legal books usually available to the public only at law school libraries or some county law libraries. The cases are also available online through the Internet from a variety of sources. Access to these cases by the average citizen is very limited, and proper analysis of such cases generally requires a law degree.

NCGS 1-538.3 Negligent Supervision of a Minor Child (for Liability to a School)

a. A parent or legal guardian of an unemancipated minor child may be liable to an educational facility if the child committed a felony involving injury to persons or property with a firearm, the offense occurred on educational property, the parent/guardian knew or should have known of the child's likelihood to commit such act, the parent/guardian had the opportunity and ability to control the child, and the parent/guardian made no reasonable effort to restrain or supervise the child.

c. The educational facility may recover damages from the parent/guardian, up to $50,000, for a violation of this statute involving discharge of a firearm.

d. "Educational facility" under this statute is defined in NCGS 14-269.2(a)(1).

e. Nothing in this statute prohibits recovery of damages under any other theory of law.

Caselaw.   No relevant cases found.

Comments.   This statute makes parents liable for damages suffered by a school because their child caused injury or damage at school with a firearm. This presumably covers not only property damage to the school (small likely magnitude of damages), but also liability of the school to those persons injured or killed at school by the child with the firearm. If so, the $50,000 is a small cap to damages. Perhaps the intent is to serve simply as a deterrent to parents, rather than as an avenue to recover all likely damages.

This statute was enacted in 1999, presumably in response to the school shootings in Littleton, Colorado, on April 20, 1999, where two students killed 12 students and a teacher at Columbine High School before killing themselves.

NCGS 7B-1701(8) Preliminary Inquiry, Filing of Petition Under Juvenile Code

A juvenile court counselor, without further inquiry, shall authorize the filing of a petition against a juvenile if the counselor believes that the juvenile committed a felony involving a firearm.

Caselaw.   None relevant.

Comments.   None.

NCGS 7B-1903 Criteria for Secure or Unsecure Custody of a Juvenile

b.2.   A juvenile may be ordered into "secure custody" if the juvenile used, threatened to use, or displayed, a firearm when committing an offense.

Caselaw.   No relevant cases found.

Comments.   None.

NCGS 7B-2510 Conditions of Probation for a Juvenile

a.10.   A court may impose, as a condition of probation for a juvenile, that the juvenile possess no firearm.

Caselaw.   No relevant cases found.

Comments.   None.

Chapter 14 – Criminal Law

NCGS 14-1 Felonies and Misdemeanors Defined

A felony is a crime which was a felony at common law, is punishable by death, is punishable by imprisonment in State prison, or is named a felony by statute. All other crimes are misdemeanors.

NCGS 14-16.6 Assault on Executive, Legislative, or Court Officer

It is a felony to assault a legislative, executive, or court officer with a firearm.

Caselaw.   No relevant cases found.

Comments.   None.

NCGS 14-27.2 First Degree Rape

It is first degree rape to rape a female by employing or displaying a firearm, or an article which the victim reasonably believes is a firearm. First degree rape is a felony.

Caselaw.   It is not required that a firearm actually be used in any particular manner, only that the firearm be employed or displayed during the rape. State v. Langford, 354 S.E.2d 523 (NC 1987). It was previously required that the firearm had been used to force submission or overcome resistance of the female. State v. Powell, 295 S.E.2d 413 (NC 1982).

Employing a firearm during a rape may mean only that the rapist merely had the firearm in his possession at the time. State v. Langford, 354 S.E.2d 523 (NC 1987); State v. White, 401 S.E.2d 106 (NC App 1991), cert.den. 407 S.E.2d 852 (NC 1991).

Display of a fake firearm which the victim reasonably believed was a real firearm violates this statute. State v. McKinnon, 293 S.E.2d 118 (NC 1982).

An unloaded firearm which was not known to be unloaded by the victim is a violation of this statute. State v. Woodard, 404 S.E.2d 6 (NC App 1990), cert.den. 407 S.E.2d 550 (NC 1991).

Possession of a firearm by one rapist may be imputed to a co-rapist who did not actually possess a firearm. State v. Haywood, 550 S.E.2d 38 (NC App 2001), cert.den. 553 S.E.2d 206 (NC 2001).

Comments.   None.

NCGS 14-32 Felonious Assault With a Firearm

a. It is a felony to assault someone with a firearm with intent to kill, and inflict serious injury.

b. It is a felony to assault someone with a firearm and inflict serious injury.

c. It is a felony to assault someone with a firearm with intent to kill.

Caselaw.   A firearm is always defined as a deadly weapon. State v. McCree, 584 S.E.2d 861 (NC App 2003). State v. Parker, 171 S.E.2d 665 (NC App 1970).

It is not required that the "serious injury" actually be caused by the perpetrator's use of a firearm. State v. McCree, 584 S.E.2d 861 (NC App 2003).

Self-Defense. A Defendant may defend himself by assaulting a person with intent to kill only if such force was necessary or reasonably appeared to him to be necessary under the circumstances to protect himself from death or great bodily harm. Likewise, the Defendant may be absolved from liability for the assault with intent to kill only if he acted in self-defense when he was in actual or apparent danger of suffering death or great bodily harm. To repel a felonious assault, a Defendant may employ deadly force in his defense, but only if it reasonably appears necessary to protect himself against death or great bodily harm. State v. Hunter, 338 S.E.2d 99 (NC 1986). State v. Barnette, 174 S.E.2d 82 (NC App 1970). State v. Dial, 248 S.E.2d 366 (NC App 1978).

Regarding the decision as to when or how a judge or jury is to determine whether a Defendant acted "reasonably" in choosing to defend himself with a firearm, courts have held that "the reasonableness of the apprehension must be determined by the jury on the basis of all facts and circumstances as they appeared to defendant at the time of the shooting. Among the circumstances to be considered by the jury are the size, age and strength of defendant's assailant in relation to that of defendant; the fierceness or persistence of the assault upon defendant; whether the assailant had or appeared to have a weapon in his possession; and the reputation of the assailant for danger and violence." State v. Tann, 291 S.E.2d 824 (NC App 1982), following the Supreme Court in State v. Ellerbe, 28 S.E.2d 519 (NC 1944).

98

The Supreme Court has stated that "although a defendant need not submit in meekness to indignities or violence to his person because the affront does not threaten death or great bodily harm, he may not resort to the use of deadly force to protect himself from mere bodily harm or offensive physical contact. The use of deadly force to prevent harm other than death or great bodily harm is therefore excessive as a matter of law." State v. Hunter, 338 S.E.2d 99 (NC 1986).

Regarding self defense, the court in State v. Hunter, 338 S.E.2d 99 (NC 1986), stated that "a person is entitled under the law of self-defense to harm another only if he is without fault in provoking, or engaging in, or continuing a difficulty with another."

Merely because a Defendant feared an adversary, and that adversary occasionally abused the Defendant, and although the adversary had threatened the Defendant only 30 minutes prior, the Defendant could not assert mere apprehension of further abuse as a defense for shooting a shotgun at his adversary. The Defendant had to show that he reasonably believed it necessary to use the firearm to protect himself from death or great bodily injury. State v. Kinney, 375 S.E.2d 692 (NC App 1989).

A Defendant may show evidence to justify his use of a firearm that the adversary against whom he used a firearm was a dangerous and violent person, a "fighting man," or a man with a reputation for violence. State v. Tann, 291 S.E.2d 824 (NC App 1982).

The court in State v. Plemmons, 223 S.E.2d 549 (NC App 1976), following the Supreme Court in State v. Watkins, 196 S.E.2d 750 (NC 1973), stated that "the right of self-defense is available only to a person who is without fault, and if a person voluntarily, that is, aggressively and willingly, without legal provocation or excuse, enters into a fight, he cannot invoke the doctrine of self-defense unless he first abandons the fight and withdraws from it and gives notice to his adversary that he has done so."

Comments.   See NCGS 14-33.1 (former threats used as evidence of self-defense). See the section on the "Common Law" below for a discussion on the right and duty to defend others.

NCGS 14-32.1   Assaults on Handicapped Persons

It is a felony to use a firearm to commit an aggravated assault or assault and battery upon a handicapped person.

99

Caselaw. The perpetrator committing the assault must have known, or had reasonable grounds to know, that the victim was handicapped to be guilty under this statute. State v. Singletary, 594 S.E.2d 64 (NC App 2004), cert.den., 608 S.E.2d 65 (NC 2004).

Comments. This statute was most recently amended in 1994. This statute generally makes it a felony to assault a handicapped person.

NCGS 14-32.4   Assault Inflicting Serious Bodily Injury

Unless the conduct is covered by some other statute providing a greater punishment, it is a felony to assault someone and inflict serious bodily injury.

Serious bodily injury is defined as bodily injury which creates or causes a substantial risk of death, serious permanent disfigurement, coma, long term extreme pain, long term impairment of function of a bodily member, or prolonged hospitalization.

Caselaw. No firearms cases found.

Courts have held that "serious bodily injury, as set forth in NCGS 14-32.4, requires proof of more severe injury than the "serious injury" element of other assault offenses." State v. Williams, 563 S.E.2d 616 (NC App 2002); State v. Hannah, 563 S.E.2d 1 (NC App 2002).

Comments. This is not a firearms statute, strictly speaking. However, use of a firearm is one of the most likely methods by which the infliction of serious bodily injury is caused. This statute was enacted in 1996.

NCGS 14-33 Misdemeanor Assaults, Batteries, Affrays, Etc.

(c.1) and (d). It is a misdemeanor if, during an assault, assault and battery, or affray, a perpetrator uses a firearm, unless another statute provides greater punishment.

Caselaw. In State v. Messick, 363 S.E.2d 657 (NC App 1988), the defendant, who was sleeping in a white supremacist church one night, believed that he overheard people in a car stopped in front of the church commenting that they planned to firebomb the church. The defendant emerged from the church in camouflage fatigues with an AR-15 rifle and fired 29 rounds at the car, stating that he did so in an attempt to disable the car as it sped off. The defendant was found guilty of this statute.

Comments.   An affray is a noisy quarrel or brawl.

NCGS 14-33.1 Evidence of Former Threats on Self-Defense Pleas

In a case of alleged assault, battery, or affray in which the defendant asserts that the victim had made threats against the defendant at some time before the assault, those prior threats are evidence of the reasonableness of the claim of apprehension by the defendant of an attack by the victim. Such prior threats shall also be relevant evidence as to the amount of force which appeared reasonably necessary to the defendant under the circumstances to repel the victim's attack.

Caselaw.   The court in State v. Graves, 196 S.E.2d 582 (NC App 1973), stated that "by statute, evidence of threats is admissible in assault cases upon a plea of self-defense. Logically, under proper factual circumstances such evidence is admissible upon a plea of defense of others."

Comments.   This statute was enacted in 1969. An affray is a noisy quarrel or brawl.

NCGS 14-34 Assault by Pointing a Gun

It is a misdemeanor to point a firearm at any other person, whether in fun or otherwise, whether such firearm is loaded or unloaded.

Caselaw.   The firearm must have been pointed not by accident to violate this statute. State v. Evans, 253 S.E.2d 590 (NC App 1979).

The firearm must have been pointed without legal justification to violate this statute. State v. Spinks, 250 S.E.2d 90 (NC App 1979). "The pointing of a gun need only be done without legal justification to constitute assault under Section 14-34." In Re: J.A., 407 S.E.2d 873 (NC App 1991).

The Supreme Court stated that "if any person intentionally points a pistol at any person, this action is in violation of NCGS 14-34 and constitutes an assault. Moreover, such action, being in violation of the statute, is negligence *per se;* and if the pistol accidentally discharges, the injured person may recover damages for actionable negligence." Lowe v. Department of Motor Vehicles, 93 S.E.2d 448 (NC 1956).

Comments.   This statute dates from 1889 in its original form. It is perhaps an attempt to codify the common law tort of brandishing a firearm.

NCGS 14-34.1 Discharging a Firearm Into Occupied Property

a. It is a felony to willfully or wantonly discharge, or attempt to discharge, a firearm into an occupied building, structure, vehicle, aircraft, watercraft, or other conveyance or enclosure.

b. It is a felony to willfully or wantonly discharge a firearm into an occupied dwelling.

b. If the conveyance described in paragraph (a) above "is in operation" when fired into, the felony grade penalty is more severe.

c. A person violating this section who causes serious bodily injury to any person is guilty of a more severe grade of felony.

Caselaw.   Standing outside an enclosure or vehicle, and reaching into the enclosure with the firearm, and then discharging the firearm, violates this statute. State v. Mancuso, 364 S.E.2d 359 (NC 1988). The firearm itself may actually be inside of the building, vehicle, etc., when fired. State v. Alexander, 568 S.E.2d 317 (NC App 2002).

To violate this statute, the shooter must know, or reasonably believe, that the building or other enclosure is occupied when shooting into the enclosure. State v. Jones, 409 S.E.2d 322 (NC App 1991). The Supreme Court stated that "this Court interpreted the statute so as to add a knowledge requirement, as follows: We hold that a person is guilty of the felony created by NCGS 14-34.1 if he intentionally, without legal justification or excuse, discharges a firearm into an occupied building *with knowledge* that the building is then occupied by one or more persons or when he has reasonable grounds *to believe* that the building might be occupied by one or more persons." State v. James, 466 S.E.2d 710 (NC 1996) (italics added).

Each of multiple shots can constitute multiple violations of this statute. State v. Nobles, 515 S.E.2d 885 (NC 1999). State v. Rambert, 459 S.E.2d 510 (NC 1995).

Interpretation of this statute by the courts used to be that it was not a violation of this statute to unlawfully fire a bullet at an occupied automobile, but miss the car, and have the bullet strike an occupied house. State v. Watson, 311 S.E.2d 381 (NC App 1984). However, subsequent courts have held that under the "doctrine of transferred intent" an unlawful shooting which results in a stray bullet impacting into a dwelling could be a violation of this statute. State v. Hughes, 2002 App. Lexis 2482 (NC App 2002). In State v. Fletcher, 481 S.E.2d 418 (NC App 1997), rev.den., 487 S.E.2d 560 (NC 1997), cert.den., 139 L.Ed.2d 299 (U.S. 1997), the Defendant

102 _____

was chasing a woman he had just raped, shooting at her, and while shooting at the woman, hit a man's house several times. The Defendant was found guilty of shooting into an occupied dwelling. Fletcher does not mean that a bullet which was not fired illegally which goes astray and strikes a house is a violation of this statute.

It is enough to violate this statute that the Defendant intended to fire *at* the building, and it need not be shown that the Defendant intended to fire *into* the building. State v. Byrd, 510 S.E.2d 410 (NC App 1999).

Discharging a firearm from one apartment through a common wall into the adjoining apartment can be a violation of this statute. State v. Cockerham, 574 S.E.2d 694 (NC App 2003), rev.den., 580 S.E.2d 702 (NC 2003).

Discharging a firearm from the outside into two separate apartments located within the same apartment building is two separate violations of this statute. It is not "double jeopardy" to be charged twice for the same offense, once for each apartment. State v. Ray, 389 S.E.2d 422 (NC App 1990). State v. Rambert, 459 S.E.2d 510 (NC 1995).

Comments.   There are many cases under this statute, illustrating many situations. A reader should take care to survey the entire body of caselaw on this statute to determine the law in a particular situation.

This statute was amended in late 2005 to make penalties more severe and to broaden the acts needed to violate the statute. The strengthened statute, informally called "Rachel's Law," is a legislative response to the shooting of Rachel Sanchez, a young girl shot while traveling along a Catawba County road in 2003.

NCGS 14-34.2 Assault With a Firearm Upon Government, Company Police, or Campus Police Officer

It is a felony to use a firearm to assault an officer or employee of the State or any political subdivision of the State, a company police officer, or a campus police officer, when the officer is performing official duties, unless another law provides greater punishment.

Caselaw.   The person using the firearm must know, or should have known, at the time of shooting that the victim was a police officer in order to violate this statute. State v. Avery, 337 S.E.2d 786 (NC 1985).

A number of cases under this statute involve situations where a police officer allegedly used excessive force in making an arrest. Some cases present an issue, perhaps intentionally unanswered, in the following statement:

> "where there is evidence tending to show the use of such excessive force by the law officer, the trial court should instruct the jury that the assault by the defendant upon the law officer was justified or excused if the assault was limited to the use of reasonable force by the defendant in defending himself from that excessive force." State v. Mensch, 239 S.E.2d 297 (NC App 1977), cert.den., 241 S.E.2d 845 (NC 1978); State v. Burton, 423 S.E.2d 484 (NC App 1992).

The unanswered question is whether, if the police officer is using deadly force excessive for the situation, may a Defendant use a firearm against a police officer to defend himself? The court in State v. Irick, 231 S.E.2d 833 (NC 1977) discussed this issue at page 846, but seemed to avoid answering the question.

Comments.   None.

NCGS 14-34.3 Teflon-Coated Bullets Prohibited

a. It is illegal to import, manufacture, possess, store, transport, sell, offer to buy or sell, purchase, deliver, give to another, or acquire a teflon-coated bullet.

b. This statute does not apply to:

1. military personnel when acting pursuant to orders; federal civil officers while acting in their official duties; State, county, or municipal officers while acting in their official duties
2. licensed importers, manufacturers, and dealers who possess such bullets for the purpose of sale to authorized law enforcement agencies
3. inventors, scientists, and other technical personnel engaged in creation, development, or manufacture of body armor for police officers.

c. Violations of this statute are misdemeanors.

Caselaw.   No relevant cases found.

Comments.   Teflon bullets are bullets which have been coated with teflon. Teflon has an extremely high ability to reduce friction between moving parts. The primary purpose for teflon is to reduce friction in the gun barrel by the passage of the bullet down the bore. Reduced friction decreases gun barrel wear, and may increase bullet velocity. Researchers find that teflon coating helps reduce bullet ricochets and deflections upon impact on hard surfaces at oblique angles, such as windshields and automobile sheet metal. Teflon bullets thus offer two safety features relative to regular bullets, namely, that the reduced barrel friction reduces air pollution from bullet lead residue, and reduced ricochets and deflections. Teflon does not increase penetration of the target by the bullet. Teflon coating has been found to *decrease* the ability of bullets to penetrate body armor.

NCGS 14-34.5 Assault With a Firearm Upon a Law Enforcement, Probation, or Parole Officer, or Upon a Detention Facility Employee

It is a felony to assault a law enforcement officer, probation officer, parole officer, or detention facility officer, with a firearm while that officer is performing his or her duties.

Caselaw.   A drunk and boisterous man trespassing on church property being handcuffed by a police officer after refusing to leave the property seized the officer's pistol and fired at the officer before being subdued. The drunk man was found guilty of violating this statute. State v. Haynesworth, 553 S.E.2d 103 (NC App 2001).

Under this statute, "an assault is an overt act or attempt, with force and violence, to do some immediate physical injury to the person of another, which *show of force or violence* must be sufficient to put a person of reasonable firmness in fear of immediate physical injury. In proving the element of assault, the State does not have to show the defendant pointed a firearm at a law enforcement officer. Furthermore, to be guilty of this offense, the defendant must have known or had reasonable grounds to know that the victim was a law enforcement officer." State v. Dickens, 592 S.E.2d 567 (NC App 2004) (italics in original).

It is no defense under this statute that the Defendant was forgetful and hard of hearing, and had diminished mental capacity. State v. Childers, 572 S.E.2d 207 (NC App 2002), cert.den., 577 S.E.2d 899 (NC 2003).

Comments.   None.

NCGS 14-34.6 Assault Upon a Firefighter, Medic, or Emergency Room Medical Personnel

It is a felony to commit an assault or affray with a firearm on a firefighter, emergency medical technician, medical responder, or an emergency room nurse or physician.

Caselaw.   No relevant case found.

Comments.   This statute was enacted in 1995.

NCGS 14-34.7   Assault Inflicting Serious Injury on a Law Enforcement, Probation, or Parole Officer, or, an Employee of a State or Local Detention Facility

a. Unless some other statute provides for a greater punishment, it is a felony to assault a law enforcement officer, probation officer, or parole officer while the officer is in performance of his duties, and inflicts serious bodily injury on the officer.

b. Unless some other statute provides for a greater punishment, it is felony to assault an employee of a detention facility operated by the State or local government, while that employee is performing his duties, and inflict serious bodily injury on the employee.

Caselaw.   No firearms case found.

Comments.   This statute was enacted in 1996. This statute is similar to NCGS 14-34.5, except that NCGS 14-34.5 requires the use of a firearm, while NCGS 14-34.7 does not. Presumably, NCGS 14-34.7 is not a firearms-related statute, since, if a firearm was involved, charges would be brought under NCGS 14-34.5.

NCGS 14-43.3 Felonious Restraint

It is a felony to unlawfully restrain someone without their consent and transport the person from the initial place of restraint in a motor vehicle or other conveyance.

Caselaw.   Only one case involving this statute was found, and the case did not state the means by which the Defendant restrained the victim..

Comments.   Felonious restraint is a "lesser included offense of kidnapping." In other words, felonious restraint is a less-serious version of kidnapping. This is expressly stated in the statute.

This statute was enacted in 1985. This statute is not, strictly speaking, a firearms statute. However, one of the ways that a person could likely violate this statute is by using a firearm to restrain a victim. However, in the 20 years since this statute was enacted, only one case seems to have been brought under this statute.

NCGS 14-51.1   Use of Deadly Force Against an Intruder (to Prevent Forcible Entry of Intruder Into Residence)

a. An occupant of a home or residence may use any degree of force, including deadly force, that the occupant reasonably believes is necessary against an intruder to prevent forcible entry into the home or residence, or to terminate the intruder's entry, if the occupant reasonably believes that the intruder: 1) may kill or inflict serious bodily harm to the occupant or others in the home, or   2) intends to commit a felony in the home.

b. An occupant in a home or other residence has no duty to retreat from an intruder in the circumstances described in this statute.

c. This statute does not expand, repeal, or limit any other common law defenses.

Caselaw.   The court in State v. Marshall, 414 S.E.2d 95 (NC App 1992), rev.den., 419 S.E.2d 576 (NC 1992), discussed the change in rules applicable to using a firearm to prevent entry into a residence by an intruder compared to using a firearm once the intruder is already in the residence, *before the enactment of NCGS 14-51.1.* The Marshall court stated that:

> "The North Carolina Supreme Court has stated the legal principles of defense of habitation as follows:
>
> A person has the right to use deadly force in the defense of his habitation in order to *prevent* a forcible entry, even if the intruder is not armed with a deadly weapon, where the attempted forcible entry is made under such circumstances that the person reasonably apprehends death or great bodily harm to himself or the occupants of the home at the hands of the assailant or believes that the assailant intends to commit a felony."
>
> "Once an intruder enters a person's home, the usual rules of self-defense replace the rules governing defense of habitation, with the exception that there is no duty to retreat."

A homeowner cannot use deadly force merely to protect residential property. State v. Hedgepeth, 265 S.E.2d 413 (NC App 1980). The Hedgepeth court stated that "although defined as defense of habitation, the defense in reality is that of defense of person, for under no circumstances is the taking of life available as a defense for protecting property."

It is not required that the defending homeowner first challenge the intruder. State v. Baker, 23 S.E.2d 340 (NC 1942).

It is not required that the intruder actually have a deadly weapon for it to be permissible for the homeowner to use a firearm to defend the residence. State v. Jones, 261 S.E.2d 1 (NC 1980).

It is not permissible to use excessive force in defense of the home. State v. Miller, 148 S.E.2d 279 (NC 1966). However, the use of excessive force is permissible if, under the circumstances, the defending homeowner reasonably believed that the amount of force used was necessary. State v. Roberson, 368 S.E.2d 3 (NC App 1988).

The North Carolina Supreme Court discussed NCGS 14-51.1 in detail in the case of State v. Blue, 565 S.E.2d 133 (NC 2002). State v. Blue is, as of 2005, the only quality case interpreting NCGS 14-51.1, which was enacted in 1994.

The court in State v. Blue defined the common law defense of defense of the person inside a habitation by stating:

> "The common law right of an individual to defend himself from death or bodily harm on his premises was stated in State v. Johnson: Ordinarily, when a person who is free from fault in bringing on a difficulty is attacked in his own home or on his own premises, the law imposes on him no duty to retreat before he can justify his fighting in self defense, regardless of the character of the assault, but is entitled to stand his ground, to repel force with force, and to increase his force, so as not only to resist, but also to overcome the assault and secure himself from all harm. This, of course, would not excuse the defendant if he used excessive force in repelling the attack and overcoming his adversary."

Interpreting that passage, the court, when stating "when a person is free from fault" he may defend himself, the court is stating that the occupant of the home, if the intruder is already in the home, must wait until the intruder attacks him, and then only "meet force with force," but could not escalate to "excessive force." This

108

reactive mode would, of course, put a defending homeowner at a severe disadvantage in a confrontation with a home invader.

The court in State v. Blue then summarized the common law right of defense of a habitation, and stated:

> "The common law defense of habitation was stated thusly in State v. Miller:
>
> When a trespasser enters upon a man's premises, makes an assault upon his dwelling, and attempts to force an entrance into his house in a manner such as would lead a reasonably prudent man to believe that the intruder intends to commit a felony or to inflict some serious personal injury upon the inmates, a lawful occupant of the dwelling may legally prevent the entry, even by the taking of the life of the intruder. Under those circumstances, the law does not require such householder to flee or to remain in his house until his assailant is upon him, but he may open his door and shoot his assailant, if such course is apparently necessary for the protection of himself or family. But the jury must be the judge of the reasonableness of defendant's apprehension. A householder will not, however, be excused if he employs excessive force in repelling the attack, whether it be upon his person or upon his habitation."

Therefore, as stated by State v. Blue, an occupant defending a home had the common law right to defend the home against an intruder, and even kill the intruder, without having to wait to first be attacked by the intruder.

The court in State v. Blue then distinguished the common law defenses of "defense of the habitation" and of "defense of the person inside a habitation" by stating:

> "The principal distinction between the common law defense of habitation and the defense of the person on or within one's own premises is that in the former, the victim is attempting to forcibly enter the defendant's dwelling; whereas, in the latter, the victim has actually attacked or assaulted the defendant in the defendant's dwelling or on the defendant's premises. In neither case is the defendant required to retreat."

The court in State v. Blue then described the practical difference between the two situations by first discussing defense of the habitation, and stated:

109

"The legal effect of the difference between the defenses is that under the defense of habitation, the defendant's use of force, even deadly force, *before being physically attacked* would be justified to prevent the victim's entry provided that the defendant's apprehension that he was about to be subjected to serious bodily harm or that the occupants of the home were about to be seriously harmed or killed was reasonable and further provided that the force used was not excessive." (italics added)

The court in State v. Blue then identified the key difference with the defense of the person within one's habitation by stating that:

"Under the defense of the person on one's premises, the defendant would have the benefit of perfect self-defense and no duty to retreat *only if the defendant had first been attacked* or assaulted." (italics added)

The court in State v. Blue then gave a rationale for the differences in the common law rules described above, by stating:

"However, once the assailant has gained entry, the usual rules of self-defense replace the rules governing defense of habitation, with the exception that there is no duty to retreat. The rationale for this distinction is that once the occupant is face-to-face with the assailant, the occupant is better able to ascertain whether the assailant intends to commit a felony or has the means to inflict serious injury."

In the passage above, the court in State v. Blue is saying that the homeowner was given extra latitude to defend the home from invasion, due to the extra uncertainty and danger involved in defending against an intruder whose intentions and weapons availability were unknown. However, once the intruder was in the home, the homeowner was then placed under a more restrictive set of rules, because the homeowner would, supposedly, then be in a better position to determine the intruder's intentions and weapons availability.

There was a contradictory belief held by many people holding that reality was the other way around, that if an intruder was still outside trying to gain entry against an alerted homeowner, then the danger was relatively low as compared to if the intruder had already gained entry, and was in the house. Once the intruder was in the home, the danger level was immediate and extreme, then justifying greater latitude in self defense by the homeowner.

The Supreme Court in State v. McCombs, 253 S.E.2d 906 (NC 1979), had stated that it was important to have these separate rules because:

> "To allow the distinctions between these rules to become blurred or to extend any of them to situations for which they were not intended would dilute the safeguards designed to protect human life."

NCGS 14-51.1 was nevertheless enacted in 1994, which apparently changed this two-rule common law scenario. Editorializing now, perhaps the Legislature in enacting this statute began to give more weight to safeguarding the rights of family members peacefully residing in their homes, and less weight to safeguarding the rights of home invaders.

The court in State v. Blue was stating that, before NCGS 14-51.1 was enacted, once the intruder was already in the home, the occupant of the premises had to actually wait until an intruder attacked the occupant first, before the occupant was authorized to defend with deadly force. The text of the court in State v. Blue is:

> "Prior to passage of NCGS 14-51.1, once the victim was inside the defendant's home, the defendant would have the benefit of perfect self-defense only if the victim made the initial attack or assault on the defendant, though the defendant would have no duty to retreat. However, if the defendant made the initial attack or assault, the defendant would be entitled only to imperfect self-defense and would be guilty at least of voluntary manslaughter."

> "The limitation that the defendant be acting to prevent forcible entry into the home for the defense of habitation to be applicable was eliminated by NCGS 14-51.1. In enacting NCGS 14-51.1, the General Assembly broadened the defense of habitation to make the use of deadly force justifiable whether to *prevent* unlawful entry into the home or to *terminate* an unlawful entry by an intruder."

This statute gives the occupant of a home the right to use a firearm to *prevent* unlawful entry, or to *terminate* an unlawful entry into the home by an intruder, determined by the court to be a broadening of the common law right to defend a habitation. State v. Blue, 565 S.E.2d 133 (NC 2002).

111

The statute could have been better written. While "preventing unlawful entry" is clearly the same as the old common law defense of habitation, what is "termination of unlawful entry"?

One inference is that "prevention" means to stop an intruder planning to enter the home, while "terminate an unlawful entry" means to stop an intruder who is actually in the process of entering the home, at the moment of entry, but who has not yet made it all the way in. This distinction seems improbable, given that the different definitions between the two phrases would seem very minor that way, and not worth the verbiage and time of the Supreme Court to discuss in State v. Blue.

The other inference is that the language in State v. Blue characterizing this new statute as having "broadened" the defense of habitation infers that the old common law of "defense of the person in the dwelling" is now called "termination of unlawful entry," and the occupant of the home now has one rule to follow, whether the intruder is outside trying to get in, or is already in, the home. Under this inference, "termination of entry" does not mean stopping the intruder when he has one leg in, and one leg out, of the home, at the moment of entry. Rather, under this inference, the phrase "termination of *entry*" is synonymous with "termination of *presence*." This inference certainly is a material broadening of the common law rules, and would be worth the verbiage and time of the Supreme Court to discuss.

The text of State v. Blue which perhaps best clarifies this point is:

> "*Prior to passage of NCGS 14-51.1, once the victim was inside the defendant's home*, the defendant would have the benefit of perfect self-defense only if the victim made the initial attack or assault on the defendant, though the defendant would have no duty to retreat. However, if the defendant made the initial attack or assault, the defendant would be entitled only to imperfect self-defense and would be guilty at least of voluntary manslaughter." (italics added)

The phrase "prior to passage of NCGS 14-51.1" can only mean that the old common law rule applying to defense of oneself against an intruder already in the dwelling existed only up to the passage of NCGS 14-51.1. The phrase "once the victim was in the defendant's home" can only mean that the common rule being discussed in that paragraph is the old common law rule applying to defense of oneself against an intruder already in the dwelling.

Taken together, then, those two phrases almost surely mean that NCGS 14-51.1 was intended to broaden the rights of self defense, so that the occupant of a dwelling had one set of rules for self defense, no matter whether the intruder was attempting entry into the home, or was already in the home.

There are no meaningful cases after State v. Blue interpreting this point.

Whether a porch, deck, patio, garage, etc., is within a home for the purposes of this statute is a question for the jury. State v. Blue, 565 S.E.2d 133 (NC 2002).

Comments.   This statute is an important statute, enacted in 1994. This statute gives powerful rights to residents to protect themselves against forcible entry and home invasions. This statute is a codification of the common law right of "defense of habitation."

Felony vs. Misdemeanor – Which Is It?

Most citizens would not know which statute a criminal's actions are violating, and even if they did, whether the violation of that statute was a felony or misdemeanor. The extent of the average citizen's knowledge is to assume that murder, rape, and kidnapping are surely felonies.

This is important since this statute, like some others, allow a firearm to be legally used in self defense only under certain circumstances, one of which is if the criminal was committing or about to commit a felony.

The Castle Doctrine

Some States require the resident to attempt escape and abandon the home to the intruder, if possible. North Carolina takes the "your home is your castle" approach, and allows defense of the home, even if escape is possible.

The North Carolina castle doctrine, which is generally representative of many other States, is stated by the Supreme Court in State v. Johnson, 136 S.E.2d 84 (NC 1964), as:

> "Ordinarily, when a person who is free from fault in bringing on a difficulty, is attacked in his own home or on his own premises, the law imposes on him no duty to retreat before he can justify his fighting in self defense, regardless of the character of the assault, but is entitled to stand his ground, to repel force with force, and to increase his force, so as not only to resist, but also to overcome the

113

assault and secure himself from all harm. This, of course, would not excuse the defendant if he used excessive force in repelling the attack and overcoming his adversary."

The text from the Johnson case above has been superseded by NCGS 14-51.1, as discussed above, but the reference concerning the castle doctrine (i.e., "no duty to retreat") remains valid. NCGS 14-51.1 makes the same point, stating that "An occupant in a home or other residence has no duty to retreat from an intruder in the circumstances described in this statute."

North Carolina's version of the castle doctrine should not be confused with the version of this doctrine enacted in Florida in 2005, which established that 1) there is a presumption that anyone who forcibly enters a home or occupied vehicle is there to cause death or great bodily harm and therefore a person may use any manner of force including deadly force in self-defense, 2) there is no duty to retreat if a person is attacked in any place they have a right to be in, and can use any amount of force they believe reasonably necessary for self-defense, 3) persons using force authorized by law shall not be prosecuted for using such force, and 4) criminals and their families cannot sue persons who shot them validly under this statute. North Carolina's version of the castle doctrine is reasonably broad, but the Florida version is broader still.

NCGS 14-72 Larceny of Property; Receiving and Possessing Stolen Goods

b.   The crime of larceny is a felony, without regard to the value of the property in question, if the larceny is of a firearm.

c.   The crime of knowingly possessing stolen goods, or of receiving stolen goods, is a felony if the property in question is a firearm.

Caselaw.   "A fair and reasonable reading of NCGS 14-71.1 together with NCGS 14-72(a), (b) and (c) leads inescapably to the conclusion that the General Assembly intended to make the possession of any stolen firearm, by anyone knowing or having reasonable grounds to believe the firearm to be stolen, a felony, regardless of the value of the firearm." State v. Taylor, 317 S.E.2d 369 (NC 1984).

Comments.   None.

NCGS 14-87 Robbery With a Firearm

Anyone who, while possessing a firearm, or while using or threatening to use a firearm, whereby the life of a person is endangered or threatened, unlawfully takes

114

or threatens to take personal property from a place of business, residence, or bank, or any other place where persons are in attendance, is guilty of a felony. Anyone who aids or abets someone in committing such crime is also guilty of the same crime.

Caselaw.   A firearm being used in a robbery other than as a firearm (such as with a rifle being used as a club to batter a victim) is still considered a firearm under this statute. State v. McNatt, 463 S.E.2d 76 (NC 1995).

Whether the Attacker Did, or Did Not, Have a Firearm

The Supreme Court stated that "whether an instrument is a dangerous weapon or a firearm can only be judged by the victim of a robbery from its appearance and manner of use. When a person perpetrates a robbery by brandishing an instrument which appears to be a firearm…in the absence of any evidence to the contrary, the law will presume the instrument to be what his conduct represents it to be—a firearm." State v. Thompson, 254 S.E.2d 526 (NC 1979).

However, somewhat in contrast to Thompson, the court in State v. Allen, 343 S.E.2d 893 (NC 1986), later held that if the perpetrator commits the robbery with an item appearing to the victim to be a firearm, but for which other evidence is later presented showing that the item *was not* a firearm (such as a cap pistol or toy pistol), then it should be put to the jury to decide whether the item was, or was not, a firearm under this statute. If the jury finds as a fact that the item was not a firearm, then it is not a firearm under this statute, no matter what it seemed to be to the victim. Specifically, the court stated "No matter what an instrument appears to be, if in fact it is a cap pistol, or a toy pistol, or some other instrument incapable of threatening or endangering life, it cannot be a firearm or other dangerous weapon within the meaning of the armed robbery statute." State v. Allen, 343 S.E.2d 893 (NC 1986).

However, the Appeals Court then seemed to shift back to the viewpoint it held in Thompson, stating that a firearm need not be actually used or displayed by the violator of this statute. It is sufficient that the victim was led to believe that the violator possessed or threatened to use a firearm in violating this statute. State v. Lee, 495 S.E.2d 373 (NC App 1998).

The court then solidified its original position following Thompson in the case of State v. Jarrett, 607 S.E.2d 661 (NC App 2004), cert.den., 611 S.E.2d 840 (NC 2005), where the court stated that someone who claims to possess a firearm, but who does not actually possess a firearm, who otherwise violates this statute, has violated this statute, if the victim reasonably believed that the violator had a firearm.

This position seems to supersede State v. Allen discussed above. The Jarrett court stated that:

> "Proof of armed robbery requires that the victim reasonably believed that the defendant possessed, or used or threatened to use a firearm in the perpetration of the crime. State v. Thompson, 254 S.E.2d 526 (NC 1979). The State need only prove that the defendant represented that he had a firearm and that circumstances led the victim reasonably to believe that the defendant had a firearm and might use it."

The Jarrett court took care to cite Thompson, apparently reverting back to its position taken earlier in Thompson.

How Certain the Victim Must be That the Attacker Actually Had a Real Firearm

In the case of State v. Quick, 299 S.E.2d 815 (NC App 1983), a man defended himself against accusations under this statute by asserting that the firearm he used in a robbery was not sufficiently confirmed by the victims to be a firearm. The victims testified that the accused man had brandished what "appeared to be" or which they "thought was" a sawed off shotgun, which the accused man asserted was not proof beyond a reasonable doubt of this element of the crime. The court held that victims are not required to "test the character of the projectile which would emanate from the barrel" of the alleged firearm. If a perpetrator threatens a victim's life with a firearm, the victim is not required to "wait and see if the trigger would be pulled."

Operability of the Firearm

The firearm must be operable to be a violation under this particular statute, according to the court in State v. Cowley, 461 S.E.2d 804 (NC App 1995). This is contrary to certain other statutes, such as NCGS 14-269.2(b) (illegal to carry firearm onto school property), where operability of the firearm is not required. Cowley. However, the Court of Appeals had earlier, in State v. Joyner, 312 S.E.2d 681 (NC App 1984), aff'd, 324 S.E.2d 841 (NC 1985), stated that inoperability of the firearm was no defense to a violation of this statute (rifle without a firing pin and thus inoperable no defense). The earlier Joyner case was affirmed by the Supreme Court, and the comments in Cowley appear to be non-controlling "dicta." Therefore, Joyner seems to control, meaning that inoperability of a firearm is not a defense to violation of this statute.

Comments.   None.

NCGS 14-88 Train Robbery

It is a felony to enter a locomotive engine or train car, and by display or discharge of a firearm, to induce or compel anyone in the engine or car to surrender anything of value.

Caselaw.   No relevant cases found.

Comments.   This statute dates from 1895 in its original form, about the time when train robberies were in vogue in the United States, especially in far reaches of the American West.

NCGS 14-160.1 Alteration or Removal of Permanent Identification Marks

a. It is a misdemeanor to alter, deface, destroy, or remove the serial number from any firearm with the intent to conceal or misrepresent the identity of the firearm.

b. It is a misdemeanor for anyone to sell, buy, or possess any firearm, not his own, on which the serial number has been altered, defaced, destroyed, or removed for the purpose of concealing or misrepresenting the identity of the firearm.

Caselaw.   No relevant case found.

Comments.   This statute, enacted in 1977, is intended to prevent removal of serial numbers from firearms, among other things. Removal of serial numbers aids in selling stolen firearms, transfer of firearms among criminals, and tracing of firearms used in crimes.

NCGS 14-258 Conveying Weapons to Convicts and Other Prisoners

It is a felony to convey a firearm to a convict or imprisoned person.

Caselaw.   None.

Comments.   This statute was most recently amended in 1994. This statute is similar to NCGS 14-258.1.

NCGS 14-258.1 Furnishing Firearms, Cartridges, or Ammunition to Inmates

a. It is a felony to give or sell a firearm or ammunition to an inmate of any charitable, mental, or penal institution, or any local confinement facility. A violator who is an officer or employee of the State or a local confinement facility, shall be dismissed from his position or office.

Caselaw.   No firearms related cases found.

Comments.   This statute is similar to NCGS 14-258. This statute was last amended in 1994.

NCGS 14-258.2 Possession of Dangerous Weapons in Prison

a. It is a felony for someone, while in custody in a prison or confinement facility, to possess a firearm without authorization.

b. It is a felony to assist someone in custody in a prison or a confinement facility to escape or attempt to escape, and who either assaults someone with a firearm and inflicts bodily injury, or, by the use of the firearm, accomplishes the escape.

Caselaw.   No relevant firearms cases found.

Comments.   This statute is related to NCGS 14-258 and 14-258.1.

NCGS 14-269   Carrying Concealed Weapons

a. It is illegal for a person to willfully and intentionally carry concealed about his person a bowie knife, dirk, dagger, metallic knuckles, stun gun, "or other deadly weapon of like kind," except when upon that person's own premises.

a.1. It is illegal for anyone to willfully and intentionally carry concealed about his person any pistol or gun, except:

　　　1) when on his own premises, or
　　　2) when the firearm is a handgun and the person has a concealed handgun permit, or
　　　3) when the person is a military permittee as defined under NCGS 14-415.10(2a) who provides proof of deployment to a law enforcement officer as required under NCGS 14-415.11(a).

b. This statute prohibiting concealed firearms does not apply to the following people:

　　　1) military personnel when on duty acting under orders
　　　2) federal law enforcement personnel

3) National Guard personnel when on duty acting under orders
4) State or local government officers when performing official duties
5) certain off-duty law enforcement officers.

b.1. A person is excused from violating the restrictions prohibiting concealed weapons cited above under certain circumstances if a firearm was not involved.

b.2. It is a defense to violation of this statute if the accused is a military permittee, the deadly weapon is a handgun, the person is a military permittee, and the accused provides to the court proof of deployment as defined in NCGS 14-415.10(3a).

c. A first violation of this statute is a misdemeanor. A second violation is a felony.

Caselaw.   The purpose of this statute is to reduce the likelihood that a concealed firearm will be resorted to in a fit of anger. State v. Gainey, 160 S.E.2d 685 (NC 1968).

The firearm may be concealed "on" or "about" someone's body to be a violation of this statute. The firearm may be concealed in close proximity to the violator, under convenient control and within easy reach, so that the violator could promptly use the firearm. State v. Gainey, 160 S.E.2d 685 (NC 1968). The Gainey court, describing the text of this statute, stated that:

> "the language is not 'concealed *on* his person,' but 'concealed about his person'; that is, concealed near, in close proximity to him, and within his convenient control and easy reach, so that he could promptly use it, if prompted to do so by any violent motive. It makes no difference how it is concealed, so it is on or near to and within the reach and control of the person charged."

A person's automobile is not their "premises" under this statute. State v. Gainey, 160 S.E.2d 685 (NC 1968).

A pistol in a bag on the back seat of an automobile within reach of the driver of the car is a concealed firearm. State v. White, 195 S.E.2d 576 (NC App 1973), cert.den., 196 S.E.2d 811 (NC 1973).

A pistol under the driver's seat in an automobile within reach of the driver is a concealed firearm. State v. Jordan, 331 S.E.2d 232 (NC App 1985).

Concerning the exception allowing people to carry concealed firearms on their own premises, the person carrying the concealed firearm under this statute need not be the owner of the premises. They can be a tenant or a hired employee of the landowner acting on the landowner's instructions. State v. Terry, 93 N.C. 585 (1885). State v. Anderson, 39 S.E. 824 (NC 1901).

It is unstated by statute or caselaw whether an employee, who is located upon his employer's premises, who is carrying a concealed handgun without his employer's instructions but not against his employer's wishes, may validly deem his jobsite as his "premises," thus entitling him to carry a concealed handgun without a permit.

The posting of notice under NCGS 14-415.11(c) invalidating the carry of concealed handguns on the posted premises does not bar carrying concealed firearms if the person is located "on their premises."

The old case of State v. Broadnax, 91 N.C. 543 (NC 1884), had an interesting ruling, stating that:

> "The mischief intended to be remedied by the statute was the practice of *wearing* offensive weapons concealed about the person, or carrying them so concealed with a purpose to be used offensively or defensively upon an emergency. We cannot believe that it was the intention of the law-makers to hold one answerable to the criminal law who carries a pistol, for instance, in his pocket to a gunsmith to be repaired, or that a gentleman residing in a city who buys a pistol to be taken to his residence, is required to carry it through the streets openly in his hand. It would certainly be an unseemly plight for some members of the community, who might yet think that a pistol was a necessary household article for protection against thieves and burglars."

Concealment is the essence of the offense. State v. Broadnax, 91 N.C. 543 (1884). Broadnax was apparently followed by State v. Harrison, 93 N.C. 605 (NC 1885).

Harrison and Broadnax were overruled by State v. Dixon, 19 S.E. 364 (NC 1894), where the court stated "in trials for this offense it should be borne in mind that the guilty intent is the intent to carry the weapon concealed, and does not depend upon the intent to use it. The object of this statute is not to forbid the carrying of a deadly weapon for use, but to prevent the opportunity and temptation to use it arising from its concealment."

The Attorney General issued an opinion that an unconcealed pistol located in an automobile is not a violation of this statute. 41 N.C.A.G. 207 (1971).

120

The Attorney General issued an opinion that a security guard employed by a security company may not carry a concealed handgun when on the job on a client's premises, unless the guard possessed a concealed handgun permit. 1979 N.C.A.G. Lexis 64 (1979).

Comments.   This key statute is the basic statutory prohibition on unauthorized carrying of concealed firearms.

Many people believe that only concealed handguns are prohibited unless a concealed handgun permit is possessed. Subsection (a.1) above definitely prohibits concealed rifles, long guns, and shotguns. Further, there is no authorization for issuance of a permit to carry concealed rifles, long guns, or shotguns.

"Officers" of the State, or of any county, city, or town in subsection (b)(4) above is not defined by the statute or in the Article in which this statute appears. It is not clear whether this means "law enforcement officers," or any "officer" of the State, however that is defined.

Subsection (b)(2) contains no stipulation that the federal officer must be on duty or acting in an official capacity to qualify for the exception. Subsection (b)(4) regarding State and local officers, however, has a stipulation that the officer, to qualify for the exception, must be acting in the discharge of official duties.

Subsection (b)(5) stipulates that, to qualify for the exception, if a sworn law enforcement officer is off-duty, the officer must not be consuming alcohol or illegal drugs (or have such remaining in their body). Subsection (b)(4) and (b)(5) seem harmonious, with an on-duty/off-duty rule for *State and local* officers.

However, (b)(2) and (b)(5) seem to conflict regarding *federal* officers. The old version of (b)(2) read like (b)(4), granting the exception only to on-duty federal officers. Subsection (b)(2) was changed in 2005, however, deleting application of the subsection only to on-duty federal officers. With the deletion of that limitation, (b)(2) now gives a blanket rule that federal officers are exempt from concealed carry rules, whether on-duty or off-duty. However, (b)(5) then seems to provide a restriction to the blanket rule, stating that the exception from coverage of the concealed carry rules do not apply if a "sworn law enforcement officer" is consuming alcohol or illegal drugs. Ordinarily, this apparent conflict would be resolved by reading all subsections as a whole, and concluding that the legislature meant that there was to be an on-duty/off-duty rule. The problem with that resolution is that subsection (b)(4) expressly states that the exception for State and local officers from the concealed carry rule covers them only when *on-duty*. The legislature expressly *deleted* the on-duty limitation for federal officers in the 2005

121

amendment to (b)(2). Therefore, this statute is somewhat unclear as to whether the concealed carry laws apply to off-duty federal officers consuming alcohol or illegal drugs.

See NCGS 14-415.10 to NCGS 14-415.24 for statutes on concealed carry permits. See NCGS 14-415.10 regarding deployed military personnel.

NCGS 14-269.1 Confiscation and Disposition of Deadly Weapons

Upon conviction for violation of NCGS 14-269, NCGS 14-269.7, or any offense involving the use of a firearm referred to in NCGS 14-269, the firearm used in the crime shall be confiscated and disposed of as ordered by the presiding judge.

The methods of disposition available to the judge are specified in this statute, and generally include return to rightful owner, turnover to the Sheriff for destruction, turnover to a local law enforcement agency for use or sale by that agency, turnover to the State Bureau of Investigation, and turnover to the North Carolina Justice Academy.

Caselaw.   No relevant case found.

Comments.   This is a general statute giving authority for confiscation and disposition of firearms seized from violators of firearms laws.

NCGS 14-269.2 Weapons on Campus or Other Educational Property

a.1. "Educational property" is defined as any school building, bus, school campus, grounds, or recreational area.

a.1.b. "School" is any public or private school, community college, college, or university.

b. It is a felony for any person to carry, concealed or openly, any gun, rifle, or pistol on any educational property or to an activity sponsored by a school. Discharging a firearm on school property is a more severe felony.

c. It is a felony to cause, encourage, or aid a minor under 18 years old to carry, concealed or openly, a gun, rifle, or pistol on any educational property or to an activity sponsored by a school.

f. Instead of the felony charge in section (b) above, it is a misdemeanor for any person to carry, concealed or openly, any gun, rifle, or pistol on any educational

122

property or to an activity sponsored by a school, if that person is not a student or employee attending or employed by the school, and the firearm is not loaded, and the firearm is in a motor vehicle, and the firearm is in a locked container or rack.

g. This statute does not apply to firearms used solely for educational programs; a person exempted by NCGS 14-269(b); emergency services personnel; guards employed by the school; home schools; or when permission has been obtained from the school's governing body.

h. The prohibition regarding possession of a firearm on school property does not apply if a person came into possession of the firearm by taking the firearm from another person or by finding the firearm, and the person delivered the firearm as soon as practical to a law enforcement officer.

Caselaw.   The firearm need not be operable to violate this statute. State v. Cowley, 461 S.E.2d 804 (NC App 1995). State v. Jackson, 546 S.E.2d 570 (NC 2001).

"Firearm" is interpreted broadly in this statute. State v. Cowley, 461 S.E.2d 804 (NC App 1995).

There is no requirement under this statute that the accused have "willfully, feloniously, and knowingly" acted to violate this statute in carrying a firearm onto school property. State v. Hester, 2004 Lexis 333 (NC App 2004).

The parking lot of a school is part of school grounds for the purposes of this statute. In Re: D.D., 554 S.E.2d 346 (NC App 2001), cert.den., 558 S.E.2d 867 (NC 2001).

The State Attorney General issued an opinion that a faculty member residing in a home on campus may keep a firearm in that home on campus without violating this statute. 41 N.C.A.G. 466 (1971).

Comments.   This is the basic statute prohibiting firearms in schools.

It is not well defined in the statute as to what constitutes an extracurricular activity off school grounds, thus creating a "bubble" of protection under this statute. Extracurricular activities, such as a school's "Food Night" fundraiser held at a local hamburger shop, may be held at places also simultaneously open to the public, and often are not advertised to the public. An armed citizen, without warning or notice, may find himself in at least technical violation of this statute. No cases address these issues.

NCGS 14-269.3 Carrying Weapons Into Assemblies of People, and Into Establishments Where Alcoholic Beverages are Sold and Consumed

a. It is a misdemeanor to carry a firearm into any assembly of people for which a fee has been charged for admission to the assembly, or into any establishment where alcoholic beverages are sold and consumed.

b. This statute does not apply to someone exempted from compliance with NCGS 14-269; the owner or tenant of the premises; a person participating in the event if he is carrying a firearm with permission of the landowner or tenant, or person organizing the event; or a security guard hired by the landowner, tenant, or person organizing the event.

Caselaw.   No relevant case found.

Comments.   This statute was enacted in 1977.

Assemblies of people for which an admission fee has been charged would presumably be events such as concerts, movie theaters, lectures by famous speakers, and nightclubs. It is unclear whether events such as art gallery exhibits, where an admission fee is charged, but where the people inside do not so much "assemble" together as "occupy" various separate parts of the gallery, would be included under this statute.

The second prohibition in the statute regards places where alcoholic beverages are sold and consumed. This refers to bars and nightclubs. The statute does not discuss whether firearms are prohibited from a place during the day, when alcoholic beverages are sold and consumed only at night.

NCGS 14-269.4 Weapons on State Property and Courthouses

It is a misdemeanor to possess or carry a firearm which is not used solely for instructional or official ceremonial purposes in the State Capitol, the Executive Mansion, the Western Residence of the Governor, or any courthouse.

This section does not apply to anyone exempted by NCGS 14-269(b) (soldiers and law enforcement officers); anyone possessing a firearm in a courthouse for evidentiary purposes; anyone delivering a firearm to a law enforcement agency in a building housing a court; anyone delivering a firearm for registration in a building housing a court.

This section also does not apply to State-owned rest areas and stops along highways; and to State-owned hunting and fishing reservations.

Caselaw.   No relevant case found.

Comments.   This statute was enacted in 1981.

The two exculpation clauses (i.e., "does not apply to public rest stops or hunting/fishing preserves") seem unnecessary, because the prohibition clause makes the statute applicable only to the Capitol, the governor's residences, and any courthouse.

NCGS 14-269.7 Prohibitions on Handguns For Minors

a. Any minor child who possesses or carries a handgun is guilty of a misdemeanor.

b. This statute does not apply to:

  - military personnel acting pursuant to orders;
  - a minor possessing a handgun for educational or recreational purposes under supervision of an adult who is present;
  - an emancipated minor who possesses the handgun in their residence; or
  - a minor who possesses a handgun while hunting outside the city limits if the minor has written authorization from their parent/guardian on their person.

Caselaw.   No relevant case found.

Comments.   This statute was enacted in 1993. Several statutes, NCGS 14-315.2, 14-269.7, and 14-315.1, were enacted in 1993 to protect children from firearms.

This statute is a companion statute of sorts to NCGS 14-315. NCGS 14-269.7 prohibits and punishes the minor child for possessing handguns, where NCGS 14-315 prohibits and punishes the person who supplied the minor child with the firearm.

NCGS 14-269.7 and NCGS 14-315 apply only to handguns, not rifles. NCGS 14-316 applies to rifles and handguns.

NCGS 14-269.8   Purchase or Possession of Firearms by Person Subject to Domestic Violence Order Prohibited

a. In accord with NCGS 50B-3.1, it is illegal, if ordered by a court under a protective order, to own, possess, purchase, or receive a firearm or ammunition.

b. Violation of this statute is a felony.

Caselaw.   No relevant case found.

Comments.   None.

NCGS 14-277.2   Weapons at Parades, Funeral Processions, Picket Lines, Health Care Facilities, or Government Property

a. It is a misdemeanor to carry or have immediate access to a firearm while participating in, or present as a spectator at, a parade, funeral procession, picket line, demonstration upon any private health care facility grounds, or on any public place owned by a governmental unit. A rifle or gun carried in a rack in a pickup truck at a holiday parade or funeral procession is allowed under this statute.

c. This statute does not apply to persons exempted by NCGS 14-269(b), to law enforcement personnel, or to anyone holding a special permit from the Sheriff or police chief to carry firearms at such event.

Caselaw.   No relevant case found.

Comments.   This statute was enacted in 1981. The rationale at prohibiting firearms in picket lines or health care facility demonstrations seems clear, because those places are known to generate extreme emotions and tension. Prohibition of firearms on government property is similar, and is a recurrent theme throughout the statutes.

However, the rationale for including parades and funeral processions into this statute is unclear because parades and funeral processions seem dissimilar to picket lines and health care facility demonstrations. Parades and funeral processions also do not seem likely to produce extreme emotions resulting in gunplay. The exception allowing firearms at parades or funeral processions, if carried in a gun rack in a pickup truck at "holiday" parades, is even more peculiar.

NCGS 14-280 Shooting at Trains or Passengers

It is a felony to shoot at or into a railroad car, locomotive, or train, while such train is underway or stopped.

126

Caselaw.   No relevant case found.

Comments.   This statute dates from 1876, about the time when train robberies were in vogue in the United States, especially in far reaches of the American West. The State Legislature has kept this statute current, however, amending it as recently as 1994.

Riots and Civil Disorders

Article 36A of Chapter 14 of the North Carolina General Statutes is entitled "Riots and Civil Disorders." Article 36A is composed of statutes NCGS 14-288.1 through 14-288.20. This Article was originally enacted in 1969, a year which saw much civil unrest, rioting, protest marching, and strife. Numerous statutes in Article 36A involve firearms and prohibitions on firearms. Article 36A is of heightened recent interest due to controversial actions taken by governmental agencies in New Orleans under similar Louisiana statutes to restrict and even confiscate firearms during Hurricane Katrina in 2005, at a time of great civil disorder.

NCGS 14-288.7 Transporting Dangerous Weapon During Emergency

a. Except as allowed by this statute, it is a misdemeanor for anyone to transport or possess a firearm off their premises anywhere a declared state of emergency exists, or near where a riot is occurring.

b. This statute does not apply to persons exempted from NCGS 14-269 (soldiers, law enforcement officers) when lawfully performing official duties.

Caselaw.   It is no defense under this statute that the firearm was disassembled when being carried. State v. Dobbins, 178 S.E.2d 449 (NC 1971).

Comments.   Definitions for this statute are in NCGS 14-288.1. This statute was enacted in 1969, a year which saw much civil unrest, rioting, protest marching, and strife.

The exceptions to this statute are limited to soldiers and law enforcement officers. Otherwise, during emergencies and riots, civilians and concealed firearm permit holders who wish to be armed must stay on their own premises.

The word "premises" is not defined. The word presumably means their residence, but it could mean their place of business. Transporting a firearm between work and home is apparently not permitted during an emergency.

NCGS 14-288.8   Weapons of Mass Death and Destruction

a. Except as allowed by this statute, it is illegal to manufacture, assemble, possess, store, transport, sell, offer to sell, purchase, deliver, give to another, or acquire a weapon of mass death and destruction.

b. This statute does not apply to certain persons, such as those exempted from NCGS 14-269; licensed importers, manufacturers, dealers, and collectors; and those lawfully engaged in development or manufacture of weapons of mass death and destruction.

c. "Weapons of mass death and destruction" include, among other things, a:

-firearm other than a shotgun with a barrel more than one-half inch in diameter;
-firearm capable of fully automatic fire;
-shotgun with a barrel less than 18 inches in length;
-shotgun with an overall length less than 26 inches;
-rifle with a barrel less than 16 inches in length;
-rifle with an overall length less than 26 inches;
-muffler or silencer for any firearm;
-combination of parts intended or designed to convert or assemble a weapon named above.

c. Weapons of mass death and destruction do not include:

-a device neither designed or redesigned for use as a weapon;
-a weapon redesigned as a signaling, pyrotechnic, line-throwing, safety, or similar device;
-surplus ordnance sold or provided by the Secretary of the Army under 10 USC 4684(2), 4685, or 4686;
-a device which the Secretary of the Treasury finds is not likely to be used as a weapon, is an antique, or is a firearm the owner intends to use solely for sporting purposes, in accord with Chapter 44 of Title 18 of the United States Code.

d. Violation of this statute is a felony.

Caselaw.   It is no defense under this statute that the firearm was disassembled. State v. Fennell, 382 S.E.2d 231 (NC App 1989).

The State Appeals Court ruled that if a firearm is "totally inoperable and incapable of being readily made operable," then the firearm is deemed not to be a weapon of mass death and destruction. State v. Fennell, 382 S.E.2d 231 (NC App 1989). However, the Supreme Court clarified Fennell in that simple inoperability was no defense, because the statute clearly states that even disassembled (and thus inoperable) pieces of a weapon of mass death and destruction are prohibited. State v. Jackson, 546 S.E.2d 570 (NC 2001). The Jackson court stated that "inoperability" in Fennell means that the weapon cannot be repaired or made to operate as a weapon of mass death and destruction.

The Secretary of the Treasury defines an antique firearm as manufactured in or before 1898. State v. Blackwell, 592 S.E.2d 701 (NC App 2004), cert.den., 597 S.E.2d 768 (NC 2004); 18 USC 921(a)(16)(A).

The burden of proof to show that a firearm was not a weapon of mass death and destruction because it was inoperable or because it was an antique is upon the accused defendant, to be raised as an affirmative defense. State v. Fennell, 382 S.E.2d 231 (NC App 1989). State v. Blackwell, 592 S.E.2d 701 (NC App 2004), cert.den., 597 S.E.2d 768 (NC 2004).

Comments.   This statute was enacted in 1969, a year which saw much civil unrest, rioting, protest marching, and strife. The most common weapon of mass death and destruction found in the caselaw is a sawed-off shotgun.

This statute has no exception for persons authorized and licensed under federal law to have some of these weapons, such as a fully automatic firearm. There are no State cases creating or acknowledging such an exception. It is presumed that State prosecutors have taken the position that authorization under a federal law permitting such activity preempts contradictory State law.

Title 18 of the United States Code is the section on crimes and criminal law. Chapter 44 is the subsection of Title 18 presenting various federal firearms laws. Chapter 44 starts with 18 USC 921, entitled "Definitions."

NCGS 14-288.9   Assault on Emergency Personnel

a. An assault under this statute is an assault upon emergency personnel (as defined below) committed where a declared state of emergency exists, or in the immediate vicinity where a riot is occurring or is imminent.

b. "Emergency personnel" are law enforcement officers, firemen, ambulance personnel, utility workers, doctors, nurses, and other persons providing essential services during an emergency.

c. Violation of this statute with a firearm is a felony.

Caselaw.   No relevant case found.

Comments.   This statute was enacted in 1969, a year which saw much civil unrest, rioting, protest marches, and strife.

NCGS 14-288.10   Frisk of Persons During Violent Disorders

a. Law enforcement officers may frisk any person in order to discover firearms on that person when the officer reasonably believes that the person may become involved in an existing riot, and where the person frisked is close enough to become immediately involved in such riot.

Caselaw.   No relevant case found.

Comments.   This statute was enacted in 1969, a year which saw much civil unrest, rioting, protest marches, and strife.

NCGS 14-288.11 Warrants to Inspect Vehicles in Riot Areas or Approaching Municipalities During Emergencies

a. and b. Warrants may be issued for law enforcement officers to inspect vehicles to discover firearms in such vehicles which are likely to be used by someone likely to become involved in a riot.

b. Warrants may authorize inspection of vehicles entering or approaching a municipality where a state of emergency exists, or which are within or approaching the immediate vicinity of an existing riot.

g. Warrants issued under this statute become invalid 24 hours after issuance.

h. Warrants issued under this statute are not considered search warrants.

Caselaw.   No relevant firearms case found.

Comments. This statute was enacted in 1969, a year which saw much civil unrest, rioting, protest marches, and strife. This statute has never been amended. See NCGS 14-288.17.

NCGS 14-288.12 Power of Municipalities to Enact Ordinances to Deal With States of Emergency

A municipality may prohibit or restrict possession, transportation, sale, purchase, storage, and use of firearms during an emergency. Violation of this statute is a misdemeanor.

Caselaw. During a period of severe civil unrest in Asheville, N.C., in 1969, the mayor prohibited carrying of firearms off the landowner's premises. The Defendant in State v. Dobbins, 178 S.E.2d 449 (NC 1971), was caught carrying a shotgun off his premises. Dobbins defended by alleging that this statute was invalid because it was excessively vague and over-broad, and failed to specify objective standards upon which a state of emergency could be declared. The court ruled otherwise.

The court in State v. Allred, 204 S.E.2d 214 (NC App 1974), cert.den., 205 S.E.2d 724 (NC 1974), cert.den., 42 L.Ed.2d 828 (US 1975), stated that the court in State v. Dobbins, 178 S.E.2d 449 (NC 1971), had held that this statute was constitutional. However, a reading of Dobbins reveals that the Dobbins court's ruling expressly did not consider a constitutional challenge to this statute based upon the accused's rights under the federal Second Amendment (right to keep and bear arms).

Comments. This statute was enacted in 1969, a time of severe social unrest, rioting, civil disobedience, and protest marches. See NCGS 14-288.16 and 14-288.17.

This statute can be broadly interpreted to apparently conflict with the right to keep and bear arms. An example is Hurricane Katrina in 2005. The City of New Orleans, during the disaster recovery period immediately after Hurricane Katrina demolished the city, issued an order under a Louisiana statute much like this North Carolina statute. The New Orleans municipal government ordered confiscation of firearms from virtually all civilians, regardless of their situation and documented right to possess firearms. This confiscation order came at a time when city police were unable to protect citizens from roving bands of looters, rapists, and thieves. The police were even unable to protect firefighter, medic, and ambulance teams working to aid injured or stranded citizens. The North Carolina statute can literally be read to give municipal authorities the right to "prohibit…the possession…of firearms." Whether a North Carolina municipality could legally impose such a draconian edict has not been tested in the North Carolina courts (see the Dobbins case discussion).

131

NCGS 14-288.13 Power of Counties to Enact Ordinances to Deal With States of Emergency

a. A county may, during an emergency, prohibit or restrict the possession, transportation, sale, purchase, storage, and use of firearms.

b. The allowable prohibitions and restrictions are as stated in NCGS 14-288.12.

c. No ordinance enacted under this statute shall apply within the corporate limits of any city, unless that city consents to its application.

d. Violation of this statute is a misdemeanor.

Caselaw.   This statute was held to be constitutional in State v. Allred, 204 S.E.2d 214 (NC App 1974), cert.den., 205 S.E.2d 724 (NC 1974), cert.den., 42 L.Ed.2d 828 (US 1975). The Allred court made a number of statements concerning this statute, and how it was to be enacted and applied.

Comments.   This statute was enacted in 1969, a time of severe social unrest, rioting, civil disobedience, and protest marches. See NCGS 14-288.16.

NCGS 14-288.14 Power of Chairman of County Commission to Impose Emergency Restrictions Imposed by a Municipality

The chairman of a county commission may extend or impose upon county residents the restrictions previously imposed by a municipality under NCGS 14-288.12. The chairman may impose such restrictions by proclamation. The restrictions may be imposed upon part or all of the county.

Caselaw.   No relevant firearms cases found.

Comments.   This statute is similar to NCGS 14-288.13. This statute was originally enacted in 1969, a time of severe social unrest, rioting, civil disobedience, and protest marches. See NCGS 14-288.16.

NCGS 14-288.15 Authority of Governor to Exercise Control in Emergencies

d. The Governor may impose restrictions on the possession, transportation, sale, purchase, use, and storage of firearms during states of emergencies.

e. Violation of this statute is a misdemeanor.

<u>Caselaw.</u>   No cases found. See NCGS 14-288.12 and 14-288.13 for similar statutes found valid.

<u>Comments.</u>   This statute was enacted in 1969, a time of severe social unrest, rioting, civil disobedience, and protest marches. See NCGS 14-288.16.

NCGS 14-288.16   Effective Time, Publication, Amendment, and Rescission of Proclamations

a. This statute applies to proclamations issued under NCGS 14-288.12, 14-288.13, 14-288.14, and 14-288.15.

b. All proclamations issued shall take effect immediately upon publication, unless a later date is specified in the proclamation. Publication may be by mass media communications or other effective means.

c. The prohibitions and restrictions in such proclamations generally last 5 days unless extended or terminated early.

<u>Caselaw.</u>   No relevant case found.

<u>Comments.</u>   This statute was enacted in 1969, a time of severe social unrest, rioting, civil disobedience, and protest marches.

NCGS 14-288.17   Municipal and County Ordinances May Be Made Immediately Effective if State of Emergency Exists or is Imminent

a. This statute controls regarding ordinances authorized by NCGS 14-288.11 and 14-288.12.

b. Upon proclamation that a state of emergency exists or is imminent, any ordinance enacted under authority of this Article shall take effect immediately unless the ordinance sets a later time.

<u>Caselaw.</u>   No relevant case found.

<u>Comments.</u>   This statute was enacted in 1969, a time of severe social unrest, rioting, civil disobedience, and protest marches.

NCGS 14-288.20   Certain Weapons at Civil Disorders

a. A civil disorder is a public disturbance involving acts or violence by assemblies of three or more persons which causes an immediate danger of damage or injury to property or persons, or results in damage or injury.

b. A person is guilty of a felony if he:

1. teaches another person to use a firearm, knowing or having reason to know or intending that the skills taught will be unlawfully used in a civil disorder;
2. assembles with one or more persons to train, practice, or be instructed in the use of any firearm, intending to use said skills in a civil disorder.

c. Nothing in this statute makes unlawful the acts of any law enforcement officer performed in the lawful performance of official duties.

Caselaw.   A person may violate this statute by causing other people to actually perform the conduct violating the statute, acting on his behalf or at his direction. Person v. Miller, 854 F.2d 656 (4th Cir. 1988).

It is not required that violation of this statute threatens immediate danger, but that the act be intended to cause future civil disorder. Person v. Miller, 854 F.2d 656 (4th Cir. 1988).

Comments.   This statute was enacted in 1981.

The title of this statute is somewhat misleading, referring to weapons *at* civil disorders, when the text of the statute refers only to training and educating people to use certain weapons, for their *later use* at a civil disorder. The aim of this statute is to criminalize the training and educating efforts *before* a civil disorder takes place, and does not affect someone who *later* actually takes a weapon to a civil disorder.

NCGS 14-315   Selling or Giving Weapons to Minors

a. It is a misdemeanor to sell, offer to sell, give, or transfer a pistol cartridge to a minor.

a.1. It is a felony to sell, offer to sell, give, or transfer any handgun to a minor child.

a.1. This statute does not apply in any of the following circumstances:

1) the handgun is only loaned to the minor and the minor's possession of the handgun is lawful under NCGS 14-269.7, NCGS 14-316, and all other statutes;

2) the handgun is transferred to an adult custodian for the minor;

3) the handgun is a devise to the minor under the Will of someone who died, and the handgun was transferred to the minor's parent or guardian.

b.1. It is a defense to violation of this statute if all of the following conditions are met:

1.   the person shows that the minor had produced an apparently valid permit to receive the firearm, if a permit was required for the transaction under NCGS 14-402 or NCGS 14-409.1 (Section 14-409.1 has since been repealed),

2.   the person reasonably believed that the minor was not a minor, and

3.   the person either shows that the minor produced identification showing that the minor was not a minor, or, shows that the minor produced evidence of other facts that reasonably indicated that the minor was not a minor.

Caselaw.   No relevant case found.

Comments.   This is the basic statute prohibiting transfer of handguns to minors. The statute does not prohibit transfer of rifles or shotguns, or ammunition for long guns, to minors. The rationale for not prohibiting sales of rifles or shotguns to children is not known.

This statute, when read in full, primarily targets the commercial sale of cartridges and handguns to minor children, and secondarily targets giving handguns to children for other reasons.

A literal reading of subsection "a" seems to prohibit a parent from supplying their child with a pistol cartridge at a shooting range during firearms safety training, while the child was continuously under the personal supervision of that parent. However, in view of NCGS 14-316, such an interpretation is too restrictive.

This statute is a companion statute of sorts to NCGS 14-269.7. NCGS 14-269.7 prohibits and punishes the minor child for possessing handguns, where NCGS 14-

315 prohibits and punishes the person who supplied the minor child with the firearm.

NCGS 14-269.7 and NCGS 14-315 apply only to handguns, not rifles. NCGS 14-316 applies to rifles and handguns.

NCGS 14-315.1   Storage of Firearms to Protect Minors

a. It is a misdemeanor for anyone residing in the same premises as a minor child to:

- own or possess a firearm,
- store or leave the firearm such that the firearm can be discharged, and,
- store or leave the firearm where the person knew or should have known that a minor child could gain access to the firearm,

and the following events occur:

- a minor gains access to the firearm without lawful permission,
- the minor exhibits the firearm in a public place in a careless, angry, or threatening manner, and,
- the minor causes personal injury or death while not acting in self-defense, or uses the firearm to commit a crime.

b. This section does not prohibit carrying a concealed firearm.

c. This section does not apply if the minor gained access to the firearm due to the unlawful entry by any person.

Caselaw.   No relevant case found.

Comments.   This statute, enacted in 1993, is North Carolina's primary safe storage law. Safe storage laws are sometimes referred to as Child Access Prevention ("CAP") laws. The intent, of course, is to create an incentive (i.e., punishment as a misdemeanor) for parents to prevent needless gun violence by reducing access by children to firearms by safe storage of those firearms.

This statute, by requiring exhibition of the firearm in a public place, is not targeted to prevent injuries to children which occur in the home due to access to firearms which were improperly stored in that home.

This statute presumably targets situations where parents leave a loaded firearm around the house where a child could obtain the firearm and cause mischief in

136

public with the firearm. It is not clear whether this statute covers situations where parents leave an *unloaded* firearm around the house, with the ammunition separately stored, and the child finds the firearm and ammunition, loads the firearm, and then performs mischief in public. Is it enough for a parent to say that they did not "leave the firearm such that the firearm can be discharged" because it was unloaded? Or, does this statute mean that parents must leave the firearm so that it cannot be discharged due to more affirmative reasons, such as because it had a trigger lock installed, or because it was locked up in a safe? There are no cases to interpret this issue.

This statute does not limit the scope of coverage to that adult's own child. The text reads such that the offending child could be a visiting child who gets possession of a firearm.

The text of this statute is lacking in that the only adults covered by this statute are adults who have a minor child *residing* in the home. This statute does not cover children visiting homes where no child resides, such as children visiting a non-custodial parent or children visiting grandparents. A better idea is to require all firearm owners to secure firearms from children in or visiting the home, regardless of whether a child happens to reside in the home.

This statute appears to limits its scope to places of residence. A better idea is to require all firearm owners to secure firearms from children, whether the place be a residence, a workplace, an automobile, etc.

Several statutes, NCGS 14-315.2, 14-269.7, and 14-315.1, were enacted in 1993 to protect children from firearms.

NCGS 14-315.2   Warning Upon Sale or Transfer of Firearm to Protect Minor

a.   The seller or transferor of any firearm, upon the retail sale or other transfer of a firearm, shall give a copy of NCGS 14-315.1 to the purchaser or recipient of the firearm.

b.   All sellers, gun shops, or sales outlets which sell firearms shall post conspicuously at each purchase counter the following message in block letters of at least one inch in size "It is unlawful to store or leave a firearm that can be discharged in a manner that a reasonable person should know is accessible to a minor."

c.   Violation of this section is a misdemeanor.

<u>Caselaw.</u>　　　No relevant case found.

<u>Comments.</u>　　　This statute was enacted in 1993. Several statutes, NCGS 14-315.2, 14-269.7, and 14-315.1, were enacted in 1993 to protect children from firearms.

NCGS 14-316　Allowing Young Children (under age 12) to Use Firearms

a.　It is a misdemeanor for a parent, guardian, or "person standing in loco parentis" to knowingly allow a child under age 12 to have the possession, custody, or use of a firearm, whether unloaded or unloaded, except when the child is under the supervision of that parent, guardian, or person in loco parentis.

a. It is illegal for anyone to furnish a firearm to such a minor child, except for the parent, guardian, or person in loco parentis of that child.

b. Air rifles or pistols, and BB guns are not "firearms" under this section except in 17 specified counties.

<u>Caselaw.</u>　　　No relevant case found.

<u>Comments.</u>　　　This is an older statute, dating back to 1913 in a prior version. This older statute uses the archaic phrase "standing in loco parentis," which is a Latin phrase meaning "in place of a parent." This phrase refers to an adult or entity which has assumed or accepted some legal responsibility for a minor child, such as a boarding school, foster parent, county custodial agency, or an appointed guardian. The legal responsibility traditionally associated with this phrase is more of a longer, not transient, duration. The legal responsibility is usually very comprehensive in extent, rather than limited to a single purpose (i.e., classroom behavior).

It is questionable, then, whether a firearms trainer conducting a firearms class, or a range officer at a Boy Scout marksmanship class, would stand in loco parentis of a child in the class.

This statute thus seems to conflict with the more recent NCGS 14-269.7, which allows possession of handguns by minors with supervision by *any* adult. These two statutes seem to conflict concerning the proper supervisory authority for children under age 12.

It is possible that the phrase "in loco parentis" in this statute would be broadened by a court as meaning supervision by *any competent adult*. If so, that would harmonize this statute with NCGS 14-269.7, and reconcile the conflict.

138

However, it is possible that this statute is intended to put a greater restriction on the use of firearms by children under age 12, by specifically limiting the only acceptable supervisory adult to be the child's parent.

It is likely that a court would interpret these two statutes to follow the more restrictive rule of NCGS 14-316 for children under age 12, and the more general rule of NCGS 14-269.7 for all other minor children.

NCGS 14-269.7 and NCGS 14-315 apply only to handguns, not rifles. NCGS 14-316 applies to rifles and handguns.

NCGS 14-402   Sale of Certain Weapons Without Permit Forbidden

a.   It is illegal to sell, give away, transfer, purchase, or receive a <u>pistol</u> in North Carolina unless: 1) a license or permit has been obtained by the purchaser or receiver from the Sheriff, or   2) the purchaser or receiver holds a concealed handgun permit issued under NCGS 14-415.10 through 14-415.24.

a.   It is unlawful to receive a pistol from a postal employee without showing the permit from the Sheriff.

a.   A violation of this statute is a misdemeanor.

b.   This section does not apply to antique firearms.

c.   An antique firearm is defined in NCGS 14-409.11.

<u>Caselaw.</u>   No relevant case found.   There is a relevant Attorney General opinion. In 1982 N.C.A.G. Lexis 55 (1982), the question was raised whether this statute, as read literally, required firearms dealers with a federal firearms license to obtain permits from the Sheriff for each firearm purchased for inventory. The Attorney General replied that dealers are not required to obtain Sheriff's permits for inventory firearms. However, a permit would be required for dealers who remove a pistol from inventory for personal use.

<u>Comments.</u>   This is a key statute requiring a permit to acquire or receive a pistol. A permit must be obtained from the Sheriff before a pistol can be purchased, unless the purchaser holds a North Carolina concealed handgun permit. The purchaser submits the permit to the seller of the pistol.

The requirement applies only to pistols, not rifles, long guns, or shotguns. The word "pistol" is not defined in this set of statutes, but is very likely synonymous with "handgun." See 14-409.39 (3).

The statute does not specify any limitation on the number of permits which may be issued at one time, or over any particular period of time.

The statute has been implemented such that a separate permit is issued for each pistol. The form of the permit specified by NCGS 14-403 expressly reads that the permit allows the applicant "to purchase one pistol."

This statute does not expressly state that the permit holder (the buyer) must give the permit or a copy of the permit to the seller of the pistol before completing the sale. Giving the seller a copy of the permit is implied because that is the only way that the seller could later prove that they sold the pistol to someone who held a permit.

One question is whether a person receiving a pistol as an inheritance must obtain a permit. Literal reading of the statute suggests that any receipt or transfer of a pistol would require a permit, even if by inheritance. Sparse literature suggests that a permit must be obtained, but no case or Attorney General opinion has been found answering that point.

This statute does not seem to apply to *loaned* or *rented* firearms.

NCGS 14-403 Permit Issued by Sheriff; Form of Permit; Expiration of Permit

Sheriffs shall issue a license or permit to any person, firm, or corporation to purchase or receive a <u>pistol</u> from anyone offering to sell, transfer, or dispose of the pistol. The permit expires 5 years from the issuance date. The permit shall be in the form specified in this statute.

<u>Caselaw.</u>   No relevant case found.

<u>Comments.</u>   This key statute, enacted in 1919, requires purchasers to obtain a permit from their local Sheriff before purchasing a pistol. The Sheriff will perform a background check on the prospective purchaser before issuing the permit as a precaution against criminals or unauthorized persons purchasing pistols. This background check is not expressly mandated in the statute itself, but is part of the prescribed text of the permit form.

This statute reads that the Sheriff "shall issue" the permit if the applicant passes the background check. North Carolina is thus known as a "shall issue" State, as opposed to "may issue" States where Sheriffs have discretion to grant or deny purchase permits. Some Sheriffs in "may issue" States take a gun control stance and decline a larger percentage of permit requests.

The mandated form of the pistol purchase permit does not have a section to specifically identify any particular pistol to be purchased by description or serial number or otherwise.

The statute has been generally implemented such that a separate permit is issued for each pistol. The form of the permit specified by NCGS 14-403 expressly reads that the permit allows the applicant "to purchase one pistol."

The permit form does not specify from whom the pistol must be purchased, simply giving the permittee the right to purchase a pistol "from any person, firm or corporation authorized to dispose of the same."

NCGS 14-404   Issuance or Refusal of Permit; Appeal; Grounds for Refusal; Sheriff's Fee

a.   Sheriffs must issue pistol purchase permits only to residents of the county where the Sheriff is located, except for collectors, when the Sheriff has verified by a criminal background check that the applicant is not barred from purchasing a pistol, and that the Sheriff is satisfied as to the "good moral character" of the applicant, and that the applicant desires the pistol for self-defense, target shooting, collecting, or hunting.

b. The Sheriff may decline to issue the permit if reasons for the rejection are supplied to the applicant in writing within 7 days of declining the permit. An applicant may appeal the Sheriff's rejection to the local District Court.

c. The Sheriff may not issue a permit to an applicant who is or has been:

-under indictment or information, or who has been convicted of, a felony
-a fugitive from justice
-an unlawful drug user
-mentally incompetent
-committed to a mental institution
-an illegal alien
-discharged from the armed forces under a less than honorable discharge
-renounced his United States citizenship
-subject to certain domestic restraining orders.

d.   The permitting requirements do not apply to a law enforcement officer authorized to carry firearms if the officer identifies himself as such an officer, and states that the firearm is needed for the officer's official duties.

e. The Sheriff may charge a processing fee of $5.00 *upon issuance* of the permit.

f. The Sheriff has 30 days to respond to an application for a permit. If the application is approved, the permit shall be immediately issued to the applicant.

Caselaw.   No relevant case found.

Comments.   This section cites procedures and eligibility for issuance by the Sheriff of a permit to purchase a handgun.

Subsection (a) specifies that the applicant must be a "resident" of the county where the application is filed. No minimum time of having been a resident is specified. No criteria to determine whether an applicant qualifies as a resident are supplied by the statute. It is not stated whether applicants can, or cannot, have "dual residency" with other States (usually Florida).

NCGS 14-404.1   Database of Denied Applications for a Permit to Purchase a Pistol

There is no such statute as of December 2005. House Bill 1415 was introduced in the 2005 Legislative Session calling for a statewide database of denied applications for a permit to purchase a pistol. The bill made it very much through the legislative process, but was not enacted before the session adjourned. This bill will presumably be seen in a future session.

NCGS 14-405   Record of Permits Kept by Sheriff

The Sheriff shall keep a record of all permits issued to purchase pistols.

Caselaw.   No relevant case found.

Comments.   This statute is self explanatory. This is a somewhat politically sensitive statute. Gun-rights groups assert that such records can be, and have been, used to identify gun owners in gun confiscation programs by the government.

NCGS 14-406   Dealer to Keep Record of Sales

Dealers in pistols and other weapons mentioned in Article 52A shall keep an accurate record of all such sales, including certain information specified in this statute. This sales record shall be open to inspection by any law enforcement officer.

Caselaw.   No relevant case found.

Comments.   This statute was enacted in 1919 and is self explanatory. See NCGS 14-408 (violation of this statute a misdemeanor). This is a somewhat politically sensitive statute. Gun-rights groups assert that such records can be, and have been, used to identify gun owners in gun confiscation programs by the government.

"Dealers" in pistols are required to keep records of pistol sales, but the word "dealer" is not defined in this statute or Article. NCGS 14-409.39(1) defines a dealer as someone licensed as a dealer under 18 USC 921 (a federal law) or NCGS 105-80, but NCGS 14-409.39 limits the application of the definition of "dealer" to the Article in which it appears, which does not include NCGS 14-406.

This statute does not specify for how long a dealer must maintain sales records.

This statute does not require non-dealers of firearms who make a firearm sale, such as with private party sales, to keep such sales records.

NCGS 14-407.1 Sale of Blank Cartridge Pistols

A permit is required for the sale or transfer of pistols designed to fire blank cartridges.

Clerks of Court, and not the Sheriff, may issue permits to purchase or receive pistols suitable for firing blank cartridges. The form of the permit is specified in this statute.

Caselaw.   No relevant case found.

Comments.   This statute was enacted in 1959. It is presumed that pistols covered by this statute are pistols designed *solely* to fire blank cartridges, and not firearms which can *also* fire blank cartridges *in addition to* firing regular ammunition.

143

NCGS 14-408 Violation of NCGS 14-406 is a Misdemeanor

Violation of NCGS 14-406 is a misdemeanor.

<u>Caselaw.</u>   No relevant case found.

<u>Comments.</u>   This statute is self explanatory.

NCGS 14-409 Machine Guns and Other Like Weapons

a. A "machine gun" or "submachine gun" is any weapon which shoots, is designed to shoot, or can be readily restored to shoot, automatically more than one shot, without manual reloading, by a single function of the trigger. The terms also include the frame or receiver of any such weapon, and any combination of parts designed to convert a weapon into a machine gun.

b. It is unlawful to sell, give away, dispose of, use, or possess machine guns or submachine guns, except for:

-banks, merchants and recognized business establishments for use on their premises, if such entities have a permit for such firearm from the local Sheriff
-United States Army soldiers on official duty
-National Guard soldiers when on actual duty
-government officers when acting on behalf of the government
-manufacturers, users, or possessors of such firearms for scientific or experimental purposes when such use is lawful under federal law, and where the firearm is registered with a federal agency, and where a permit for the firearm has been obtained from the local Sheriff.

A State resident who "now owns" a machine gun used in "former wars" as a relic or souvenir, does not violate this statute if the machine gun is reported to the local Sheriff.

c. Violation of this statute is a felony.

<u>Caselaw.</u>   The only once relevant case on this statute was <u>State v. Lee</u>, 176 S.E.2d 772 (NC 1970), which was invalidated by substantial change in the statute in 1989.

In an Attorney General opinion, 1982 N.C.A.G. Lexis 56 (1982), the question was raised as to what standards and criteria a Sheriff should apply in deciding whether to issue a permit for a machine gun, since the statute is silent on the subject. The

Attorney General's opinion discussed the issue at length, concluding that the Sheriff's decision was a matter of judgment at the Sheriff's discretion.

Comments.   This statute generally prohibits ownership of machine guns by civilians. The authority given by this statute for certain civilians to possess and use machine guns is significantly limited by federal law.

It is presumed that the exception allowing residents to own a machine gun obtained as a war souvenir was intended to avoid criminalizing the uncounted war veterans who brought back captured enemy automatic firearms. This statute does not require that the owner of the firearm necessarily be the veteran who originally captured the firearm, or that the owner be a veteran at all.

NCGS 14-409.10 Purchase of Rifle and Shotguns Out of State

It is legal for North Carolina citizens to purchase rifles, shotguns, or ammunition for such firearms in States contiguous to North Carolina.

Caselaw.   No relevant case found.

Comments.   This statute was enacted in 1969. This statute does not expressly permit North Carolina residents who purchased a firearm or ammunition out of state to import the items into North Carolina, but that right is presumed. Some jurisdictions have laws which prohibit the importation of firearms and/or ammunition into that jurisdiction except by dealers. Such laws may be an attempt to protect local merchants, to hinder the firearms industry, or to insulate the jurisdiction from the effects of a neighboring jurisdiction which has less restrictive gun laws.

The protections of this statute does not extend to handguns. The intention and meaning of the Legislature in omitting handguns from this statute is unknown.

14-409.11 Antique Firearm Defined

An antique firearm is any firearm manufactured in or before 1898, any matchlock, flintlock, percussion cap, or similar weapon, or any replica of such weapon regardless of when manufactured. An antique firearm is also any weapon using fixed ammunition manufactured in or before 1898, for which ammunition is no longer manufactured in the United States and is also not readily available.

Caselaw.   No relevant case found.

Comments.   This statute is useful because some firearms are exempt from firearms laws if they are an antique.

NCGS 14-409.39 Definitions

1. A "dealer" is any person licensed under 18 USC 921 or NCGS 105-80.

2. A "firearm" is a handgun, shotgun, or rifle which expels a projectile by action of an explosion.

3. A "handgun" is a pistol, revolver, or other gun which has a short stock and is designed to be held and fired by the use of a single hand.

Caselaw.   Merely because a firearm cannot "expel a projectile" because the firearm is inoperable, disassembled, or unloaded does not mean that such a firearm is not a firearm under the statutes. State v. Jackson, 546 S.E.2d 570 (NC 2001).

Comments.   This statute is self-explanatory.

NCGS 14-409.40   Statewide Uniformity of Local Regulation

a.   The entire field of regulation of firearms is preempted from regulation by local governments except as provided by this section.

a.1. The lawful design, marketing, manufacture, distribution, sale or transfer of firearms or ammunition to the public is not an unreasonably dangerous activity and does not constitute a nuisance per se. It is the unlawful use of firearms and ammunition, rather than their design, marketing, manufacture, distribution, sale or transfer that is the cause of injuries arising from their unlawful use. This subsection applies only to lawsuits brought under subsection "g" below.

b.   No county or city may regulate in any manner the possession, ownership, storage, transfer, sale, purchase, licensing, or registration of firearms, ammunition, components of firearms, or dealers, unless otherwise permitted by statute.

c.   A county or city may regulate by zoning or other ordinances the sale of firearms at a location only if there is a lawful, general, and similar regulation or prohibition of commercial activities at that location.

d.   No county or city may, by zoning regulation or otherwise, regulate firearms shows (i.e., "gun shows") more stringently than shows of other items.

146 _____

e.   A county or city may regulate transport, carrying, or possession of firearms by employees of that government in the course of those employees' employment with that government.

f.   Nothing in this statute limits the application of authority of local governments under the following statutes:

NCGS 36A (governmental powers in states of emergency)
NCGS 153A-129 (county regulation of discharge and display of firearms);
NCGS 160A-189 (city regulation of discharge and display of firearms);
NCGS 14-269 (carrying concealed firearms);
NCGS 14-269.2 (firearms on school campuses prohibited);
NCGS 14-269.3 (firearms where alcoholic beverages are sold or consumed);
NCGS 14-269.4 (carrying firearm onto State property or courthouses);
NCGS 14-277.2 (firearms at parades, funeral processions, picket lines, health care facilities, or government property);
NCGS 14.415.11 (carrying concealed handguns);
NCGS 14-415.23 (statewide uniformity of concealed handgun laws);
and related to possession of firearms in publicly-owned buildings or in public parks or recreational areas.

Nothing in this subsection prohibits a person from storing a firearm in a motor vehicle while the vehicle is located upon these grounds or areas.

g.   The authority to bring a lawsuit and the right to recover against any firearms or ammunition marketer, manufacturer, distributor, dealer, seller, or trade association by or on behalf of any governmental unit for any remedy related to the lawful design, marketing, manufacture, distribution, sale, or transfer of firearms or ammunition to the public is reserved exclusively to the State. Any action brought by the State pursuant to this section shall be brought by the Attorney General.

Caselaw.   No relevant case found.

Comments.   This statute, enacted in 1995, is important in several ways. A key part is that the State preempts all County and municipal governments from making local laws concerning firearms. This generally makes firearms law statewide in scope in North Carolina. Some States allow counties and cities to make local firearms law, and that results in a bewildering patchwork of local laws about which residents are often ill-informed.

An Attorney General opinion, 1981 N.C.A.G. 66 (1981) opined that cities and counties could require registration of handguns, despite the federal Second

147

Amendment and the corresponding State constitutional right. That Attorney General opinion was invalidated by this statute in 1995.

NCGS 14-409.40(a.1) and (g), NCGS 99B-1.1, and NCGS 99B-11, are intended to prevent the types of lawsuits being asserted by some other States, or cities or counties outside North Carolina, or by private parties in those other States, who are suing the manufacturers of firearms and ammunition under various novel legal theories. The policy of North Carolina, as stated in these statutes, is to hold the criminal who used a firearm to commit a crime accountable, not the manufacturer of the firearm or ammunition. The persons bringing such lawsuits in those other States do not seriously hope to win such lawsuits against firearm or ammunition manufacturers, but have the ulterior aim of putting the manufacturer out of business by forcing them to incur heavy legal fees in defending against the lawsuits.

NCGS 14-409.45 Definitions for the Sport Shooting Range Protection Act

A sport shooting range is an area designed and operated for the use of rifles, shotguns, pistols, or any other similar sport shooting.

Caselaw.   No relevant case found.

Comments.   NCGS 14-409.45 to 14-409.47 is Article 53C, the Sport Shooting Range Protection Act of 1997.

This statute does not necessarily require that the shooting range be commercially operated or open to the public. This statute does not prohibit gun clubs from coming under its protections.

NCGS 14-409.46   Sport Shooting Range Protection Act

a. Owners, operators, or users of a shooting range shall not be subject to civil or criminal liability for excessive noise or noise pollution if the range was in use at least 3 years before the effective date of Article 53C (which was 1997), and the range was then in compliance with all noise control laws which existed *at the time the range began operation.*

b. This subsection is the same as subsection (a) above, except that the owner, operator, or user of the shooting range is not liable for *nuisance* on account of noise.

c. Rules adopted by any State department or agency limiting outdoor decibel noise levels shall not apply to a shooting range protected by this statute.

d. A person who acquires title to a tract of real estate which is burdened by the noise of a pre-existing shooting range is not allowed to bring a nuisance lawsuit against the range for noise violations, unless the shooting range had a substantial change in use after that person acquired title.

e. A shooting range that was in compliance with existing law when a new ordinance is enacted (or existing ordinance was amended), and where the range was in existence at least 3 years before the enactment of this Act in 1997, is not required to comply with the new ordinance or amendment.

Caselaw.   No relevant case found.

Comments.   This statute was enacted in 1997. A shooting range, then, had to be in operation in <u>1994</u> to come under the protections of this statute. There are questions about this statute. Does the shooting range have to continuously operate a shooting range to maintain eligibility under this statute? If a shooting range expands operations with new acreage, is the new acreage also covered under this statute? If the shooting range acreage remains the same, but the amount of shooting increases for whatever reason, is the increased shooting protected under this statute? Is police training, which is not "sport shooting," protected?

Senate Bill 1137 was introduced in March 2005 to add a section to this statute stating that if a qualifying shooting range had to be relocated due to condemnation, road construction, rezoning, or development, then the shooting range could keep its qualification under this statute at its new location. This bill never made it out of committee.

Protection under this statute does not appear to be affected by a change in ownership of the shooting range, so long as range operations take place as specified by the statute.

It is common that a shooting range is built in the rural outskirts of a town on inexpensive land. Years pass, and city development expands out to the shooting range. The new residents complain, and the shooting range sells its now expensive acreage, and moves outward to a new rural site. That common story became more complicated with the passage of this statute, because the protections granted by this statute are not transferable to the new acreage. The value of the old shooting range acreage increased due to its new proximity to expanding development, perhaps increased in value even more due to its right of protection under this statute.

NCGS 14-409.47 Application of Article 53C (NCGS 14-409.45 to .47)

NCGS 14-409.45 and 14-409.46 do not prohibit a local government from regulating the location and construction of a shooting range after the effective date of this statute, which is 1997, except as stated in those two statutes.

Caselaw.   No relevant case found.

Comments.   None.

Article 54A – The Felony Firearms Act (NCGS 14-415.1 to 415.9)

NCGS 14-415.1 Possession of Firearms, Etc., by a Felon Prohibited

a. It is a felony for a convicted felon to purchase, own, possess, or have in his custody or control a firearm or any weapon of mass death and destruction as defined by NCGS 14-288.8(c). For the purposes of this statute, silencers are defined to be firearms.

b. The prior felony conviction, to be counted under the preceding subsection, can have occurred any time in the felon's life.

Caselaw.   While North Carolina law may allow convicted felons to possess firearms in their home or place of business, this does not bar federal law which may prohibit felons from possessing firearms in those places. U.S. v. King, 119 F.3d 290 (4th Cir. 1997). This case became moot with the 2004 amendment, because felons can no longer possess a firearm even in their own home.

A felon's "home" can be a rented residence. State v. Locklear, 465 S.E.2d 61 (NC App 1996). This case became moot with the 2004 amendment, because felons can no longer possess a firearm even in their own home.

It is likely that a felon's home can also be a motel room in which he is staying. State v. Cloninger, 350 S.E.2d 895 (NC App 1986). This case became moot with the 2004 amendment, because felons can no longer possess a firearm even in their own home.

A felon's home does not include common areas in an apartment community. State v. McNeill, 337 S.E.2d 172 (NC App 1985). This case became moot with the 2004 amendment, because felons can no longer possess a firearm even in their own home.

It is no defense to a violation of this statute that the firearm was not working or operable. State v. McCree, 584 S.E.2d 861 (NC App 2003). State v. Jackson, 546 S.E.2d 570 (NC 2001).

Comments.   This is a key criminal statute, generally prohibiting a felon from possessing firearms.

Prior to 2004, felons were not prohibited from owning or possessing a rifle with a barrel longer than 18 inches, and did not prohibit a felon from possessing a firearm on his own home or place of business. The 2004 amendment to this statute tightened the restrictions upon felons, generally prohibiting possession of firearms by felons.

NCGS 14-415.3   Possession of a Firearm or Weapon of Mass Destruction by Insane or Incompetent Persons

a. It is illegal for anyone acquitted of certain specified crimes by reason of insanity, or who has been determined to "lack capacity to proceed" regarding those crimes, to purchase, own, possess, or have in their custody a firearm or weapon of mass death and destruction.

b. Violation of this statute is a felony. Firearms seized under this statute shall be forfeited to the State.

Caselaw.   No relevant case found.

Comments.   This statute was enacted in 1994. This statute contains a paradox. The sole circumstances where this statute would be relevant, namely, where a person cannot be found guilty of a crime because they are either insane or lack capacity to proceed to trial, would also be the exact circumstances which would prevent a felony conviction under *this* statute as well. Convictions aside, at least this statute allows seizure of the firearms from the insane person.

Article 54B – Concealed Handgun Permits (NCGS 14-415.10 to 14-415.24)

Article 54B is a significant firearms statute. The statutes included in Article 54B are NCGS 14-415.10 through 14-415.24. The concealed handgun statutes were enacted in 1995, as North Carolina was following a national trend of expanding concealed handgun statutes. This trend also featured making issuance of concealed handgun permits mandatory if an applicant met specified criteria, rather than leaving the decision on issuance up to the discretion of a government employee.

151

The concealed handgun statutes passed both houses of the State General Assembly with wide margins, and enjoyed bi-partisan support.

See NCGS 14-269 for the basic prohibition on carrying concealed firearms.

NCGS 14-415.10 Definitions

1. The phrase "to carry a concealed handgun" also means to have "possession of a concealed handgun."

2. A handgun is a firearm that has a short stock and is designed to be held and fired by the use of a single hand.

1a. The term "deployed" or "deployment" is any military duty that removes a military permittee from the permittee's county of residence during the date on which the permittee's concealed carry license expires.

2a. The term "military permittee" means anyone who holds a concealed carry license who is also a member of the federal armed forces or the State national guard.

3a. The term "proof of deployment" means a copy of a military permittee's deployment orders, or other written notification from the permittee's command, indicating the start and end date of deployment and that orders the permittee to travel outside the permittee's county of residence.

Various other definitions are given.

Caselaw.   No relevant case found.

Comments.   This statute was originally enacted in 1995. A concealed handgun permit under NCGS 14-415.11 is different from a permit to purchase a pistol under NCGS 14-403. The holder of a concealed handgun permit also had to obtain a permit to purchase a handgun until a law change in 2005.

Deployed Military Personnel Act.   The statutes were amended in 2005 to provide extra time for military personnel who are concealed carry license holders to renew their licenses, if the permittee was deployed on military duties at the time. This amendment, Session Law 2005-232, entitled "An Act to Grant Deployed Military Personnel an Extension of Time Within Which to Renew a Concealed Handgun Permit," was enacted in response to the large numbers of military personnel based in North Carolina who were deployed in Afghanistan and Iraq. See NCGS 14-

415.10, 14-415.11(a), 14-415.16A, and 14-269(a1) for specific references to this Act.

NCGS 14-415.11   Permit to Carry Concealed Handgun; Scope of Permit

a. Anyone who has a concealed handgun permit may carry a concealed handgun unless otherwise prohibited by law.

a. A person shall carry the concealed handgun permit with identification whenever that person carries a concealed handgun.

a. A person carrying a concealed handgun shall disclose to a police officer that he or she is carrying a concealed handgun permit and a concealed handgun when approached or addressed by the officer.

a. A person shall display both his or her concealed handgun permit and identification to any police officer upon request of the officer.

a. A military permittee whose permit expired during deployment may carry a concealed handgun during the 90 days following the end of his deployment before the permit is renewed provided the permittee also displays proof of deployment to any law enforcement officer. See NCGS 14-415.10.

b. The Sheriff shall issue a permit to carry a concealed handgun to a person who qualifies for a permit under NCGS 14-415.12.

b. Concealed handgun permits are valid for 5 years.

c. A concealed handgun permit does not authorize a person to carry a concealed handgun in the following places:

      -schools, universities, private schools, educational properties
            NCGS 14-269.2
      -assemblies where a fee is charged for admission NCGS 14-269.3
      -places where alcoholic beverages are sold and consumed NCGS 14-269.3
      -State government property or courthouses NCGS 14-269.4
      -parades NCGS 14-277.2
      -picket lines NCGS 14-277.2
      -funeral processions NCGS 14-277.2
      -demonstrations upon private health care facilities NCGS 14-277.2
      -public places owned or operated by State or local governments
            NCGS 14-277.2

-State legislative building grounds NCGS 120-32.1
-school grounds 18 USC 922
-any area prohibited by federal law
-law enforcement facilities
-correctional facilities (jails, prisons)
-buildings housing only State or federal offices
-State or federal offices in commercial office buildings
-financial institutions (banks, credit unions, etc.)
-premises posted with notice prohibiting concealed firearms.

c. It is illegal for a person to carry a concealed firearm while consuming alcohol, or when that person has in his blood any remaining alcohol or controlled substance previously consumed, unless the controlled substance was lawfully obtained and taken in therapeutically appropriate amounts.

d. The holder of a concealed handgun permit shall notify the Sheriff who issued the permit of any change in the person's permanent address within 30 days after the change of address.

d. If a permit is lost or destroyed, the permit holder shall notify the Sheriff who issued the permit of the loss or destruction. A person may obtain a replacement permit by making a notarized application and paying the required fee.

Caselaw.   No relevant case found.

Comments.   This is a key statute, and was originally enacted in 1995. See NCGS 14-269 for the general prohibition on carrying concealed firearms.

A concealed handgun permit allows the holder to carry only a concealed handgun, as the name implies. The permit does not authorize carrying concealed carbines, rifles, or shotguns.

A literal reading of the statute indicates that the concealed carry permit authorizes the carry of only one concealed handgun at a time, because the statute reads that a permit holder "may carry a concealed handgun," with the word "handgun" being written in the singular, not plural. There were no cases found where this has ever been tested in court.

A concealed handgun permit is not tied to or valid for any one particular handgun. The holder of a permit may carry one handgun one day, and another handgun the next day.

The notice to be posted declaring concealed handgun permits invalid on their premises must be a "conspicuous" notice. "Conspicuous" is not defined by statute or caselaw. The contents of this notice are unstated. It is not stated by statute or caselaw whether *all* entrances to the premises must be posted before this prohibition would be valid. These notices are extremely rare for two reasons. First, most people do not know of their right to declare an area upon which concealed handgun permits are invalid. Second, as the only people who would obey the notice are law-abiding people, the effect of the notice is to put disarmed law-abiding people at the mercy of armed criminals.

The person entitled to post the notice invalidating concealed carry permits is "the person is legal possession or control of the premises," which usually means the landowner or a tenant.

The sentence structure of sub-section (c) above is a little awkward, but probably means that concealed firearms may be carried at state-owned rest stops on public highways.

NCGS 14-415.12 Criteria to Qualify for Issuance of a Concealed Handgun Permit

a. The Sheriff shall issue a concealed handgun permit to an applicant if the applicant:

1. is a United States citizen residing in the State for at least 30 days before applying,

2. is 21 years of age or older,

3. has no physical or mental infirmity preventing safe handling of a handgun,

4. completed an approved firearms safety training course, and

5. is not disqualified under subsection (b) following.

b. The Sheriff shall deny a permit to any applicant who:

1. is ineligible to own, possess, or receive a firearm under State or federal law,

2. is under indictment for a felony,

3. has been found guilty of a felony,

4. is a fugitive from justice,

5. is an unlawful user of alcohol or any controlled substance or drug,

6. lacks mental capacity or is mentally ill,

7. has been discharged from the military with a less than honorable discharge,

8. has been found guilty of, has received a prayer for judgment continued for, or received a suspended sentence for, certain specified misdemeanor crimes,

9. has had entry of a prayer for judgment continued for any crime in this statute,

10. is free on bond or personal recognizance for any crime in this statute, or

11. has been convicted of an impaired driving offense under specified statutes within three years before applying for the concealed handgun permit.

Caselaw.   No relevant case found.

There is an Attorney General opinion, 1997 N.C. A.G. 11 (1997), where a concealed handgun permittee had his permit revoked for breach of law. The ex-permittee then moved to another county in North Carolina, and applied there for a concealed handgun permit. The Attorney General gave the opinion that a permittee whose permit had been revoked could not re-apply for a new permit in that county or any other county in North Carolina. The Attorney General went on to say that nothing would prohibit the permittee from re-applying for a permit after the old permit which had been revoked would have expired.

Comments.   North Carolina has no provision for issuance of non-resident concealed carry permits, unlike some other States. This becomes less of an issue with the steady increase of reciprocity laws. This statute was enacted in 1995.

NCGS 14-415.12A Firearms Course Exemption for Current or Former Law Enforcement Officers

a. A current or former law enforcement officer, as defined in NCGS 14-415.10(4) or (5), is exempt from taking the firearms safety and training course required for a concealed handgun permit.

b. Certain private security guards are exempt from taking the firearms safety and training course required for a concealed handgun permit.

Caselaw.   No relevant case found.

Comments.   None.

NCGS 14-415.13 Application for Concealed Handgun Permit

a. Applicants shall apply to the Sheriff of the county in which the applicant resides to obtain a concealed handgun permit.

The applicant shall submit to the Sheriff all of the following:

    1. an application, under oath, on a form provided by the Sheriff

    2. a nonrefundable permit fee

    3. a set of fingerprints taken by the Sheriff

    4. a certificate of completion of the firearms safety and training course required by NCGS 14-415.12(a)(4)

    5. A release authorizing disclosure to the Sheriff of any medical records of the applicant concerning mental health or capacity of the applicant.

b. The Sheriff shall submit the fingerprints to the State Bureau of Investigation for a records check of certain databases, which fingerprints will also be submitted to the Federal Bureau of Investigation as needed. The applicant pays the cost of processing the fingerprints.

Caselaw.   No relevant case found.

Comments.   This statute was enacted in 1995.

NCGS 14-415.14 Application Form to be Provided by the Sheriff; Information to be Included on the Application Form

a. The Sheriff shall make applications readily available to applicants. The form shall be prescribed by the Administrative Office of the Courts.

b. The form shall contain a specified warning stating that federal and State laws on possession of a handgun differ, and possession of a State handgun permit is not a defense to violation of federal handgun law.

b. Any person or entity (presumably, a mental health facility or physician) that is presented with the release specified by NCGS 14-415.13(a)(5) shall promptly disclose to the Sheriff medical records they have on the applicant named in the release.

Caselaw.   No relevant case found.

Comments.   None.

NCGS 14-415.15 Issuance or Denial of a Concealed Handgun Permit

a. The Sheriff shall issue or deny a concealed handgun permit to the applicant within 90 days of the application date, except as otherwise allowed by subsection (b). The Sheriff may conduct any investigation necessary to determine the qualification or competency of the applicant for the permit.

b. The Sheriff may issue a temporary concealed handgun permit to the applicant in what is deemed by the Sheriff to be an emergency situation. The temporary permit is valid for a maximum of 90 days. The temporary permit may not be renewed. The temporary permit may be revoked by the Sheriff without a hearing. The applicant may submit a protective order issued under NCGS 50B-3 (protective orders in domestic violence situations) as evidence of an emergency situation.

c. The Sheriff may deny the application for a concealed handgun permit only if the applicant fails to qualify under the criteria specified by statute. If the Sheriff denies the application, the Sheriff shall, within 90 days, notify the applicant in writing of the grounds for denial.

c. An applicant may appeal the denial, revocation, or nonrenewal of a permit by petitioning a District Court judge in the judicial district where the application was filed. The determination of the court shall be final.

<u>Caselaw.</u>　　No relevant case found.

<u>Comments.</u>　　This statute was originally enacted in 1995. The statute was amended in 2005 by Session Law 2005-343 to make it easier for people to be protected under a domestic protective order to obtain a temporary concealed carry permit from the Sheriff. See subsection (b) above, and NCGS 50B-3.

NCGS 14-415.16 Renewal of a Concealed Handgun Permit

The holder of a concealed handgun permit shall apply to renew the permit at least 30 days before the expiration date of the permit by filing a renewal application with the Sheriff of the county where the applicant resides.

New fingerprints are required in certain cases.

A renewal fee is charged. The standards specified by NCGS 14-415.12 apply for renewals. A criminal background check will be performed.

The Sheriff may waive the firearms safety and training course for renewals.

If the applicant remains qualified, the Sheriff shall issue the renewal permit.

<u>Caselaw.</u>　　No relevant case found.

<u>Comments.</u>　　This is a straightforward procedural statute. The statute again states that the Sheriff "shall issue" a renewal permit if the applicant remains qualified.

NCGS 14-415.16A　　Concealed Handgun Permit Extensions and Renewals for Deployed Military Permittees

a. Military personnel who will be deployed when their concealed handgun permit will expire may personally or by an agent apply to the local Sheriff for an extension of the permit to a date 90 days after the deployment is scheduled to end.

b. The concealed handgun permit of a military person which is <u>not</u> extended under subsection (a) above is nevertheless valid during the deployment and up to 90 days after the deployment ends. The military person may carry a concealed firearm provided the permit holder meets the requirements of subsection (a) above.

c. A military permittee under subsection (a) or (b) has until 90 days after the end of deployment to renew the concealed handgun permit.

Caselaw.   This statute, enacted in mid-2005, is too new for any cases.

Comments.   This statute was enacted to assist the many military personnel deployed out of North Carolina for extended periods during the Second Iraqi War. See NCGS 14-415.10.

NCGS 14-415.17 Form of the Permit; List of Permit Holders Available to Law Enforcement Agencies

The concealed handgun permit form is prescribed by the Administrative Office of the Courts, and shall be approximately the same size as a drivers license. The content of the permit form is prescribed by this statute.

The Sheriff shall maintain a list of concealed handgun permits issued, which data shall be made available to other law enforcement agencies.

Sheriffs shall notify the State Bureau of Investigation of permits issued, which shall make permit data available to law enforcement agencies and Clerks of Court on a statewide system.

Caselaw.   No relevant case found.

Comments.   The "statewide system" where the database of permit information is maintained is not described in the statute. Identities of persons and agencies authorized to access the database are not specified. The statute does not specify limits on how the database information may be used by the persons entitled to access the database.

NCGS 14-415.18 Revocation or Suspension of Concealed Handgun Permit

a. The Sheriff of the county where a concealed handgun permit was issued may, after a hearing, revoke a permit for specified reasons:

1. fraud or intentional misrepresentation in applying for the permit,

2. misuse of a permit, lending a permit to another, duplicating a permit, or using a permit to cause harm to another person,

3. the doing of an act, or existence of a condition, which would have been grounds to deny the application for the permit,

160

4. the applicant is found guilty of, or receives a prayer for judgment continued for, a crime which would have disqualified the applicant when initially applying for the permit.

A permit holder may appeal the revocation or non-renewal of a permit by petitioning the District Court in the judicial district where the permit holder resides.

b. A court may suspend a permit as part of an order issued under NCGS 50B.

Caselaw.   No relevant case found.

Comments.   This is a straightforward procedural statute. Procedure for the hearing required before revocation is not described.

The statute does not specify when an ex-permittee can re-apply for a new permit. The Attorney General said, in his opinion of 1997 N.C. A.G. 11 (1997), that nothing prohibits an ex-permittee from re-applying for a permit after the old permit which was revoked would have expired. That implies that some permittees whose permits are about to expire have little at risk from having their permit revoked, and thus implies that the severity of the penalty one suffers from revocation of a permit will arbitrarily vary depending upon when their original permit would have expired.

NCGS 14-415.19   Fees For Concealed Handgun Permit

a. Fees specified by this statute are paid to the Sheriff. The fees are $80.00 for the initial application, $75.00 for the renewal fee, and $15.00 for a replacement permit fee, as of 2004. Use and sharing between government agencies of these fees are specified.

a.1. Fees for retired law enforcement officers are reduced to $45.00 for the application fee and $40.00 for the renewal fee.

b. Additionally, a $10.00 fee for fingerprinting may be charged.

Caselaw.   No relevant case found.

Comments.   None.

NCGS 14-415.20 No Liability For Sheriff For Issuing or Refusing to Issue Concealed Handgun Permits

A Sheriff who issues or refuses to issue a permit to carry a concealed handgun shall not incur any civil or criminal liability for the performance of the Sheriff's duties.

Caselaw.   No relevant case found.

Comments.   Enacted in 1995, this statute seems reasonable so long as denials of permits are on a case by case basis for reasonable cause, rather than a general refusal to grant any permits.

NCGS 14-415.21   Violation of This Article Is a Misdemeanor

a. Anyone issued a concealed handgun permit found to be carrying a concealed handgun without the permit in their possession, or who fails to disclose to a law enforcement officer that they hold a permit and is carrying a concealed handgun as required by NCGS 14-415.11, shall be punished in accordance with NCGS 14-3.1. In lieu of paying a fine for the first offense, the permittee may surrender the permit. Violations subsequent to the first violation shall be punished under subsection (b).

b. A violation of this statute other than as cited in subsection (a) is a misdemeanor.

Caselaw.   No relevant case found.

Comments.   NCGS 14-3.1 states that an "infraction" is a non-criminal violation of law not punishable by imprisonment. The penalty is a fine of not more than $100.00. This statute does not specify when or if, and under what circumstances, the permittee may get the permit back. This statute does not distinguish between the effects of "surrendering" a permit and having the permit "revoked," if there is a difference.

NCGS 14-415.22 Construction of This Article

Article 54B, the Concealed Handgun Permit group of statutes, does not require that a person who is authorized to carry a concealed handgun under NCGS 14-269(b) (i.e., military, police) to obtain a concealed handgun permit.

A person who is authorized to carry a concealed handgun under NCGS 14-269(b) (i.e., military, police) is not prohibited by this Article from carrying a concealed handgun onto property posted with a conspicuous notice prohibiting concealed handguns.

Caselaw.   No relevant case found.

Comments.   None.

NCGS 14-415.23 Statewide Uniformity

No county, city, town, political subdivision, State board or agency, or any department or agency, may enact an ordinance, rule, or regulation concerning legally carrying a concealed handgun.

Local governments may enact ordinances to allow posting of prohibitions against carrying a concealed handgun, in accord with NCGS 14-415.11(c), in government buildings and parks.

Caselaw.   No relevant case found.

Comments.   This is an important statute which preempts local jurisdictions from making ordinances regarding concealed carry. In other words, the State has made a uniform statewide set of laws for concealed carry. Uniformity makes it easier for citizens moving from jurisdiction to jurisdiction to know the rules.

Some political groups advocate allowing local jurisdictions to make their own rules on concealed carry. These political groups often assert that local people making local rules to address local problems is better than rules forced upon them from a distant State capital. However, if the State is a patchwork of conflicting concealed carry rules, more citizens would choose not to carry concealed firearms, or decide not to purchase firearms at all, because carrying and using firearms would be so problematical. These political groups see reduced carrying of concealed firearms and reduced purchasing of firearms, which were their ulterior motives, as good things, and generally see the possession of firearms by civilians as a bad thing.

Other political groups applaud statewide uniformity of concealed carry rules, which promotes the legal carry of concealed firearms. Statewide uniformity of firearms laws means no fragmented patchwork of differing laws. This uniformity gives the average citizen a much better chance to understand State firearms law. Further, travel with a firearm within the State becomes less problematical with uniform State laws, because the law is basically the same everywhere within the State. These political groups base their support for statewide uniformity on their belief that legal carrying of concealed firearms by citizens reduces crime.

Statewide uniformity laws are a battleground between gun-rights groups and anti-gun groups.

NCGS 14-415.24 Reciprocity; Out-of-State Concealed Handgun Permits

a. A valid concealed handgun permit issued in another State is valid in North Carolina if that other State accepts North Carolina permits in their State.

b. The North Carolina Attorney General shall maintain a list of States meeting the reciprocity requirements of North Carolina.

c. The North Carolina Department of Justice shall annually update its list of reciprocal States accepting North Carolina permits. The Department of Justice shall strive to increase reciprocity with other States.

Caselaw.   No relevant case found.

Comments.   Reciprocity is a valuable aid to persons carrying concealed firearms from State to State. Some political groups oppose reciprocity for the same reasons that such groups oppose statewide uniformity of concealed carry laws, discussed in NCGS 14-415.23 above. North Carolina has an express public policy of striving to increase reciprocity, per paragraph (c) above.

The key item to remember is that the holder of a North Carolina concealed handgun permit, when present in some other State accepting North Carolina's permit through reciprocity, must nevertheless follow the State laws of that other State regarding concealed carry.

A North Carolinian expecting to spend much time in some other State carrying a concealed handgun with a North Carolina permit is well advised to study that State's concealed weapons laws.

North Carolina does not issue concealed carry permits to non-residents, unlike some other States. This becomes less of an issue with the steady increase of reciprocity laws.

North Carolina only recently joined the growing number of States exchanging reciprocity privileges with other States, as this statute was enacted in 2003.

Chapter 15 (Criminal Procedure), Article 2 (Record and Disposition of Seized Items)

NCGS 15-11.1 Seizure, Custody, and Disposition of Certain Property

(This statute applies to Mecklenburg County only.)

a. If a law enforcement officer seizes a firearm under lawful authority, the property shall be held under the direction of the court as long as is necessary to assure that the firearm may be used as evidence at trial.

b.1. If the District Attorney determines that the firearm is no longer needed as evidence, the District Attorney, after notice to interested parties (including the owner of the firearm) shall apply to the court for an order of disposition of the firearm.

b.1. The judge, after hearing on the District Attorney's request for an order on disposition of a firearm, may order the disposition of the firearm, including, among other things, return to its rightful owner, return to the defendant, destruction of the firearm, delivery of the firearm to a local police agency for their use or sale.

b.1. Subsection (b1) is not applicable to seizures under NCGS 113-137 of firearms used only in connection with a violation of Article 22 of NCGS 113, or any local wildlife hunting ordinance.

Caselaw. Violation by the police or government of this statute does not require dismissal of charges against a criminal. State v. Ysut Mlo, 440 S.E.2d 98 (NC 1994).

Comments. Section 3 of Session Law 2005-106 states that this "act" (presumably, NCGS 15-11.1) applies to Mecklenburg County only. This statute is an example of a codified session law which affects only one county.

NCGS 15-11.2 Disposition of Unclaimed Firearms not Confiscated or Seized as Trial Evidence

a. An "unclaimed firearm" is a firearm found or received by a law enforcement agency that remains unclaimed by the person entitled to it for 30 days after publication of notice required by subsection (b) below. This phrase does not include a firearm obtained under NCGS 15-11.1 or NCGS 14-269.1.

b. When a law enforcement agency finds or receives a firearm, and the firearm remains unclaimed for 180 days, the agency shall publish a notice concerning the firearm in the newspaper, stating, among other things, that the firearm will be disposed of if not claimed within 30 days.

c. If no one claims the firearm within 30 days, then the person who found the firearm and turned the firearm over to the law enforcement agency may claim the firearm, if that person is eligible to possess a firearm.

d. If the person who found the firearm does not claim the firearm, then the chief of the law enforcement agency holding the firearm may apply to the local District Court for an order of disposition of the firearm.

e. The District Court may order turnover of the firearm to the law enforcement agency for destruction, or official use or sale by that agency.

Caselaw.   None.

Comments.   None.

Chapter 15A (Criminal Procedure Act), Article 16 (Electronic Surveillance)

NCGS 15A-290 Offenses for Which Electronic Surveillance Orders May be Granted

c.4. An order for the interception of wire, oral, or electronic communications may be granted when the interception may provide evidence of a felony offense involving assault with a firearm upon a governmental officer or employee in violation of NCGS 14-34.2.

Caselaw.   No relevant cases found.

Comments.   None.

Chapter 15A (Criminal Procedure Act), Article 20 (Arrest)

NCGS 15A-401 Arrest by Law Enforcement Officer

d.2. A law enforcement officer is authorized to use a firearm to make an arrest in certain circumstances specified in NCGS 15A-401(d)(1), if the officer reasonably believes it necessary to:

- defend against the imminent use of deadly force against the officer,
- defend against the imminent use of deadly force against another person,
- arrest or prevent escape of a person the officer reasonably believes
    is attempting to escape by using deadly force;
- arrest or prevent escape of a person the officer reasonably believes
    presents an imminent threat of death or serious physical injury
    to others unless apprehended without delay; or
- prevent escape of a person from custody held as a result of conviction
    for a felony.

f. A person is not justified in using a firearm to resist arrest by a law enforcement officer who is using reasonable force, when the person knows or has reason to know that the officer is a law enforcement officer, and the person knows or has reason to know that the officer is attempting to make an arrest.

f. Nothing in this statute justifies unreasonable or excessive use of force by a law enforcement officer making an arrest.

Caselaw.   No relevant cases found.

Comments.   None.

NCGS 15A-404   Detention of Offenders by Private Persons

a. No private person may <u>arrest</u> another person except as provided in NCGS 15A-405. A private person may <u>detain</u> another person as provided in this section.

b. A private person may detain another person when he has probable cause to believe that the other person committed, in his presence, a felony, a breach of the peace, a crime involving physical injury to another person, or a crime involving theft or destruction of property.

c. The manner of detention must be in a reasonable manner considering the offense involved and the circumstances.

d. The time period of the detention may be no longer than that needed to determine that no offense was committed, or to surrender the person detained to a law enforcement officer, whichever is sooner.

e. A private person who detains someone must immediately notify a law enforcement officer and surrender the person to the law enforcement officer.

<u>Caselaw.</u>   This statute and the concept of "detaining" a criminal were enacted in 1973 to replace the concept of the "citizen's arrest." The definition of "detain" means to "hold or keep in or as if in custody." <u>State v. Wall</u>, 286 S.E.2d 68 (NC 1982). Discussed, N.C. Atty. Gen. Opinion, 2001 N.C.A.G. (Lexis 5).

A private citizen cannot use a firearm to detain a person fleeing from committing a misdemeanor if a police officer is not authorized to use a firearm in that situation. <u>State v. Wall</u>, 286 S.E.2d 68 (NC 1982).

Use of a firearm to detain an alleged criminal may be permissible in certain situations. <u>State v. Ataei-Kachuei</u>, 314 S.E.2d 751 (NC App 1984), rev.den., 321 S.E.2d 146 (1984). The <u>Ataei-Kachuei</u> case was on appeal where the lower court had refused to allow the Defendant, a business owner, to use this statute as a defense for his shooting and killing the victim. The business owner asserted that he had just been robbed and was also present when the victim apparently tried to assault a person on the company premises with a deadly weapon (an automobile) when he made his escape, both felonies. The business owner fired two warning shots into the air, then shot and killed the victim with his third shot. The court found that a jury could find in that situation that the necessary events described in subsection (b) of the statute were present. As to whether the business owner acted

168

"in a reasonable manner" in shooting the victim to prevent his escape, and thus satisfy subsection (c) of the statute, the court found that a jury could have found that he acted reasonably. Therefore, the Ataei-Kachuei court stated that it is possible that a jury could find that it was reasonable for a citizen to enforce detention under this statute, upon pain of being shot with a firearm, under the facts of this case. The State appealed Ataei-Kachuei, but the Supreme Court refused to review the court's decision.

One such situation was where a father attempted to detain two thieves from theft of personal property and possible bodily harm to his daughter and/or wife. It is also possible that the criminals, escaping in a truck, may have endangered the father. The father apparently gave a warning shout to the fleeing criminals, then fired a warning shot from his rifle. The criminals then likely returned heavy fire from a pistol at the father. The father then began shooting at the criminals, hitting one. The trial court found that the father acted appropriately under this statute in attempting to detain the criminals, even by the shooting at the fleeing criminals. The appeals court affirmed the trial court's ruling. State v. Gilreath, 454 S.E.2d 871 (NC App 1995).

Comments.   This statute is most relevant in situations such as when a private person defending their home or residence with a firearm, or a person legally carrying a concealed handgun, catches a perpetrator committing a crime. This statute was enacted in 1973 to replace repealed statute NCGS 15-39, which allowed citizen's arrest in certain situations.

This statute is especially useful to those persons who carry concealed handguns, or keep firearms at their home or business for self defense. The question often raised is to what extent can a citizen detain a perpetrator caught committing certain crimes.

The change in terminology from "arrest" to "detention" is only semantics. This is especially odd since "arrest" connotes more sweeping powers than "detention," however, as discussed in the Official Commentary below, a citizen's detention powers seem to be broader in scope than what were a citizen's arrest powers.

The "Official Commentary" from NCGS 15A-404 reads as follows:

> "This section would replace the old concept of "citizen's arrest" with a concept of "citizen's detention." North Carolina has authorized the private citizen to make arrests in certain limited circumstances -- essentially felonies and breaches of the peace in his presence. To those two situations are added crimes involving physical injury to another person and a general authorization with regard to crimes involving theft or destruction of property.

169

The important conceptual change is from "arrest" to "detention." The notion of a private citizen "arresting" another in certain circumstances had led persons at times to act without authority and at times to place themselves or others in unjustified danger. Perhaps a safer idea is that the private citizen may detain the offender sufficiently long to turn him over to a law-enforcement officer. Though there may be little or no difference in the physical actions taken, it is hoped that this will be a clearer and safer concept for the private citizen."

It is a common question as to when a citizen can legally use a firearm to detain a suspected criminal. Several cases addressing this issue are discussed below.

Another guide may be NCGS 15A-401(d)(2), described in the statute above, which describes the situations when a police officer may use a firearm. The court in State v. Wall, 286 S.E.2d 68 (NC 1982), made this analogy, without explicitly stating it as a rule, that one could look to the rules on law enforcement officers using their firearms to detain a fleeing suspect as a guide as to what a civilian could do.

The three relevant firearms cases found for this statute, all discussed below, are not totally conclusive. Wall is a case where firearms use was not authorized because the crime was a minor misdemeanor. In State v. Ataei-Kachuei and State v. Gilreath, the facts offered the possibility that the shooter was acting in self-defense from the criminal's assault with a deadly weapon (in both cases, assault with an automobile as the criminals attempted to flee). In other words, neither State v. Ataei-Kachuei or State v. Gilreath was a situation where the suspect was merely fleeing without threatening danger to the armed civilian on the scene.

The pointed question is, then, assuming all the elements of the statute are otherwise met, whether a citizen would ever be justified in shooting a fleeing criminal where the criminal's flight posed no danger to the citizen making the detention, or to other people in the area. This question is directly relevant to a homeowner detaining home invaders, to a concealed handgun carrier who stumbles into a felony street robbery, or to the armed shopkeeper thwarting a brutal robbery.

The part of the statute that best addresses this issue about when a civilian can legally use a firearm to detain a suspect is subsection (c), which authorizes detention that is of a "reasonable manner" under the circumstances and considering the offense involved. If an armed citizen witnessed a brutal murder on the street, or an armed homeowner confronted home invaders who had just attacked his family, both high felonies, it would seem that "detention" at the point of a firearm would be a

170

"reasonable manner" under the circumstances. This is the author's opinion and observation in lieu of clear statutory or caselaw guidance.

It has been observed that very rarely will there be a situation where a suspect has just committed a felony, and then simply tries to run away without causing further threats to anyone as the suspect is confronted by the armed civilian. The suspect would usually still be threatening in some manner to the others present at the altercation. In that situation, then, the right of the armed civilian to use his or her firearm is based more so in the need for self defense or the defense of others, rather than being based in this statute.

NCGS 15A-405 Assistance to Law Enforcement Officer to Make Arrest

A private person, upon request for assistance by a law enforcement officer, has the same powers of arrest or to prevent escape as the law enforcement officer.

Caselaw.   No relevant cases found.

Comments.   None.

Chapter 15A (Criminal Procedure Act), Article 56 (Incapacity to Proceed)

NCGS 15A-1001.   Defendants who are mentally incapacitated may not be tried, sentenced, or punished.

NCGS 15A-1003 Referral of Incapable Defendant for Civil Commitment Proceeding

a. Defendants who are incapable of being prosecuted for a criminal offense due to mental incapacity may generally be committed to a mental health facility. If a Defendant was charged with a crime involving a firearm, the judge's custody order shall require a law enforcement officer to take the Defendant directly to a 24-hour facility described in NCGS 122C-252.

Caselaw.   No relevant cases found.

Comments.   None.

Chapter 15A (Criminal Procedure Act), Article 81B (Structured Sentencing of Persons Convicted of Crimes)

NCGS 15A-1340.16 Aggravated and Mitigated Sentences

d.10.   Sentences for crimes committed generally must fall within the range specified in NCGS 15A-1340.17(c)(2), unless certain aggravating circumstances exist, in which case a more severe sentence may be imposed. One of the aggravating factors is whether the perpetrator was armed with a firearm during the crime.

Caselaw.   It is not necessary to have actually used the firearm in committing the crime, only that the perpetrator was armed with the firearm while committing the crime. State v. Rios, 369 S.E.2d 576 (NC 1988).

Possession of a firearm during a crime by one co-criminal is imputed to all other co-criminals. State v. Smaw, 384 S.E.2d 304 (NC App 1989).

Comments.   None.

NCGS 15A-1340.16A   Increased Sentencing For Crimes Where Firearm Used

c. If a person is convicted of certain felonies, and the person committed the felony by using, displaying, or threatening to use a firearm, and the person actually possessed a firearm about their person, then the person shall have the minimum term of imprisonment to which the person is sentenced for that felony increased by 60 months. The maximum term of imprisonment shall be that term equal to the minimum term after it is increased by 60 months.

f. Section (c) above does not apply if the use, display, or threatened use of the firearm is needed to prove an element of the felony.

f. Section (c) above does not apply if the person is not sentenced to an active term of imprisonment.

Caselaw.   There are various caselaw examples.

Comments.   This statute, enacted in 1994, is North Carolina's version of similar State laws increasing prison time arbitrarily if the criminal uses a firearm in committing certain crimes. It is obviously intended to be a deterrent to using firearms to commit crime. The statute, as originally written, gave the authority to impose the additional prison time to the court and not the jury, which was found unconstitutional in State v. Guice, 541 S.E.2d 474 (NC App 2000), cert.den., 551 S.E.2d 112 (NC 2001). The replacement statute cited above was enacted in 2003.

Chapter 15A (Criminal Procedure Act), Article 82 (Probation)

NCGS 15A-1343(b)(5) Conditions of Probation

As a regular condition of probation, a defendant must possess no firearm without written permission of the court.

Caselaw.   No relevant cases found

Chapter 15A (Criminal Procedure Act), Article 84A (Post-Release Supervision)

NCGS 15A-1368.4(e) Controlling Conditions for Post-Release Supervision

e.4. Appropriate controlling conditions, violation of which may result in revocation of post-release supervision, includes the condition that the person not possess a firearm without written permission is granted by the Commission or a post-release supervision officer.

Caselaw.   No relevant cases found.

Comments.   The post-release supervision program is a program which allows conditions to be placed upon an inmate after release from prison.

The "Commission" means the Post-Release Supervision and Parole Commission.

Chapter 15A (Criminal Procedure Act), Article 85 (Parole)

NCGS 15A-1374 Conditions of Parole

b.5. Appropriate controlling conditions, violation of which may result in revocation of parole, includes the condition that the parolee not possess a firearm without written permission granted by the Commission or a parole officer.

Caselaw.   No relevant cases found.

Comments.   The "Commission" is the Post-Release Supervision and Parole Commission.

Chapter 19 (Offenses Against Public Morals), Article 1 (Abatement of Nuisances)

NCGS 19-1 Nuisances

Pursuant to NCGS 19-1.1(1), "breach of the peace" means repeated acts that disturb the public order including discharging firearms and unlawful possession of firearms.

Pursuant to NCGS 19-1(b), the use, ownership, etc., of any building or place where breaches of the peace take place is a nuisance.

Caselaw.   No relevant cases found.

Comments.   Charging that noise generated by firing weapons was a nuisance was perhaps the most common legal theory under which offended persons brought charges against users of firearms. These two statutes are the basis for that common charge. The filing of charges under these statutes has probably declined since the enactment of the Sport Shooting Range Protection Act at NCGS 409.45, which protects some shooting ranges against charges of noise as a nuisance.

NCGS 20-11(n.1) Loss of Motor Vehicle Drivers License or Permit

d.2.   If certain students or minors bring, possess, or use a firearm on school property, which resulted in disciplinary action under NCGS 115C-391(d1), or that which could have resulted in that disciplinary action if the conduct had occurred in a public school, may have their drivers license or permit suspended or revoked.

Caselaw.   According to the State Attorney General, this statute does not require that a home school student lose his drivers license due to his use of a firearm under his parent's supervision on land owned by the parents. 20 N.C.A.G Lexis 11 (2000).

Comments.   This statute was enacted in 2000 as part of the Legislature's "Lose Control, Lose Your License" program.

NCGS 20-79.4(b)(28)   License Plates, National Rifle Association

This statute was passed in 2004 authorizing a special automobile license plate displaying the National Rifle Association logo.

Chapter 50B (Domestic Violence)

NCGS 50B-3(a)(11)   Relief in Domestic Violence Protective Orders

Courts may grant any protective order to bring about cessation of domestic violence prohibiting a party from purchasing a firearm for a time fixed in the order. The maximum term of such an order is one year, but the order can be renewed.

NCGS 50B-3(a1)(2)(c)   Temporary Custody and Visitation Rights of Children

The court may take into account whether firearms were used or threatened to be used in considering setting custody or visitation rights.

Caselaw.   None.

Comments.   None.

NCGS 50B-3(c1)   Notice of Right to Apply for Temporary Concealed Handgun Permit

When a protective order in a domestic violence case is issued under NCGS 50B-3, the Clerk of Court shall also notify the recipient of the protective order of their right to apply for a temporary concealed handgun permit under NCGS 14-415.15(b).

Caselaw.   None.

Comments.   NCGS 50B-3(c1) was enacted in August 2005. Session Law 2005-343 (s.3) states that the Administrative Office of the Courts shall develop an informational flyer to explain the right to apply for a temporary concealed firearms permit.

NCGS 50B-3.1 Surrender and Disposal of Firearms

a. A person (the "Defendant") may be ordered by a court to surrender to the local Sheriff all firearms, ammunition, permits to purchase firearms, and permits to carry concealed firearms possessed by or in the care of the Defendant.

a. Before issuing such an order compelling surrender of firearms, etc., the court must find that at least one of the following factors exists:

1. the use or threatened use of a deadly weapon by the Defendant, or a pattern of prior conduct involving the use or threatened use of a firearm, against other persons

176

2. threats to seriously injure or kill an aggrieved party or minor child by the Defendant

3. threats to commit suicide by the Defendant

4. serious injuries inflicted upon an aggrieved party or a minor child by the Defendant.

b. and c. Before issuing the order, the court must hold an emergency or ex-parte hearing, and the court shall inquire as to presence or ownership of firearms, etc., by the Defendant.

d. Upon delivery of the court order by the Sheriff, the Defendant shall immediately surrender the ordered items to the Sheriff. If the firearms, etc., cannot be surrendered immediately to the Sheriff, the firearms shall be surrendered to the Sheriff within 24 hours. The Sheriff shall store the firearms, or contract with a licensed dealer to store the firearms.

d.1. The protective order authorized by this statute may also prohibit the Defendant from owning, possessing, purchasing, or receiving a firearm. The order shall include instructions on how the Defendant may request return of the items surrendered to the Sheriff.

d.2. The Sheriff may charge a reasonable fee for the storage of firearms, etc. The Sheriff may not release firearms without a court order. The Sheriff shall not be liable for damage or deterioration due to storage or transport of firearms.

e. The Defendant may retrieve the items surrendered to the Sheriff upon expiration of the protective order, or upon final disposition of any pending criminal charges committed against the person who is protected by the protective order.

f. The Defendant may initiate the process to retrieve the firearms by filing a motion with the court. A hearing shall be held. The approved form for this motion is Form AOC-CV-319. The court order on this motion is entered on Form AOC-CV-320.

g. If the firearms which are surrendered by the Defendant are owned by a third party, that third party may petition the court for delivery of the firearms to that owner. The approved form for this motion is Form AOC-CV-319. The court order on this motion is entered on Form AOC-CV-320.

h. If no motion is made for recovery of the firearms by the Defendant or third party owner, then the Sheriff shall dispose of the firearms as directed by the court, after hearing and notice. The Sheriff may deduct costs of the sale of the firearms from the sale proceeds. The approved form for this motion is Form AOC-CV-321. The court order on this motion is entered on Form AOC-CV-322.

i. It is illegal for anyone to violate a protective order to fail to surrender all firearms, ammunition, etc., cited in the order; to fail to provide all information pertaining to firearms, etc., as requested by the court; or provide false information to the court pertaining to any of these items.

j. It is a felony under NCGS 14-269.8 to own, possess, or receive a firearm, ammunition, or permits to purchase or carry a concealed firearm if prohibited by a protective order.

k. This statute does not prohibit law enforcement officers or military personnel from possessing firearms.

Caselaw.   This statute, effective December 1, 2003, is too new for caselaw.

Comments.   There will likely be cases brought in the future challenging the broad sweep of this statute at infringing upon the right to keep and bear arms.

Subsection (e) is somewhat vague due to incorrect grammar as written regarding the addition made by Session Law 2005-423 regarding pending criminal charges. Also, it seems excessively broad, apparently allowing a firearm to be withheld from its rightful owner, despite no protective order prohibiting that owner from possessing the firearm, and despite no requirement of any connection between the "pending criminal charges" and the owner of the firearm or the firearm itself. This ambiguity is improved by the 2005 amendment to subsection (f), which adds the proviso that the pending criminal charges must have been committed by the owner of the firearm.

Firearms Law of North Carolina
www.ncfirearmslaw.com

NCGS 74C-13 Armed Security Guard to Have Firearm Registration Permit

a. It is illegal for an armed security guard to carry a firearm when serving as a guard without first having met the qualifications cited in this statute, and without having been issued a registration permit by the Private Protective Services Board, a branch of the North Carolina Department of Justice.

b. It is illegal for any person, firm, association, or corporation to employ an armed security guard and knowingly authorize or allow him to carry a firearm while serving in the employ, if the State Board has not issued the guard a firearm registration permit. The guard may carry the firearm directly to and from work. The firearm must be a .32 or .38 caliber revolver, or any other firearm approved by the Board.

c. Applicants for a firearm registration permit shall apply to the State Board on a form provided by the State Board.

d. The firearm registration permit shall be in the form of a pocket card with contents specified by this statute. The permit is valid for one year, and can be renewed.

e. If the holder of the firearm registration permit ceases employment with the security guard company, the permit expires, and must be returned to the State Board.

f. Temporary firearm registration permits are authorized.

g. Firearm registration permits may be suspended or revoked under certain specified circumstances.

h. The State Board and the State Attorney General shall establish basic and refresher training programs for armed security guards. The general contents of these classes are specified.

i. The State Board may not issue a firearm registration permit to an applicant until the applicant completes an approved basic training course, meets all qualifications specified in this statute, and that he is physically and mentally capable of handling a firearm.

j. The State Board and Attorney General may establish rules to implement this statute.

l. The State Board and Attorney General shall establish training programs for certified trainers.

m. The State Board and Attorney General shall establish a training program for unarmed security guards.

Caselaw.   No relevant cases found.

Comments.   None.

NCGS 74D-6(3) Denial of a License as an Alarms System Professional

An application for licensing or registration as an alarms systems professional may be denied due to prior conviction of the applicant for illegal use, possession, or carrying of a firearm.

Caselaw.   No relevant cases found.

Comments.   NCGS 74D is the Alarm Systems Licensing Act. NCGS 74D-2 requires that no one may operate as an alarm system professional without being licensed under this statute.

NCGS 74E-6(c) Company Police Officers

b. "Company police officers" are divided into three categories:

    1) certain college campus police officers,
    2) railroad police officers, and
    3) "special police officers."

c. Company police officers, if authorized by their superior officer, are authorized to carry concealed firearms when off-duty pursuant to NCGS 14-269(b)(5) (i.e., the authority to carry concealed firearms when off-duty).

<u>Caselaw.</u>   No relevant cases found.

<u>Comments.</u>   Also see Chapter 74G, the Campus Police Act.

NCGS 74E-7 Company Police Officer Weapons (and Other Matters)

Company police agencies are responsible for ensuring their employees comply with Chapter 74E regarding carrying firearms.

<u>Caselaw.</u>   No relevant cases found.

<u>Comments.</u>   None.

NCGS 74F-16(11) Applicability of Act to Sellers of Gun Locks and Gun Safes

The Locksmith Licensing Act does not apply to sellers of gun safes or locking devices for firearms when those sellers are acting in the routine course and scope of selling such items.

Caselaw.   None.

Comments.   None.

The statutes were amended in 2005 to add in a new chapter, namely, Chapter 74G, entitled the Campus Police Act.

In addition to creating a new chapter of statutes expressly for campus police officers, this Act amended several other statutes in various other Chapters which reference campus police officers, particularly NCGS 74E-6.

NCGS 74G-6(d) Concealed Weapons

Campus police officers shall have the authority to carry concealed firearms pursuant to NCGS 14-269(b)(5), if authorized by their campus police agency and the County Sheriff.

Caselaw.   None.

Comments.   None.

NCGS 74G-7 Badges, Uniforms, Weapons, and Vehicles

Campus police agencies shall be responsible for ensuring that all employees comply with the law on the carrying of firearms.

Caselaw.   None.

Comments.   None.

NCGS 77-35 Powers of the Lake Wylie Marine Commission

The Commission is authorized to lease or purchase firearms.

Caselaw.   No relevant cases found.

Comments.   None.

NCGS 77-75(a)(5) Powers of the Mountain Island Lake Marine Commission

The Commission is authorized to lease or purchase firearms.

Caselaw.   No relevant cases found.

Comments.   None.

NCGS 90-21.20 Reporting by Physicians and Hospitals of Wounds and Injuries

a. Certain wounds and injuries specified in subsection (b) below must be reported. The physician or the medical facility has the responsibility to make the report. The report is made to the Chief of Police if located in a municipality, otherwise to the Sheriff. The report must be made "as soon as it becomes practicable before, during or after completion of treatment of a person suffering such wounds."

b. Some of the injuries and wounds which must be reported are bullet wounds, gunshot wounds, and powder burns from discharge of a firearm.

c. The contents of the report are specified in this sub-section.

d. Medical providers making reports shall have no legal liability for making such reports.

Caselaw.   No relevant cases found.

Comments.   This is the basis of the requirement that medical professionals report firearm wounds to the police. The police, of course, use such reports as an aid to solving crimes.

Chapter 99B – Products Liability

NCGS 99B-1.1. Strict Liability in Product Liability Cases

There shall be no strict liability in tort in product liability actions.

Caselaw.   No relevant case found.

Comments.   This statute was enacted in 1995. This is actually a very important statute, despite the dry language of the statute.

In a common product liability lawsuit, the victim must prove that he was injured by the product, and also prove that the manufacturer of the product was negligent in some way in manufacturing the product which caused the victim's injuries.

In a "strict liability" product liability lawsuit, the victim only has to prove that he was injured by the product. Strict liability is usually only imposed on people engaged in inherently dangerous or ultrahazardous activities.

A victim has an incentive to convince a court that the product which injured him is inherently dangerous, because that eliminates the need to prove that the manufacturer was somehow negligent in making the product.

Litigants in some courts have tried to convince judges and juries that firearms are ultrahazardous products which should be governed by the principles of strict liability. Victims of shootings usually have no effective monetary recourse against a penniless criminal who shot them, and they turn their sights instead upon the manufacturer of the firearm which the criminal used to shoot them.

The firearm itself usually did not have any type of defect, and the manufacturer was not negligent in manufacturing the firearm. Victims would have a hard time under the usual product liability laws, because no manufacturer negligence can be shown. Victims want to simply have to prove the manufacturer of the firearm used against them to be able to hold that manufacturer financial responsible for their injuries.

North Carolina prohibited strict liability for product liability cases by caselaw before this statute was enacted. This statute simply codifies pre-existing case law.

NCGS 14-409.40(a.1) and (g), NCGS 99B-1.1, and NCGS 99B-11, are intended to prevent the types of lawsuits being asserted by some other States, or cities or counties outside North Carolina, who are suing the manufacturers of firearms and ammunition under various novel legal theories. The policy of North Carolina, as

187

stated in these statutes, is to hold the <u>criminal</u> who used a firearm to commit a crime accountable, <u>not the manufacturer</u> of the firearm or ammunition.

NCGS 99B-11   Claims Based on Defective Design of Firearms

a. In a products liability lawsuit involving firearms or ammunition, whether a firearm or shell casing is defective in design shall not be based on weighing the benefits of the product against the risk of the product causing injury, damage, or death.

b. In a products liability lawsuit brought against a firearm or ammunition manufacturer, importer, distributor, or retailer, which lawsuit alleges a design defect, the burden is on the plaintiff to prove that the actual design of the firearm or ammunition was defective causing it not to function in a manner reasonably expected by an ordinary consumer of firearms or ammunition, and that the alleged defective design was the actual cause of the injury, damage, or death.

<u>Caselaw.</u>   No relevant cases found.

<u>Comments.</u>   This statute was enacted in 1987.

NCGS 14-409.40(a.1) and (g), NCGS 99B-1.1, and NCGS 99B-11, are intended to prevent the types of lawsuits being asserted by some other States, or cities or counties outside North Carolina, who are suing the <u>manufacturers</u> of firearms and ammunition under various novel legal theories. The policy of North Carolina, as stated in these statutes, is to hold the <u>criminal</u> who used a firearm to commit a crime accountable, <u>not the manufacturer</u> of the firearm or ammunition.

NCGS 103-2 Hunting on Sunday

It is a misdemeanor for anyone to hunt on Sunday while possessing a firearm, except in defense of their own property. Excepted from this statute are military reservations and field trials authorized by the Wildlife Commission.

Caselaw.　　　There is only one reported case of a violation of this statute since it was enacted in 1868. In that case, State v. Howard, 67 N.C. 24 (NC 1872), a Mr. Isaac Howard was found with a shotgun in a place off his premises one Sunday in 1870.

Comments.　　　The sentence fragment "except in defense of their own property" is odd. It is unclear how someone can hunt "in defense of their own property." Perhaps this means hunting predatory animals which are attacking one's sheep or cows.

The Wildlife Commission reports about one dozen people arrested per year for violating this statute.

This statute is apparently controversial. Governor Easley requested in August 2005 that the Wildlife Commission study revising the statute, for consideration by the legislature in its 2006-2007 session.

Chapter 106 - Agriculture

NCGS 106-549.34 Interference With Agriculture Inspector

It is a misdemeanor to, while using a firearm, interfere with, assault, oppose, impede, etc., any agricultural inspector performing duties specified in Article 49C. Article 49C involves meat inspection programs.

Caselaw.   No relevant cases found.

Comments.   It is unclear why this statute, enacted in 1969, is needed against threatening meat inspectors with firearms. Meat inspecting does not seem to be an activity which compels a call to arms.

Chapter 113 – Conservation and Development

The North Carolina Wildlife Resources Commission (the "Commission") is a State agency charged with the management, wise use, and conservation of North Carolina's wildlife and fish resources. The Commission's Internet web page is at www.ncwildlife.org.

The Commission, pursuant to authority granted by several statutes below, has enacted a large body of rules governing hunting with firearms in North Carolina. These rules carry the force of law. The Commission's rules on hunting with firearms are not itemized in this book, as they are very extensive, often County-specific or region-specific, and change much more rapidly than statutes. Hunters will generally obtain copies of the current rules prior to an upcoming hunting season.

NCGS 113-270.1A(b) Licenses and Permits Issued by the Wildlife Resources Commission

The Commission shall institute a statewide course of instruction for, among other things, competency and handling of firearms. The Commission shall certify trainers, conduct classes, issue certificates of competency and safety, and adopt rules regarding classes and procedures.

Caselaw.   No relevant cases found

NCGS 113-270.3(e) Primitive Weapons Hunting Season and Firearms

Muzzle-loading firearms are defined as a "primitive weapon" pertaining to the primitive weapons hunting season pursuant to NCGS 113-291.2(a).

Caselaw.   No relevant cases found

Article 21B – Criminally Negligent Hunting – NCGS 113-290 to 113-290.1

NCGS 113-290 Unlawful Use of Firearms

It is illegal for anyone while hunting wild animals or wild birds to discharge a firearm:

1. carelessly and heedlessly in wanton disregard for the safety of others; or
2. without due caution or circumspection and in a manner so as to endanger any person or property;

and resulting in property damage or injury.

Caselaw.   No relevant cases found.

Comments.   None.

NCGS 113-290.1 Penalties

a. Anyone who violates Article 21B is guilty of a misdemeanor as specified in the statute.

b. An additional fine or imprisonment may be imposed if the person violating this Article 21B was impaired at the time of the violation. "Impaired" means being under the influence of an impairing substance, or having a blood alcohol level of 0.10 or above.

c. As an additional penalty, the Commission may suspend hunting privileges of the violator.

d. Anyone convicted hunting wild animals or birds while their hunting license is suspended under this statute is guilty of a misdemeanor, and shall have hunting privileges suspended for 5 additional years.

Caselaw.   No relevant cases found.

Comments.   None.

Article 22 – Regulation of Wildlife

NCGS 113-291.1 Manner of Taking Wild Animals and Wild Birds

a. Except as otherwise provided, game may be taken only by certain specified methods, two of which are with a rifle and a shotgun. Use of taking game with pistols is governed by NCGS 113-291.1(g).

c. It is a misdemeanor for any person taking wildlife to have in his possession any:
1. firearm equipped with a silencer, or when the silencer is reasonably accessible for attachment, or
2. weapon of mass death and destruction as defined in NCGS 14-288.8.

d. Hunters may conduct "field trials" with dogs in hunting areas at times both authorized by the Wildlife Commission, using firearms and ammunition approved by the Wildlife Commission.

d.1. Hunters may train dogs during the closed season with the use of firearms and ammunition approved by the Wildlife Commission, except in areas closed to protect sensitive wildlife populations.

e.2. The Wildlife Resources Commission may by rule modify provisions of this Article to achieve conformity with applicable federal law and rules, to include the use of rifles and unplugged shotguns. In the absence of Commission rules, rules of the United States Department of the Interior prohibiting the use of rifles and unplugged shotguns shall apply, and violation of such rules is illegal.

g. During open season which permits the following, hunters may take certain varmints (rabbits, squirrels, etc.) with a pistol of .22 caliber with a barrel length of at least 5-1/2 inches in length. A hunter may use a pistol to kill an animal already taken. The Wildlife Commission may restrict or prohibit the carrying of firearms during special seasons or in special areas.

g.1. The Wildlife Resources Commission may prescribe rules regarding the types of handguns and handgun ammunition that may be used in taking big game animals other than wild turkey. The Commission may not provide any special season for the exclusive use of handguns in taking wildlife.

h. The Commission may relax its rules in certain controlled situations.

Caselaw.   No relevant cases found.

Comments.   None.

NCGS 113-291.1A   Computer Assisted Remote Hunting Prohibited

Computer assisted remote hunting is defined by this statute as using a computer, software, and/or other equipment to allow the aiming and discharge of a firearm to be controlled by a person located at some place other than where the firearm is emplaced. It is illegal to engage in computer assisted remote hunting in North Carolina.

Violation of this statute is a misdemeanor. See NCGS 113-294(q).

Caselaw.   No relevant cases found.

Comments.   This statute was enacted in 2005.

NCGS 113-291.2 Seasons, Bag Limits, Etc.

Special or extended hunting seasons may be established by the Wildlife Commission for primitive firearms.

Where there is a muzzle-loading firearm season for hunting deer with a bag limit of five or more, one antlerless deer may be taken.

Caselaw.   No relevant cases found.

Comments.   None.

NCGS 113-291.4 Regulation of (Hunting) Foxes

c. Foxes may not be taken with firearms except:

1. as provided in subsection (f) or (i) below, or NCGS 113-291.4A(a),
2. as an incidental method of killing them after otherwise lawfully taken, or
3. when they are lawfully shot under laws pertaining to the destruction of animals committing depredations to property.

f. The Wildlife Commission may, under certain circumstances, allow a hunting season for foxes with the use of firearms.

i. The Wildlife Commission may allow the hunting and killing of foxes as a population control measure when notified by the North Carolina State Health Director of the presence of a contagious animal disease in the local fox population.

Caselaw.   No relevant cases found.

Comments.   None.

NCGS 113-291.4A Open Seasons for Taking Foxes With Firearms

a. There is an open season for the taking of foxes with firearms in all areas east of Interstate 77, and in Mitchell and Caldwell Counties, which starts with the open season for rabbits and quail, and ends on the following January 1st.

Caselaw.   No relevant cases found.

194

Comments.   None.

NCGS 113-291.8 Requirement to Display Hunter Orange

a. Any person hunting game animals other than foxes, bobcats, raccoons, and opossum, or hunting upland game birds other than wild turkeys, with the use of a firearm, must wear a cap or hat made of hunter orange material or an outer garment of hunter orange visible from all sides. This section does not apply to a landowner hunting on land owned by that landowner.

Caselaw.   No relevant cases found.

Comments.   This law is the statutory basis for hunters wearing blaze orange in the field, other than the perhaps more important basis of common sense.

NCGS 113-291.9 Taking of Beaver

a. There is an open season for taking beaver with firearms during any open season for the taking of wild animals, notwithstanding any other law.

f. Landowners whose property is or has been damaged by beaver may kill beaver by any lawful method without obtaining a depredation permit from the Wildlife Commission, or may hire others to actually take the beaver under those circumstances.

Caselaw.   No relevant cases found.

Comments.   None.

NCGS 113-294(q)   Violations of NCGS 113-291.1A

Violations of NCGS 113-291.1A are a misdemeanor.

Caselaw.   None

Comments.   None

NCGS 113-302 Prima Facie Evidence Provisions

b. The flashing or display of any artificial light at night in areas frequented by deer by any person who has access to a firearm constitutes prima facie evidence of taking

195

deer with an artificial light. This subsection does not apply to headlights of a vehicle driven normally along a roadway.

Caselaw.   No relevant cases found.

Firearms Law of North Carolina
www.ncfirearmslaw.com

The Attorney General shall create a division in the Department of Justice designated as the Division of Criminal Statistics (the "DCS"). The DCS shall, among other things, collect data necessary to trace all firearms seized, forfeited, found, or coming into the possession of any State or local law enforcement agency believed to have been used to commit a crime. The DCS may also maintain a database of firearms registrations.

Caselaw.   No relevant cases found.

Comments.   This statute requires mandatory tracing of all firearms used in crimes.

This statute also requires the DCS to maintain a database of registrations of firearms, if so ordered by the Attorney General. However, this statute seems to imply that the DCS shall collect and interpret firearms registration data maintained by some other government agency, and does not seem to grant to the DCS the independent authority for itself to require firearms registration. There is no registration requirement in North Carolina as of 2005, and hence no such database exists from which the DCS may draw data.

Chapter 115C – Elementary and Secondary Education;

NCGS 115C-288(g) Powers and Duties of School Principals

g. When a school principal becomes aware that an assault with a firearm, or possession of a firearm, in violation of law occurs at school, the principal must report the incident to the local law enforcement agency, and must notify the school system superintendent, who must notify the school board. Failure to report is a misdemeanor.

<u>Caselaw.</u>   No relevant cases found.

<u>Comments.</u>   None.

Firearms Law of North Carolina
www.ncfirearmslaw.com

Chapter 122C – Mental Health, Developmental Disabilities, and Substance Abuse Act

NCGS 122C-62(b)(4)(a) Additional Rights in 24-Hour Mental Health Facilities

Adults receiving treatment or rehabilitation in a 24-hour facility have the right to make visits outside of custody of the facility unless commitment proceedings were initiated because the adult was charged with assault with a firearm, and the adult was found not guilty by reason of insanity or being incapable of proceeding.

Caselaw.   No relevant cases found.

NCGS 122C-263 First Examination by Physician

a. New patients involuntarily committed to certain mental health institutions must be examined by a physician or eligible psychologist as soon as possible after being taken into custody by law enforcement authorities, unless the exception in subsection (b) below applies.

b. The examination by a physician required by subsection (a) above is not required for a new patient whose custody order states that the patient was charged with a violent crime, including a crime involving assault with a firearm, and he was found incapable of proceeding.

Caselaw.   No relevant cases found.

NCGS 122C-266 Inpatient Commitment; Second Physician's Examination

a. Within 24 hours of arrival at a 24-hour mental health facility, the patient shall be examined by a physician, who shall not be the same physician who examined the patient under NCGS 122C-263. Except as stated in subsection (b) below, if the physician finds that the patient does not meet the criteria for commitment, the physician shall release the patient.

b. If the custody order states that the patient was charged with a violent crime involving use of a firearm, and the patient was found incapable of proceeding, the physician shall not release the patient until the district court so orders.

Caselaw.   No relevant cases found.

NCGS 122C-268(c) Inpatient Commitment; District Court Hearing

A court hearing shall be held within 10 days after a person is committed into custody for mental health problems. If the order committing someone into custody states that he was charged with a crime involving assault with a firearm, the Clerk of Court shall give additional notice of the district court hearing as provided in NCGS 122C-264(d).

Caselaw.   No relevant cases found.

NCGS 122C-271(b) Disposition by Court Upon Hearing

If a person was initially committed into custody because they were charged with a crime involving assault with a firearm, and the person was not tried in court because the person was incapable of proceeding, then the commitment order ordering continued commitment shall state these facts.

Caselaw.   No relevant cases found.

NCGS 122C-273(a)(4) Duties For Follow-up on Commitment Order

If a mental health patient was placed on outpatient treatment, and the outpatient physician determines that the patient no longer needs mental health care, and if the patient was initially committed because they were charged with a crime involving assault with a firearm, then the physician shall notify the Clerk of Court that discharge of the patient is recommended. The Clerk shall schedule a court hearing on the matter.

Caselaw.   No relevant cases found.

NCGS 122C-275(a) Outpatient Commitment

If a mental health patient was placed on outpatient treatment, and the outpatient physician determines that the patient no longer needs mental health care, and if the patient was initially committed because they were charged with a crime involving assault with a firearm, then the physician shall notify the Clerk of Court that discharge of the patient is recommended. The Clerk shall schedule a court hearing on the matter.

Caselaw.   No relevant cases found.

NCGS 122C-276 Inpatient Commitment

If a mental health patient was placed on inpatient treatment, and the term of treatment specified in the commitment order is due to expire, and if the patient was initially committed because they were charged with a crime involving assault with a firearm, then the physician shall notify the Clerk of Court that discharge of the patient is recommended. The Clerk shall schedule a court hearing on the matter.

Caselaw.   No relevant cases found.

NCGS 122C-277(b)   Release and Judicial Review of Patients

Inpatients who no longer need mental health facility treatment must be released. If they were committed in connection with being charged with a crime involving assault with a firearm, then the mental health facility shall notify the Clerk of Court, who shall schedule a hearing to review the matter.

Caselaw.   No relevant cases found.

The North Carolina State Militia

Many discussions about firearms and the right to keep and bear arms turn to talk of the militia. This is presumably because the federal and State constitutional rights to keep and bear arms refer to the militia. Therefore, a brief background on North Carolina militia statutes may be helpful to a reader.

The federal Militia Act of 1903 created the modern national guard system.

Chapter 127A of the North Carolina statutes was enacted in 1917, a time of much fear and uncertainty in the United States and North Carolina. There was open warfare on the Mexican border in 1916-1917, with Pancho Villa raiding American towns, and American troops under General John J. Pershing raiding Mexico. Pancho Villa was rumored to have had German support to destabilize the region and divert American attention from Europe. The Battle of the Somme had ended in November 1916, with 300,000 men killed. The Battle of Verdun ended in December 1916, with 260,000 men killed. Britain, already desperate from German submarine attacks in late 1916, faced surrender by summer 1917 after Germany began unrestricted submarine warfare in early 1917. Germany was discovered discussing a military alliance with Mexico early in 1917 against the United States. The United States entered World War I in April 1917. Russia, a major Allied power, revolted in early 1917, leading to Russia's exit from the war, allowing Germany to concentrate against the Allies in a one-front war. Much of the French army, comprising the bulk of the Allied army, mutinied in May 1917. The Germans won the Battle of Cambrai in late 1917, but 90,000 soldiers were killed. A very large percentage of the United States Army and National Guard was sent to Europe in 1917.

Thus, there was much fear and uncertainty in North Carolina when Chapter 127A was enacted.

NCGS 127A-1 Composition of the Militia

The State militia consists of able-bodied citizens of the State who have been drafted into the militia or who voluntarily accepted a commission or assignment to the militia.

Caselaw.   No relevant cases found.

Comments.   This statute does not distinguish between male and female. Presumably, females may be called upon to defend North Carolina.

Citizens are not automatically part of the militia according to this statute. Citizens must volunteer or be drafted. But see NCGS 127A-7.

NCGS 127A-2   Classification of the Militia

The militia is divided into the organized and unorganized militia.

The organized militia is divided into four classes:

- the national guard,
- the naval militia,
- the State defense militia, and
- the historic military commands.

Caselaw.   None.

Comments.   NCGS 127A-1 and 127A-2 make it clear that in North Carolina the militia is organized by the State. There is no authority under these statutes for groups of citizens to band together outside of sanction by the State, and call themselves the "militia" or a "militia unit," at least not as a *State* militia unit.

NCGS 127A-7 Composition of the Unorganized Militia

The unorganized militia consists of all able-bodied citizens of the State other than in the organized militia who are at least 17 years old, except those convicted of a felony or those discharged from the military under less than honorable conditions.

Caselaw.   No relevant cases found.

Comments.   NCGS 127A-1 requires that a citizen must volunteer or be drafted into the militia to be a member of the militia. NCGS 127A-2 defines the unorganized militia as part of the militia. But, NCGS 127A-7 states that *all* citizens, except for citizens in the organized militia and some other exception, are in the unorganized militia, and does not limit membership in the militia to those citizens who have volunteered or been drafted. Therefore, there seems to be a conflict between these statutes.

This apparent conflict does not amount to a pressing legislative issue given the remote likelihood of the unorganized militia ever being mobilized, and given that if there was ever a situation such that the unorganized militia would need to be mobilized, that the State would necessarily be facing such a dire threat to sheer existence that a conflict in the text would be of small importance.

NCGS 127A-16 Governor as Commander in Chief

The Governor is the commander in chief of the militia.

Caselaw.   None.

Comments.   None.

NCGS 127A-19 Adjutant General

The military head of the militia shall be the Adjutant General, who shall be a Major General. The Adjutant General is appointed by the Governor. The Adjutant General must have at least five years commissioned active service in any component of the armed services of the United States.

Caselaw.   None.

Comments.   None.

NCGS 127A-41 Uniforms, Arms, and Equipment

The national guard portion of the organized militia shall be, as far as practicable, armed with the same type of firearms as the appropriate regular military service.

Caselaw.   None.

Comments.   None.

NCGS 127A-80 Authority to Organize the State Defense Militia

The Governor may create the State defense militia from volunteers from the unorganized militia. The State defense militia is intended for defense of the State.

Comments.   This statute is vague about how the State Defense Militia is to be armed, stating that the Governor may request arms from the federal government, or to otherwise equip the units from whatever funds might be available.

During the Revolutionary War, troops taken from the States and "federalized" (using modern terminology) and formed into the American army were called "Continentals." States formed military units in addition to those units sent to the federal army as Continentals. These additional State units were called the "militia."

204

Continentals were as a rule better equipped, trained, led, and supplied than militia units. Often, the militia units would stay within their States' borders to provide internal security.

In today's terminology, federalized National Guard units would be the equivalent of the old Continental units, and the State Defense Militia would be the equivalent of the old militia. Theoretically, their roles would be the same, where the National Guard supplements the regular federal army, and the State Defense Militia, as the name implies, remains in-State to provide local security. This is theoretical, because the author has been able to find no record that the State Defense Militia has ever been activated.

NCGS 127A-87 Unorganized Militia Ordered Out for Service

The Governor may call out as much of the unorganized militia as necessary to defend the State or to respond to disasters. The statute infers that the unorganized militia will be ordered out only if federal troops, National Guard troops, and the state defense militia are insufficient to address the situation.

Caselaw.   No relevant cases found.

Comments.   This statute is even more vague than NCGS 127A-80, making no reference at all concerning how unorganized militia units would be armed. Perhaps the legislature, by placing NCGS 127A-91 (governmental promotion of civilian marksmanship programs) into Article 6 ("Unorganized Militia"), implies a desire and expectation by the State that individual citizens maintain their marksmanship skills with their own firearms.

NCGS 127A-88 Manner of Calling Out the Unorganized Militia

The Governor may call out the unorganized militia by calling for volunteers or by imposing the draft. The Governor may distribute unorganized militia troops to existing National Guard or State defense militia units, or may form unorganized militia units.

Caselaw.   None.

Comments.   None.

NCGS 127A-91 Promotion of Marksmanship

The Adjutant General may appoint a National Guard officer to promote marksmanship in the State defense militia and unorganized militia. The general goal is to organize and supervise rifle clubs to make them acceptable for membership into the National Rifle Association.

Caselaw.   No relevant cases found.

Comments.   This statute, enacted in 1937, is an oddity, mandating governmental support and sanction for groups desiring to join a political association. Also see the comments to NCGS 127A-87.

NCGS 143-63.1 Sale, Disposal, and Destruction of Firearms

a. It is illegal for any State employee, officer, or official to sell or dispose of any firearm, except as provided in this statute.

b. It is legal for the Department of Administration to sell firearms to State, county, or municipal government agencies if the purchasing agency makes the written statement that the firearm is needed in law enforcement

c. All firearms described in subsection (a) above which are declared as surplus must be sold within one year or destroyed.

d. The Highway Patrol, the Department of Corrections, and the State Bureau of Investigation may sell, trade, or dispose of surplus firearms to federally licensed dealers in a manner prescribed by the Department of Administration.

Caselaw.   No relevant cases found.

Comments.   None.

NCGS 143-143.4 Door Lock Exemption for Certain Businesses

(Chapter 10 of Volume 1 of the North Carolina State Building Code mandates certain door lock requirements.)

a. A business licensed to sell automatic firearms as a federal firearms dealer, that sells firearms or ammunition, and that operates a firing range which rents firearms and sells ammunition, is exempt from the State Building Code requirements when issued a permit to that effect by the Department of Justice under this statute.

b. The Department of Insurance shall issue a permit described in subsection (a) above when the conditions specified in the text of this statute are met.

c. The Department of Insurance shall file a copy of the permit with all law enforcement agencies local to the applicant.

Caselaw.   No relevant cases found.

Comments.   None.

NCGS 143B-146.15 Duty to Report Certain Acts to Law Enforcement

When the principal of a "residential school" has knowledge of assault involving the use of a firearm or possession of a firearm in violation of the law, the principal shall immediately report the incident to the appropriate local law enforcement agency. Failure to make such report is a misdemeanor.

The principal should also notify the Secretary of Health and Human Services, and the Superintendent of the Office of Education Services of the Department of Health and Human Services.

Caselaw.   No relevant cases found.

Comments.   None.

NCGS 147-33.2(8)(e) Emergency War Powers of the Governor

The Governor may, during time of war, whenever the General Assembly is not in session, suspend or modify any law or rule regarding the sale, use, and handling of firearms.

Caselaw.   No relevant cases found.

Comments.   This statute was adopted in 1943 during World War II.

This statute gives sweeping powers to the Governor to rule by edict. Edicts issued by the Governor supersede any other conflicting State law, according to NCGS 147-33.3. Statutory powers are, of course, subject to the State constitutional right to keep and bear arms.

NCGS 153A-129   Regulation by a County of Discharge and Display of Firearms

A county may regulate, restrict, or prohibit the discharge of firearms at any time or place except when used to hunt birds under NCGS 113, Subchapter III; when used in the defense of person or property; or when used at the lawful direction of law enforcement officers.

A county may regulate the display of firearms on public roads, sidewalks, alleys, or other public property.

Caselaw.   No relevant cases found.

Comments. This statute allows counties to regulate the *discharge* and *display* of firearms, not the *possession* of firearms. Note that the statute prohibits counties from regulating the discharge of firearms when used in defense of person or property. See NCGS 160A-189.

NCGS 153A-152(a) Privilege License Taxes

A county may levy privilege license taxes upon firearms dealers.

Caselaw. No relevant cases found.

NCGS 160A-189 Regulation by a City of Discharge and Display of Firearms

A city may regulate, restrict, or prohibit the discharge of firearms at any time or place within the city, except when used in the defense of person or property; or when used at the lawful direction of law enforcement officers.

A city may regulate the display of firearms on public roads, sidewalks, alleys, or other public property.

Caselaw. No relevant cases found.

Comments. This statute allows cities to regulate the *discharge* and *display* of firearms, not the *possession* of firearms. Note that the statute prohibits cities from regulating the discharge of firearms when used in defense of person or property. See NCGS 153A-129.

"Public display" is not the same thing as "brandishing" a firearm. Public display generally means carrying a pistol in a holster, carrying a rifle on one's shoulder by its sling, transporting a pistol by placing the pistol on a car seat in plain view while driving on a public road, etc. Brandishing a firearm means to wave or flourish the firearm menacingly or threateningly, or to display the firearm ostentatiously.

There is a spectrum of sorts, with public display being the least offensive, then moving to brandishing a firearm as more offensive, and moving to the tort of "going to the terror of the public" (discussed below) as the most offensive form of displaying a firearm in public.

Going to the terror of the public has been illegal since before the Civil War. Brandishing a firearm is less distinct as a crime called as such in modern times, perhaps because it was apparently codified in 1889 as NCGS 14-34 ("assault by pointing a gun").

Mere display of a firearm in public was never a State crime. Indeed, the open display of a handgun was effectively *required* by law to avoid the crime of carrying a *concealed* handgun, at least up until the enactment of the concealed carry handgun statutes in 1995. Open display of rifles and shotguns remains the required rule to avoid a charge of carrying a concealed rifle or shotgun, since concealed carry permits are not valid for rifles and shotguns.

Granted, there may be a gray area where public display ends and brandishing begins. Further, some people are so emotionally sensitive and unfamiliar with firearms that the merest sight of a firearm sends them into paroxysms of agitated fear.

This statute gained notoriety in October 2005 when the Charlotte-Mecklenburg Police Department proposed that the Charlotte City Council adopt a city ordinance prohibiting the public display of firearms on city streets, sidewalks, and public areas by civilians, even those with a concealed carry permit. Public display of firearms being so rare in Charlotte, except by criminals in the process of committing far more serious crimes, the need for such an ordinance is questionable.

Uncodified Local Laws, Also Known as Session Laws

Session laws which apply to only one county, or to a small number of counties, are called "local laws," and generally are not codified with a statute number. The session law number is the permanent identification number for most local laws. Local laws, not being codified, are relatively difficult to locate. Some local laws may be codified with a statute number. Local laws are very real and very enforceable in the county or counties to which they apply. Local laws, although enacted at the State level, are effectively the equivalent of local ordinances. Therefore, local laws are not listed in this book.

The North Carolina Administrative Code

The North Carolina Administrative Code ("NCAC") is a set of rules created to provide a systemized procedure for administering the requirements of the statutes, so that State agencies charged with administering any particular function will have a standard operating procedure. Many statutes dictate *what* is to occur; the NCAC spells out *how* it is to occur.

Chapter 150B of the North Carolina General Statutes is entitled the "Administrative Procedures Act." The NCAC is authorized by NCGS 150B-21.18.

Generally, the NCAC cannot "impose criminal liability or a civil penalty for an act or omission, including the violation of a rule, unless a law specifically authorizes the agency to do so or a law declares that violation of the rule is a criminal offense or is grounds for a civil penalty." NCGS 150B-19(3).

The NCAC will not be a relevant body of law for the average non-employee of a government agency.

The NCAC may very well be a relevant body of law for a government employee if there is a law relevant to that employee's function. If the employee's function involves the carrying, permitting, or licensing of firearms, then the NCAC may very well be relevant.

Common Law

Common law, as discussed above, is a body of law where past court decisions have created or documented a set of rules accepted and enforced by society. Common law is not numbered or codified like statutes. There is no official publication published by the government listing common laws. The best practical manner to identify relevant common law is to locate caselaw where the court acknowledges that a certain common law exists. Various cases illustrating acknowledged common law appear following.

NCGS 4-1, enacted in the year 1715, and amended in 1778 during the Revolutionary War, states as follows:

> **"Common law declared to be in force.**
> All such parts of the common law as were heretofore in force and use within this State, or so much of the common law as is not destructive of, or repugnant to, or inconsistent with, the freedom and independence of this State and the form of government therein established, and which has not been otherwise provided for in whole or in part, not abrogated, repealed, or become obsolete, are hereby declared to be in full force within this State."

"Going to the Terror of the People"

It is illegal for anyone to arm himself with a firearm to terrify others, and go about the public highways, and cause terror to the public. The North Carolina Supreme Court in State v. Huntly, 25 N.C. 418 (NC 1843), acknowledged this common law and discussed it in detail. The court cited a famous legal writer who said "the offense of riding or going armed with dangerous or unusual weapons is a crime against the public peace, by terrifying the good people of the land..." The case summary stated that "a man may carry a gun for any lawful purpose of business or amusement, but he cannot go about with that or any other dangerous weapon, to terrify and alarm, and in such a manner as naturally will terrify and alarm a peaceful people." The Supreme Court then went on to hold that a firearm was an "unusual weapon" for purpose of common law.

The North Carolina Supreme Court revisited the issue in modern times in State v. Dawson, 159 S.E.2d 1 (NC 1968), upholding Huntly and noting that Huntly had never been criticized in 124 years. Dawson examined whether it was the mere carrying of a firearm in public, whether it was that the firearm was carried for a wicked or mischievous purpose, or whether the person actually used the firearm in an improper manner, which constituted the crime. The <u>Dawson</u> court, citing <u>Huntly</u> frequently, held that:

> "the carrying of a gun, per se, constitutes no offense. For any lawful purpose—either of business or amusement—the citizen is at perfect liberty to carry his gun. It is the wicked purpose, and the mischievous result, which essentially constitute the crime."

The <u>Dawson</u> court then contrasted North Carolina's version of this common law with that of Tennessee, which required the person carrying the firearm to actually *attempt to use* the firearm to commit the crime.

The court in <u>State v. Staten</u>, 232 S.E.2d 488 (NC App 1977), stated:

> "In <u>State v. Dawson</u>, 159 S.E.2d 1 (NC 1968), the court enumerated the four essential elements to charge the common law offense of intentionally going about armed with an unusual and dangerous weapon to the terror of the people, namely: (1) armed with unusual and dangerous weapons, (2) for the unlawful purpose of terrorizing the people of the named county, (3) by going about the public highways of the county, (4) in a manner to cause terror to the people."

The conduct constituting this common law crime varies depending upon the context. Openly wearing of pistols on a shooting range may not be out of the ordinary, but might be terrifying if worn by an angry customer at a suburban shopping mall.

Common law is recited in caselaw and not in statute books. Different versions of a common law may exist in different cases, not by intention, but merely where text is not recited verbatim from case to case. For example, is it a required element of this common law that the person carrying the firearm travel on the public highway while inappropriately armed? Some cases require this, but other cases do not. Perhaps coincidentally, perhaps not, the North Carolina cases all seem to involve travel on a road, usually by an aggrieved person traveling to seek out his intended victim.

This common law remains relevant in modern times. There are many places where carrying firearms is prohibited by statute, but there are innumerable places where carrying firearms is *not* expressly prohibited. A person carrying a firearm must be careful to avoid carrying a firearm in such circumstances, time, place, or manner that other citizens are terrorized.

Duty to Retreat

Killing an attacker with a deadly weapon in self defense was no defense under old English law; it was only used in an attempt to win a pardon. More recent English law allowed killing in self defense, but only if there were no means of retreat or escape to being assaulted. The American Colonies took a mixed view of the rule requiring retreat before defense. Many Southern and Western states rejected the rule requiring retreat after the Revolutionary War. Southern and Western states, which held a strong code of personal honor, believed that flight was dishonorable.

North Carolina law, like English law in effect at the time of the Revolution, required retreat as late as 1839, as held in a case of that time, State v. Hill, 20 N.C. 629 (NC 1839). North Carolina had by 1876 renounced the requirement of retreat when one was attacked by someone intent on committing a felony. State v. Dixon, 75 N.C. 275 (NC 1876). The court, in State v. Musselwhite, 283 S.E.2d 149 (NC App 1981), aff'd, 287 S.E.2d 897 (NC 1982), stated:

"The common law doctrine that the right of self defense does not arise until the person assaulted has retreated to the wall has been supplanted in this State by the following doctrine: If a person is assaulted in a place where he has a right to be, he may stand his ground, meet force with force, and if need be, kill his assailant."

"If one is in his own home, he, in effect, has his back to the wall and is under no duty to retreat from an assault be it felonious or non-felonious. This exception was later extended to include both the curtilage of the home as well as one's place of business. In 1976, this Court went a step further and held that no duty to retreat from the home exists even if the assailant is another lawful occupant of the premises."

Right of Self Defense, Generally

The State Supreme Court stated in State v. Pearson, 215 S.E.2d 598 (NC 1975), that:

"The right to act in self-defense is based upon necessity, real or apparent, and a person may use such force as is necessary or apparently necessary to save himself from death or great bodily harm in the lawful exercise of his right of self-defense. A person may kill even though it be not necessary to kill to avoid death or great bodily harm if he believes it to be necessary and he has

217

reasonable grounds for such belief. The reasonableness of his belief is to be determined by the jury from the facts and circumstances as they appeared to the accused at the time of the killing."

The State Appeals Court held in State v. Browning, 221 S.E.2d 375 (NC App 1976), that:

"Ordinarily, when a person who is free from fault in bringing on a difficulty, is attacked in his own home or on his own premises, the law imposes on him no duty to retreat before he can justify his fighting in self defense, regardless of the character of the assault, but is entitled to stand his ground, to repel force with force, and to increase his force, so as not only to resist, but also to overcome the assault and secure himself from all harm. This, of course, would not excuse the defendant if he used excessive force in repelling the attack and overcoming his adversary. This rule applies not only to attacks made upon a person within his own dwelling house, but applies as well to attacks made within the curtilage of the home. And the curtilage of the home will ordinarily be construed to include at least the yard around the dwelling house as well as the area occupied by barns, cribs, and other outbuildings."

The Court of Appeals in State v. Martin, 506 S.E.2d 260 (NC App 1998), citing the Supreme Court in State v. Marsh, 237 S.E.2d 745 (NC 1977), stated that:

"Our Supreme Court has set forth the law of self-defense as follows:

The right to act in self-defense rests upon necessity, real or apparent, and a person may use such force as is necessary or apparently necessary to save himself from death or great bodily harm in the lawful exercise of his right of self-defense. A person may exercise such force if he believes it to be necessary and has reasonable grounds for such belief. The reasonableness of his belief is to be determined by the jury from the facts and circumstances as they appeared to the accused at the time. However, the right of self-defense is only available to a person who is without fault, and if a person voluntarily, that is aggressively and willingly, enters into a fight, he cannot invoke the doctrine of self-defense unless he first abandons the fight,

218

withdraws from it and gives notice to his adversary that he has done so."

The North Carolina Supreme Court stated in State v. Maynor, 417 S.E.2d 453 (NC 1992), and State v. McAvoy, 417 S.E.2d 489 (NC 1992), a more specific rule, that:

"It is well settled that perfect self-defense which excuses a killing altogether arises where, at the time of the killing:

(1) it appeared to defendant and he believed it to be necessary to kill the deceased in order to save himself from death or great bodily harm; and

(2) defendant's belief was reasonable in that the circumstances as they appeared to him at the time were sufficient to create such a belief in the mind of a person of ordinary firmness; and

(3) defendant was not the aggressor in bringing on the affray, i.e., he did not aggressively and willingly enter into the fight without legal excuse or provocation; and

(4) defendant did not use excessive force, i.e., did not use more force than was necessary or reasonably appeared to him to be necessary under the circumstances to protect himself from death or great bodily harm."

In a particular incident, a person may have used a firearm defensively when only *some* of these elements exist, but not all of the elements. The person using the firearm may then have only a *partial* defense. The North Carolina Supreme Court discussed this situation in State v. Ross, 449 S.E.2d 556 (NC 1994) and State v. Locklear, 505 S.E.2d 277 (NC 1998), by stating:

"There are two types of self-defense: perfect and imperfect. Perfect self-defense excuses a killing altogether, while imperfect self-defense may reduce a charge of murder to voluntary manslaughter. For a defendant to be entitled to an instruction on either perfect or imperfect self-defense, the evidence must show that the defendant believed it to be necessary to kill his adversary in order to save himself from death or great bodily harm. In addition, the defendant's belief must be reasonable in that the circumstances as they appeared to him at the time were sufficient to create such a belief in the mind of a person of ordinary firmness."

Right to Use a Firearm in Self-Defense of a Sexual Assault

The caselaw above states the general rule that "a person may use such force as is necessary or apparently necessary to save himself from death or *great bodily harm* in the lawful exercise of his right of self-defense." State v. Pearson, 215 S.E.2d 598 (NC 1975) (italics added).

The court in State v. Hunter, 286 S.E.2d 535 (NC 1982), stated that an assaulted person "may not resort to the use of deadly force to protect himself from *mere bodily harm or offensive physical contact.*" (italics added)

The question is whether sexual assault or rape constitutes "great bodily harm" so as to allow a potential victim to kill a sexual aggressor with a firearm to prevent a rape, or whether rape is "mere bodily harm or offensive physical contact."

The court in State v. Hunter, 286 S.E.2d 535 (NC 1982), quoted from North Carolina Pattern Jury Instruction 308.70, which then stated:

> "A killing would be entirely excused on the grounds of self-defense, if:
> *First*, it appeared to the defendant and she believed it to be necessary to kill (name the victim) in order to **save** herself from death, great bodily harm *or sexual assault...*" (italics added)

Hunter involved an attempted homosexual assault. The Hunter court took the position that although the North Carolina standardized jury instructions were written to reflect the right of a female to kill in self-defense of an attempted sexual assault, there was no reason that the concept should not also apply to a male threatened with sexual assault.

Right of a Battered Spouse to Kill Their Spouse Using a Firearm

Battered spouses have no right to kill their spouse with a firearm unless the immediate threat of death or great bodily harm exists under the general rule in State v. Hunter, 286 S.E.2d 535 (NC 1982).

In the Supreme Court case of State v. Norman, 378 S.E.2d 8 (NC 1989), a battered wife fired three bullets into the head of her husband as he lay sleeping. The court found that years of serious spousal abuse do not give rise to a right to kill the

220

abusive spouse without the immediate threat of death or great bodily harm. The Norman court stated that "we decline to expand our law of self-defense beyond the limits of immediacy and necessity which have heretofore provided an appropriately narrow but firm basis upon which homicide may be justified."

In the Supreme Court case of State v. Grant, 470 S.E.2d 1 (NC 1996), a battered wife mortally stabbed her husband as he lay sleeping on a sofa, and then shot him three times with a .357 Magnum revolver. The wife asked the Supreme Court to overrule Norman, asking for the recognition of a battered spouse syndrome defense to homicide, but the court refused.

Defense of the Person in a Dwelling vs. Defense of Habitation

At common law, there was a distinction between the "defense of a habitation" and the "defense of the person in one's habitation." The North Carolina Supreme Court stated, in State v. Blue, 565 S.E.2d 133 (NC 2002), that:

> "the principal distinction between the common law defense of habitation and the defense of the person on or within one's own premises is that in the former, the victim is attempting to forcibly enter the defendant's dwelling; whereas, in the latter, the victim has actually attacked or assaulted the defendant in the defendant's dwelling or on the defendant's premises. In neither case is the defendant required to retreat."

> "The legal effect of the difference between the defenses is that under the defense of habitation, the defendant's use of force, even deadly force, before being physically attacked would be justified to prevent the victim's entry provided that the defendant's apprehension that he was about to be subjected to serious bodily harm or that the occupants of the home were about to be seriously harmed or killed was reasonable and further provided that the force used was not excessive."

> "Whereas, under the defense of the person on one's premises, the defendant would have the benefit of perfect self-defense and no duty to retreat only if the defendant had first been attacked or assaulted."

These common law defenses were greatly affected by the enactment of NCGS 14-51.1. Please see the caselaw and comments for that statute. Also, see each defense discussed below.

Right of Self-Defense in a Dwelling or Premises

A leading case is the North Carolina Supreme Court case of State v. Blue, 565 S.E.2d 133 (NC 2002). See the caselaw section under NCGS 14-51.1 for a detailed examination of this case. The court in State v. Blue stated that:

> "The common law right of an individual to defend himself from death or bodily harm on his premises was stated in State v. Johnson, 136 S.E.2d 84 (NC 1964).

> Ordinarily, when a person who is free from fault in bringing on a difficulty is attacked in his own home or on his own premises, the law imposes on him no duty to retreat before he can justify his fighting in self defense, regardless of the character of the assault, but is entitled to stand his ground, to repel force with force, and to increase his force, so as not only to resist, but also to overcome the assault and secure himself from all harm. This, of course, would not excuse the defendant if he used excessive force in repelling the attack and overcoming his adversary. Further, defense of the person within one's premises includes not only the dwelling, but also the curtilage and buildings within the curtilage. The curtilage includes the yard around the dwelling and the area occupied by barns, cribs, and other outbuildings."

The phrase "repel force with force" is legalese for defending against an attack by the intruder, but not acting proactively against an intruder in the house.

However, enactment of NCGS 14-51.1 eliminated the requirement that the occupant of the dwelling had to wait and be attacked by the intruder before responding with force.

The court in State v. Blue, 565 S.E.2d 133 (NC 2002), stated that:

> "The limitation that the defendant be acting to prevent forcible entry into the home for the defense of habitation to be applicable was eliminated by NCGS 14-51.1. In enacting NCGS 14-51.1, the General Assembly broadened the defense of habitation to make the use of deadly force justifiable whether to *prevent* unlawful entry into the home or to *terminate* an unlawful entry by an intruder."

222

That summarizes the common law rule of defense of the person inside a habitation. NCGS 14-51.1 codified the common law rule. NCGS 14-51.1 did not so much change the common law rule of defense of the habitation, but expanded the common law rule of defense of the person inside a habitation to be the same rule as defense of the habitation.

Summarizing, the old common law rules of "defense of the habitation" and "defense of the person inside a habitation" have, for all practical purposes, been merged together by NCGS 14-51.1 into one rule. Therefore, for the occupants of a dwelling, the rules are the same, whether the occupant is acting to stop an intruder from unlawful entry, or whether the occupant is defending against an intruder already inside of the dwelling. That rule is codified as NCGS 14-51.1.

Defense of the Habitation

This common law right was, strictly speaking, not a defense of the actual structure of the habitation or dwelling. The defense is more correctly a defense of the occupants of the habitation by a defense of the protective enclosure of the habitation. A homeowner cannot use deadly force merely to protect residential property. State v. Hedgepeth, 265 S.E.2d 413 (NC App 1980). The Hedgepeth court stated that "although defined as defense of habitation, the defense in reality is that of defense of person, for under no circumstances is the taking of life available as a defense for protecting property."

The State Supreme Court stated, in State v. Miller, 148 S.E.2d 279 (NC 1966), that:

> "Reasonable apprehension of future injury is an essential prerequisite to the right to take life in defense of one's habitation. It was for the jury to say whether (the) defendant shot to *punish* (the) deceased for damaging his (entry door) screen, or to *prevent* an intruder, whom he had reason to believe intended to commit a felony or to inflict personal injury upon him or some other member of his household, from forcibly entering his dwelling. If it were the latter, there was the further question whether defendant used force excessive under all the circumstances."

> "When a trespasser enters upon a man's premises, makes an assault upon his dwelling, and attempts to force an entrance into his house in a manner such as would lead a reasonably prudent man to believe that the intruder intends to commit a felony or to inflict some serious personal injury upon the inmates, a lawful occupant of the dwelling may legally prevent the entry, even by

the taking of the life of the intruder. Under those circumstances, the law does not require such householder to flee or to remain in his house until his assailant is upon him, but he may open his door and shoot his assailant, if such course is apparently necessary for the protection of himself or family. But the jury must be the judge of the reasonableness of defendant's apprehension. A householder will not, however, be excused if he employs excessive force in repelling the attack, whether it be upon his person or upon his habitation."

The State Supreme Court stated, in Edwards v. Johnson, 152 S.E.2d 122 (NC 1967), that:

"The right to defend one's home against forcible entry by an intruder is well settled in this State. A householder, however, may not intentionally shoot even a trespasser until he attempts to force an entry in a manner sufficient to lead a reasonably prudent person to believe that he intended to commit a felony or to inflict some serious personal injury upon the occupants of the house. State v. Miller, 148 S.E.2d 279 (NC 1966). In other words, one may not shoot first and investigate later. There must be actual or apparent necessity to shoot; otherwise, shooting at a human being is unlawful. State v. Phillips, 138 S.E.2d 626, 628 (NC 1964)."

The North Carolina Supreme Court in State v. McCombs, 253 S.E.2d 906 (NC 1979), discussed the desire of the courts to maintain separate rules on the use of deadly force in self defense in the defense of habitation and defense of the person in the habitation. The court in State v. McCombs held that:

"The use of deadly force in defense of the habitation is justified only to *prevent* a forcible entry into the habitation under such circumstances (e.g., attempted entry accompanied by threats) that the occupant reasonably apprehends death or great bodily harm to himself or other occupants at the hands of the assailant or believes that the assailant intends to commit a felony."

"Once the assailant has gained entry, however, the usual rules of self-defense replace the rules governing defense of habitation, with the exception that there is no duty to retreat. This is so because the occupant is then better able to ascertain whether the assailant intends to commit a felony or possesses the means with which to inflict serious personal injury upon the occupants of the dwelling."

"The previously cited cases (in McCombs) dealing with defense of habitation are factually limited to the *prevention* of a forcible entry. Moreover, the rules governing defense of habitation, self-defense, defense of property, and eviction of trespassers are designed to allow an individual to defend his family, home and property in virtually any situation which might arise with respect to an invasion of his home while at the same time affording maximum protection of human life. To allow the distinctions between these rules to become blurred or to extend any of them to situations for which they were not intended would dilute the safeguards designed to protect human life."

That summarizes the common law rule of defense of the habitation.

However, NCGS 14-51.1 subsequently codified the common law rule. NCGS 14-51.1 did not so much change the common law rule of defense of the habitation, but expanded the common law rule of "defense of the person inside a habitation" to be the same rule as defense of the habitation.

Summarizing, the old common law rules of "defense of the habitation" and "defense of the person inside a habitation" have, for all practical purposes, been merged together by NCGS 14-51.1 into one rule. Therefore, for the occupants of a dwelling, the rules are the same, whether the occupant is acting to stop an intruder from unlawful entry, or whether the occupant is defending against an intruder already inside of the dwelling. That rule is codified as NCGS 14-51.1. NCGS 14-51.1 is a very important statute for homeowners planning to defend their homes and themselves with a firearm.

The Right to Use Firearms in Defense of Another Person

A person has the right to use deadly force in defense of another person in certain circumstances.

The Supreme Court of North Carolina, in State v. McKoy, 422 S.E.2d 713 (NC 1992), following the earlier Supreme Court case of State v. McLawhorn, 155 S.E.2d 198 (NC 1967), stated:

"A person has the right to kill not only in his own self-defense but also in the defense of another. A person may lawfully do in

225

another's defense, however, only what the other might lawfully do in his own defense."

The Supreme Court followed the McLawhorn line of cases, and stated, in State v. Terry, 447 S.E.2d 720 (NC 1994), that:

> "The elements of perfect defense of another are essentially the same as those for perfect self defense. In general, one may kill in defense of another if one believes it to be necessary to prevent death or great bodily harm to the other and has a reasonable ground for such belief, the reasonableness of this belief or apprehension to be judged by the jury in light of the facts and circumstances as they appeared to the defender at the time of the killing. The right to kill in defense of another cannot exceed such other's right to kill in his own defense as that other's right reasonably appeared to the defendant."

These rules for self defense are cited above, as stated in the Maynor and McAvoy cases.

The Duty to Defend Others

There are a number of cases holding that persons not only have the *right* to defend others, but the *duty* to defend others under certain types of attack. This is an important distinction, especially for concealed firearms carriers.

The Supreme Court held, in State v. Robinson, 195 S.E. 824 (NC 1938), that:

> "If the defendant …. had a well-grounded belief that a felonious assault was about to be committed on the (other) defendant…., he had the right and it was his duty as a private citizen to interfere to prevent the supposed crime. The principle of law is well settled in this State."

The Supreme Court in State v. Hornbuckle, 144 S.E.2d 12 (NC 1965), followed its earlier ruling in Robinson by stating:

> "The law with respect to the right of a private citizen to interfere with another to prevent a felonious assault upon a third person is well stated in State v. Robinson, 195 S.E. 824, where Justice Winborne, later Chief Justice, said: "If the defendant... had a well-grounded belief that a felonious assault was about to be

226

committed on the (other) defendant...., he had the right and it was his duty as a private citizen to interfere to prevent the supposed crime. The principle of law is well settled in this State."

The appeals court in State v. Graves, 196 S.E.2d 582 (NC App 1973), following the Robinson line of cases, stated that:

"A private citizen has a right to go to the defense of another if he has a well grounded belief that a felonious assault is about to be committed upon such other person. In fact, it is his duty to interfere to prevent the supposed crime."

The Robinson line of cases was followed in State v. Patterson, 272 S.E.2d 924 (NC App 1981), quoting Hornbuckle and Robinson.

No case was located where someone was found guilty of, or liable for, failing in this duty to defend another person despite the consistent and explicit holding that citizens have a duty to defend others under felonious assault.

No case was found stating that a person defending another against felonious assault was required to use all methods of defense at his disposal, such as use of a concealed firearm.

No mention of this duty to defend others was found in caselaw since Patterson in 1981, even though the Supreme Court repeatedly stated that this duty is "well settled" in North Carolina. The cases specifying this "duty" have not been overruled. Sometimes a court "recedes" from a ruling, where the ruling is not expressly overruled, but the court intentionally ceases mentioning the rule, and the rule falls into disuse, an artifact of the past. There is no clear court guidance on the current viability of this duty.

It is also a twist that while the cases provide no stated duty to defend *oneself*, there is this duty to defend *other people* against felonious assault.

Use of Firearms to Defend Against Simple Assault

Firearms may not be used to defend against simple assaults.

The North Carolina Supreme Court stated in State v. Pearson, 215 S.E.2d 598 (NC 1975):

"that deadly force is not privileged against nondeadly force. But, even this rule is qualified where there is a great disparity in strength between the defendant and his assailant, or where the defendant is attacked by more than one assailant. Under these circumstances, death or great bodily harm is possible without the use of any weapons by the assailant or the assailants, and the defendant therefore may be justified in employing deadly force to repel such an attack."

"It is true, as a general rule, or under ordinary conditions, that the law does not justify or excuse the use of a deadly weapon to repel a simple assault. This principle does not apply, however, where from the testimony it may be inferred that the use of such weapon was or appeared to be reasonably necessary to save the person assaulted from great bodily harm -- such person having been in no default in bringing on or unlawfully entering into the difficulty."

"In such case a defendant's right of self-defense is usually a question for the jury; and it is not always necessary to the existence of this right that the first assault should be with a deadly weapon. It may, in exceptional instances, arise when the fierceness of this assault, the position of the parties and the great difference in their relative sizes or strength show that the danger of great bodily harm is imminent."

Reinforcing this decision, the North Carolina Supreme Court then held in State v. Hunter, 338 S.E.2d 99 (NC 1986):

"to repel a felonious assault, a defendant may employ deadly force in his defense but only if it reasonably appears necessary to protect himself against death or great bodily harm. Deadly force has been defined as "force likely to cause death or great bodily harm." Although a defendant need not submit in meekness to indignities or violence to his person because the affront does not threaten death or great bodily harm, he may not resort to the use of deadly force to protect himself from mere bodily harm or offensive physical contact. The use of deadly force to prevent harm other than death or great bodily harm is therefore excessive as a matter of law."

This concept was followed more recently by the court in State v. Wills, 429 S.E.2d 376 (NC App 1993), rev.den. 433 S.E.2d 184 (NC 1993), which stated:

"A defendant may use deadly force to repel a felonious assault only if it reasonably appears necessary to protect himself from death or great bodily harm. However, a defendant may not use deadly force to protect himself from mere bodily harm or offensive physical contact, and use of deadly force to prevent harm other than death or great bodily harm is excessive as a matter of law. An assault with intent to kill is justified under self defense if a defendant is in actual or apparent danger of death or great bodily harm."

These cases are very clear. However, they suffer from a common fault: they depend upon hindsight. How is a person being assaulted supposed to know when the assault starts that the assault will only be a simple assault, or whether the assailant intends more than a simple assault? Sometimes, the assailant, possibly mentally unbalanced or under the influence of drugs or alcohol, has no clear plan of attack. In those circumstances, the attack could spiral unpredictably out of control. It appears that the cases mean that if a criminal is inflicting a simple assault upon a victim, the victim must suffer the simple assault (or defend with non-deadly means) until the assault escalates to something which creates actual or apparent danger of death or great bodily harm, at which point the victim may use his or her firearm in self defense.

Right to Use Firearms in Defense of Property

The North Carolina Supreme Court stated in State v. Lee, 127 S.E.2d 774 (NC 1962), that:

"As an incident to the indubitable right to acquire and own property, recognized by the Constitution of North Carolina and the Constitution of the United States, a person in possession of property, either as owner, or as the agent or servant of the owner, has the legal right to defend and protect it from threatened and impending injury or destruction at the hands of an aggressor, or if it is personal property, to prevent it from being unlawfully taken, or injured, or destroyed by another, and in doing so he may use such force as is reasonably necessary, and no more than is reasonably necessary, to accomplish this end, subject to the qualification that, in the absence of a felonious use of force on the part of the aggressor, *human life must not be endangered or great bodily harm inflicted.*" (italics added)

229

Right to Use Firearms Against Trespassers

This section refers to trespass of someone's property or premises other than their dwelling. Examples would be a trespasser walking across the property of another, or perhaps hunting on another's land. The archaic attitude of many rural folks in times past is to post "Trespassers Will Be Shot on Sight" signs.

The North Carolina Supreme Court in State v. McLawhorn, 155 S.E.2d 198 (NC 1967), plainly stated the relevant rule that:

> "A mere trespass or entry upon one's premises *other than his dwelling*, not amounting to a felony, is not considered sufficient provocation to warrant the owner's using a deadly weapon in its defense, or sufficient provocation to arouse the degree of passion requisite to reduce from murder to manslaughter his crime in slaying the intruder, notwithstanding the killing may have been necessary to prevent the trespass." (italics added)

The implication of McLawhorn is that the rule against the use of deadly force to prevent mere trespass applies to the occupant's premises *other than his dwelling*. Presumably, in 1967, when McLawhorn was decided, the two common law rules of defense of the habitation and defense of the person in the habitation then applied if the trespasser tried to (or did) gain access into the dwelling.

The Appeals Court in State v. Clegg, 542 S.E.2d 269 (NC App 2001), then addressed the subject. The facts in the Clegg case are not totally relevant to this firearms law book, since the "weapons" involved were a heavy ashtray and a boxcutter (not a firearm), and because there was no "trespass." The facts in Clegg consisted of a domestic dispute where a boyfriend and girlfriend began fighting in the man's dwelling while watching television, and the "defense" was said by the court to be more of self defense against an attacker rather than an attempt to thwart a trespasser.

The Clegg court, following the Supreme Court in State v. McCombs, 253 S.E.2d 906 (NC 1979), stated that:

> "It is a well-established principle that when a trespasser invades the premises of another, the latter has the right to remove him, and the law requires that he should first request him to leave, and if he does not do so, he should lay his hands gently upon him, and if he resists, he may use sufficient force to remove him, taking care, however, to use no more force than is necessary to accomplish

230

that object. However, a person may not use deadly force or force likely to cause great bodily harm against a trespasser already in his home."

The relevance of McCombs, upon which Clegg is based, however, is questionable, since after McCombs was decided, NCGS 14-51.1 was enacted, which substantially altered the common law upon which McCombs was based.

Further, the text of the Clegg case states the facts in Clegg are more of self defense against an attacker rather than an attempt to thwart a trespasser. In fact, the trial court in Clegg refused to allow a jury instruction on the defendant's right to evict a trespasser.

Further, Clegg is even less relevant, because Clegg involved an altercation *inside of a dwelling*, and this section involves trespass *outside of a dwelling*.

The comments in Clegg relate only to a "mere" trespass not accompanied with danger to the occupants. If the trespass is accompanied by other facts, such as demonstration of intent by the trespasser to commit a felony, then other rules may apply. The court in McCombs stated:

> "Our conclusion that defense of habitation is available only in limited circumstances is further supported by the fact that different rules apply to invasions *not accompanied by danger to the occupants*. In this regard, it is well settled that a person is entitled to defend his property by the use of reasonable force, subject to the qualification that, in the absence of a felonious use of force on the part of the aggressor, human life must not be endangered or great bodily harm inflicted." (italics added)

The Clegg court did not mention NCGS 14-51.1, presumably because that statute deals with home invaders, which is not the fact pattern in Clegg.

Therefore, the wording in Clegg seems to sweep in all forms of trespass, rather than only trespass within a dwelling. The rules on defending against a trespass on a person's premises out beyond their dwelling and curtilage (the immediate area around their dwelling) are simply not the same as defense on or about the dwelling, either before or after enactment of NCGS 14-51.1. It is the author's belief that Clegg should have been worded more so to limit its relevance to altercations inside of a dwelling.

Neither Clegg nor NCGS 14-51.1 apply to a mere trespass to one's premises which is not their dwelling. McLawhorn would still apply in that situation.

Therefore, McLawhorn still seems to be the controlling law on defense against mere trespassers upon one's premises except for their dwelling or curtilage. If the trespass is upon someone's dwelling or curtilage, then NCGS 14-51.1 applies.

County or City Ordinances

Counties and cities may in some cases enact ordinances regarding firearms. Pursuant to NCGS 14-409.40, local firearms laws are generally preempted by State statutes. Some local ordinances pre-dating NCGS 14-409.40 may thus be effectively unenforceable. Some local ordinances may be permissible under the exceptions to NCGS 14-409.40.

Obtaining access to local firearms ordinances is a common problem. It may be difficult for a citizen to locate or access copies of local ordinances. Local firearms ordinances may not be centralized or compiled for easy identification. Compilations which do exist may not be available to the public. Ordinances outdated by NCGS 14-409.40 may not have been repealed or deleted, thus misleading citizens. Local ordinances, unlike statutes, do not have a published body of caselaw available to citizens or the courts to better interpret the ordinances. The process for a citizen to obtain copies of ordinances varies greatly from city to city and county to county. The timetable for amending existing ordinances or enacting new ordinances will vary from city to city and county to county.

The fragmented nature of local ordinances is a primary reason for enacting the statute on statewide uniformity of firearms laws, NCGS 14-409.40.

This book does not attempt to amass local firearms ordinances. A citizen seeking local ordinances should start the discovery process by contacting their local county and city government. One valuable resource is the North Carolina Wildlife Commission's Internet web page at www.ncwildlife.org. The Commission has a county-by-county compilation of firearms laws related to hunting.

Torts

A tort is a civil wrong other than breach of contract for which the law will provide a remedy. Intentional torts and negligence are two types of torts. Intentional torts and negligence are mutually exclusive. Negligence presumes a failure to act when necessary, or to act in a careless manner. An intentional tort presumes the intention to act to someone's detriment. Lynn v. Burnette, 531 S.E.2d 275 (NC App 2000). Firearms law involving negligence and intentional torts are discussed below.

Negligence

Negligence is the failure of one person to perform or observe a duty owed to another person, which injures that second person. Negligence is generally a failure of someone to take reasonable action, such as to observe safety rules appropriate to the situation. Generally, negligence is not an "intentional tort," such as assault or battery, which requires intent to commit the wrongful behavior which results in injury.

Generally, a person may be found liable for injury or damage to another by their negligent use of a firearm. Key v. Burchette, 517 S.E.2d 667 (NC App 1999). N.C. Farm Bureau v. Mizell, 530 S.E.2d 93 (NC App 2000). Edwards v. Johnson, 152 S.E.2d 122 (NC 1967).

Negligence in a criminal action is a higher standard than in a civil situation. The Supreme Court stated in State v. Everhart, 231 S.E.2d 604 (NC 1977), that "culpable negligence in criminal law requires more than the negligence required to sustain a tort recovery. It must be such reckless or careless behavior that the act imports a thoughtless disregard of the consequences of the act or the act shows a heedless indifference to the rights and safety of others."

The Supreme Court stated that "if any person intentionally points a pistol at any person, this action is in violation of NCGS 14-34 and constitutes an assault. Moreover, such action, being in violation of the statute, is negligence *per se;* and if the pistol accidentally discharges, the injured person may recover damages for actionable negligence." Lowe v. Department of Motor Vehicles, 93 S.E.2d 448 (NC 1956).

A rule of strict liability in civil cases was historically followed in North Carolina, as discussed in the Lowe case, where a person discharging a firearm was responsible and liable for the results or effect of the bullet fired. A leading legal text summarized this rule as follows:

"If a person is violating the law by shooting a weapon, he is civilly liable for any injury, even an accidental injury, inflicted by him with such weapon, the question of negligence being immaterial. The fact that defendant's motive in discharging the weapon is laudable is immaterial where his act is illegal." 94 C.J.S., Weapons, § 28, pp. 527, 528."

The Supreme Court in Belk v. Boyce, 138 S.E.2d 789 (NC 1964), rather than continue with the Lowe strict liability standard, stated in this 1964 case that:

"the courts are now inclined to modify the rule and enlarge the scope of exceptions to this rule of absolute liability. Clearly, the modern tendency of the court is to apply the general rule of negligence where injury or death has been inflicted by missiles from a firearm, and to permit the defendant in an action for damages to show in defense his freedom from negligence in causing the injury complained of. 56 Am. Jur., Weapons and Firearms, § 22, p. 1005."

At issue in Belk v. Boyce was the concept that a person discharging a firearm may be liable on the basis of negligence to someone injured by the firearm, separate from and in addition to violation of a statute or the common law.

The court in Belk v. Boyce held that a landowner firing a pistol on his land who injured a trespasser who was on the land unknown to the landowner was not liable under the facts of that particular case to the injured trespasser based on negligence.

Firearms owners are required to use a high degree of care in operating and using firearms. As stated by the Supreme Court in Belk v. Boyce, 138 S.E.2d 789 (NC 1964),

"Persons having possession and control over dangerous instrumentalities are under duty to use a high degree of care commensurate with the dangerous character of the article to prevent injury to others. This rule applies to firearms. 3 Strong: N. C. Index, Negligence, § 4, pp. 445, 446."

However, the Supreme Court subsequently offered the following comment in the 1967 case of Edwards v. Johnson, 152 S.E.2d 122 (NC 1967), stating:

"Any loaded firearm is a highly dangerous instrumentality and, since its possession or use is attended by extraordinary danger,

236

any person having it in his possession or using it is bound to exercise extraordinary care. A person handling or carrying a loaded firearm in the immediate vicinity of others is liable for its discharge, even though the discharge is accidental and unintentional, provided it is not unavoidable. Kuhns v. Brugger, 135 A.2d 395."

This comment in Edwards v. Johnson suggests a shift back towards a strict liability standard.

The courts revisited this issue in the 1980 case of Davis v. Siloo, 267 S.E.2d 354 (NC App 1980), where the court stated:

"There are a few exceptions where strict liability has been imposed upon activity associated with a "dangerous instrumentality" and this occurs most often where explosives or blasting operations are involved. In other cases, however, liability associated with dangerous instrumentalities is predicated upon "negligence" instead of strict liability. Other cases have noted that even though a negligence standard is applied, the duty of care is nonetheless commensurate with the degree of danger involved and that a highly dangerous substance, product or instrumentality requires the "highest" care or the "utmost" caution," citing Belk v. Boyce as an example.

Davis v. Siloo thus seems to confirm that injuries from firearms may be remedied under a negligence cause of action, but that the standard of care required when firearms are concerned is exceptionally high. At some point, as the standard of care for negligence is increased, in effect the standard becomes one of strict liability.

Thus, Davis v. Siloo seems to be the current position on firearms negligence in North Carolina. The firearm operator will be liable for damage or injury caused by his or her negligence, unless the "highest care" or "utmost caution" was exercised.

NCGS 99B-11 was enacted in 1987, which limited liability based on negligence in a products liability lawsuit against manufacturers of firearms. NCGS 99B-1.1 was enacted in 1995, which stated that "there shall be no strict liability in tort in product liability actions." NCGS 99B-1.1 thus eliminated strict liability at least regarding product liability lawsuits.

Negligent Storage

There are a number of cases outside North Carolina where a gun owner negligently stored a firearm and an unauthorized user obtained the firearm and caused injury or death. There is a risk that the gun owner may be found liable for negligent storage of the firearm, and held liable to some degree for the injuries caused by the unauthorized user of the firearm.

Negligent Entrustment

The well-known case of Kitchen v. K-Mart, 697 So.2d 1200 (Florida, 1997), is a case where a retailer sold a rifle and ammunition to an obviously intoxicated purchaser. The purchaser immediately went out and shot his ex-girlfriend with the rifle, leaving her a quadriplegic. The Florida Supreme Court ruled that the retailer was guilty of negligent entrustment in selling a firearm to an intoxicated purchaser. There is no North Carolina case directly on point, but the court in Hutchens v. Hankins, 303 S.E.2d 584 (NC App 1983), implied the existence of this cause of action in North Carolina when it stated that "the person who would put into the hands of an obviously demented individual a firearm with which he shot an innocent third person would be amenable in damages to that third person for unlawful negligence."

Intentional Torts

An intentional tort is a tort resulting from an intentional act of the one who commits the tort, who is called the tortfeasor. Common intentional torts are assault, battery, false imprisonment, and intentional infliction of emotional distress. Some intentional torts, such as assault or battery, may also separately exist as a criminal act, with different types of penalties or remedies than the civil law version. At common law, assault is the threat to offensively make contact with another person, and battery is the actual making of the offensive contact.

A person may be found liable to another person for an intentional tort involving a firearm.

Assault and Battery

A shooter who intended to shoot out the tire of another person's automobile but who failed to aim properly and hit that other person's body may be liable for assault and battery. Lynn v. Burnette, 531 S.E.2d 275 (NC App 2000).

A shooter shot at the floor around a victim's feet, intending to scare the victim. One of the bullets ricocheted, hitting the victim. The shooter may be liable for assault and battery. Vernon v. Barrow, 383 S.E.2d 441 (NC App 1989).

False Imprisonment

The court in Ayscue v. Mullen, 336 S.E.2d 863 (NC App 1985), stated that:

> "False imprisonment is the illegal restraint of the person of any one against his will. Force is essential only in the sense of imposing restraint. There is no legal wrong unless the detention was involuntary. False imprisonment may be committed by words alone, or by acts alone, or by both; it is not necessary that the individual be actually confined or assaulted, or even that he should be touched. Any exercise of force, or express or implied threat of force, by which in fact the other person is deprived of his liberty or compelled to remain where he does not wish to remain is an imprisonment. The essential thing is the restraint of the person. This may be caused by threats, as well as by actual force, and the threats may be by conduct or by words. If the words or conduct are such as to induce a reasonable apprehension of force, and the means of coercion are at hand, a person may be as effectually restrained and deprived of liberty as by prison bars."

239

This tort is cited because one of the ways in which a Defendant can falsely imprison a victim is through the use of a firearm.

False imprisonment is a lesser included offense of kidnapping, such as is felonious restraint. State v. Wilson, 497 S.E.2d 416 (NC App 1998). See NCGS 14-43.3.

Lack of North Carolina Statutes

There are certain subjects on which other States or cities have statutes, but North Carolina does not. Many times, North Carolinians have heard of these other laws and mistakenly believe that they apply in North Carolina. A selection of these subjects are included in this book to educate the public about these issues which exist elsewhere, but do not exist in North Carolina.

Further, a person carrying a firearm into another State *generally* must follow the laws of that State. Interstate carry of firearms has become much more common, as was intended, due to the expansion of reciprocity between States of concealed carry handgun permits. Travelers who will be spending any significant time at all in another State are well advised to determine that State's firearms laws.

Registration of Firearms

Some jurisdictions require or are considering laws requiring firearms to be registered with the local police or Sheriff. Firearms registration is an extremely hot topic in firearms law. There is no North Carolina law requiring firearms to be registered, although handgun purchasers must generally obtain a permit to purchase handguns. NCGS 14-409.40 prohibits cities or counties from registering firearms. Persons bringing firearms into the State are not required to register their firearms.

"Safety Checks"

Some jurisdictions require or are considering laws requiring owners to have newly purchased firearms pass a "safety check" upon purchase. According to persons desiring to restrict gun rights, such safety checks are needed to ensure that firearms in civilian hands function safely. According to gun rights groups, the safety checks, which includes governmental documentation of the firearm and purchaser, is merely firearms registration by another name. North Carolina has no such law.

Registration of Firearm Owners

Some jurisdictions require or are considering laws requiring owners of firearms to be registered. There is no North Carolina law requiring firearm owners to be registered, although handgun purchasers must generally obtain a permit to purchase handguns.

Identification Cards for Firearm Owners

Some jurisdictions require or are considering laws requiring that firearms owners have a firearm owner's identification card on their person when in possession of a firearm. Some jurisdictions require such an identification card to merely own a firearm, whether or not it is in their possession. There is no such North Carolina law.

Junk Guns (Saturday Night Specials)

Saturday Night Specials or junk guns are cheap guns, usually poorly made, but definitions vary. They usually have a barrel length less than 3 inches, or an overall length of 6 inches. They may lack "essential safety features," however defined. Some jurisdictions specify "functionality tests" or safety tests to screen firearms for junk status.

There are two alleged rationales for banning junk guns. First, junk guns are firearms of choice for criminals, and a State can disarm criminals by banning junk guns. Second, junk guns are unsafe to use, and by banning them, the State can protect citizens. Gun-rights groups claim that these reasons are bogus, merely a façade to ban yet another class of firearms. There is no North Carolina law regarding junk guns or Saturday Night Specials.

One-Gun-per-Month Purchasing Limits

There is no North Carolina law limiting the purchase of firearms to one firearm per month per person. The primary purpose behind such laws is to limit the trafficking of firearms from State to State. A purchaser might buy a large quantity of guns in a State with liberal purchasing laws and illegally sell the firearms in nearby States with stricter purchasing laws. Secondarily, this type of law would limit the ability of someone (say, a mentally disturbed person) to suddenly decide to heavily arm themselves by purchasing multiple firearms. Virginia and South Carolina have a one gun per month law.

Personalized or Smart Guns

Personalized or "smart" guns are guns which, using some type of electronic feature, can determine whether the person attempting to fire the firearm is an "authorized user." The method used to verify the identity of the user varies. Technology has not approached mainstream for smart guns. Smart guns are, at best, experimental. Debate rages, however, whether smart technology should be required for firearms, or merely an owner's option, when and if the technology arrives. North Carolina has no State law on smart guns.

Shell Casing Fingerprinting

Shell casings are cylindrical brass casings which hold the gunpowder and bullet before firing of the bullet. The shell casing may remain inside the firearm after firing (as with a revolver) or may be automatically ejected from the firearm (as with a semiautomatic handgun). Advocates assert that firing of the cartridge may mark the casing is a manner unique to the gun, much like fingerprints are unique to a person. Advocates call for a database of shell casing fingerprints, based on the expectation that shell casings left at the scene of a crime could be traced to a particular gun. The premise and science for shell casing fingerprinting has not yet been proven. North Carolina has no State law on the subject.

Ballistic Fingerprinting

Firing a bullet from a firearm leaves certain unique marks on the bullet, which in some cases can be tied with accuracy to the particular firearm which fired the bullet. A very few States require that all guns sold be test-fired to create a database of ballistic fingerprints. North Carolina has no law requiring ballistic fingerprinting.

Waiting Period to Purchase Firearms

As of 2004, approximately 17 States mandated a "cooling off" period before a purchaser would be allowed to purchase a gun. Some States mandate a waiting period between completion of the application to purchase a gun and being allowed to physically take possession of the firearm. A stated purpose of cooling off periods is to reduce violence and suicides by people who are experiencing a sudden surge of anger or emotional distress, by delaying the time in which they can get possession of a firearm.

North Carolina has no such express State law. However, North Carolina's requirement that most prospective handgun purchasers must first obtain a permit from the Sheriff to purchase a handgun is a de facto cooling off period of a varying time period, for some people, for one type of firearm.

Physical Handling Tests for Firearm Purchases

Some States require a test for ability to physically handle a firearm before being allowed to purchase a firearm. North Carolina has no such State law.

Written Tests For Firearm Purchases

Some States require a purchaser to pass a written test before being allowed to purchase a firearm. North Carolina has no such State law.

Class Attendance For Firearm Purchasers

Some States require a purchaser to attend a firearms class before being allowed to purchase a firearm. The classes usually focus on firearms safety and State laws. North Carolina has no such law.

Trigger Locks, Child Safety Locks, Locked Storage Containers

Trigger locks are devices which lock onto a firearm and prevent the trigger from being pulled. This renders the firearm safe from accidental pulling of the trigger. Trigger locks are a safe-storage device. There are many styles of trigger locks, using a variety of locking mechanisms. Child safety locks are some form of locking device intended to render a firearm unable to fire.

Some jurisdictions have laws requiring trigger or child safety locks to be used any time a firearm is not in use (under certain circumstances), or that firearms be supplied with such a lock when sold.

Some jurisdictions allow, as one option for mandatory locked storage of firearms, the use of locking containers.

These laws are generically referred to as Safe Storage Laws in the firearms industry.

North Carolina has no such law specifically requiring one form of safe storage over another. North Carolina does not even expressly require safe storage except in cases where children are present in the home.

Chambered Round Indicator

Some States require that handguns or firearms sold new in their State be equipped with some type of mechanical device on the firearm which visually indicates if a round is loaded into the chamber. The theory is that, since so many people are shot by an "unloaded" firearm, it increases safety to make it more obvious that a firearm is loaded. North Carolina has no chambered round indicator law.

Some laws exist in other States prohibiting manufacture of firearms with outer surfaces (i.e., hand grips or sides of the receiver) which are resistant to retaining fingerprints. North Carolina has no such law.

Sniper Rifles

Some jurisdictions have laws prohibiting "sniper rifles," which are variously defined. Other jurisdictions occasionally define a sniper rifle to be a rifle firing a bullet of .50 caliber or larger. North Carolina has no such law, although North Carolina defines firearms of larger than .50 caliber as "weapons of mass death and destruction" under NCGS 14-288.8.

Minimum Trigger-Pull Pressures

Firearms are manufactured so that it takes a certain amount of pressure, measured in pounds, in pulling on the trigger to fire the firearm. A low pressure trigger might be 2 pounds, a medium pressure trigger might be 4 pounds, and a high pressure trigger might be 8 pounds. Some people see a high-pressure trigger as a safety feature, since the firearm is less likely to be accidentally fired, and children are less likely to be able to fire the firearm. Other people see a high pressure trigger as a safety flaw, since even adults have less ability to accurately fire a firearm with a heavy trigger pull.

Some jurisdictions have enacted, or have discussed enacting, laws mandating heavy trigger pull for firearms sold in their jurisdiction, as a safety measure. North Carolina has no such law.

Cosmetic Features (Bayonet Lugs, Flash Suppressors, etc.)

Certain features or accessories available for certain firearms are seen by some people as socially undesirable. Examples of such features are bayonet lugs, flash suppressors, and pistol grip stocks on rifles. Bayonet lugs are metal fixtures on a rifle which allow a bayonet to be affixed to the front of the rifle. These features are termed "cosmetic" because they do not affect the basic functioning of the firearm. These cosmetic features usually mimic similar features on military firearms. Some jurisdictions ban firearms with one or more of these cosmetic features. North Carolina has no such law.

Magazine Disconnect Feature

The magazine is the metal box inserted into the firearm which holds and feeds ammunition into the firing chamber as needed for firing. The issue is that some people remove the magazine from a firearm, thinking that they have fully unloaded the firearm, when one cartridge remains loaded into the chamber of the firearm, ready for firing.

Some jurisdictions have enacted, or have discussed enacting, a law which requires firearms to have a magazine disconnect feature. This feature prevents the firearm from being fired if no magazine is present in the firearm. This is intended to be a safety feature. Thus, a cartridge accidentally left in the chamber cannot be fired. Revolvers and single-shot firearms have no magazines, and so cannot have magazine disconnects.

Opponents of this feature assert that it could be dangerous in a situation where the shooter, perhaps a police officer engaged in a desperate gun battle with a criminal, or a soldier fighting in the semi-darkness of a cave in Afghanistan, ejects and loses his last magazine, but still has loose cartridges in an ammunition pouch. Without a magazine disconnect feature, the police officer or soldier could still feed cartridges into his firearm manually, and continue to fire. The firearm would be useless with a magazine disconnect feature.

North Carolina has no magazine disconnect law.

Serial Numbers on Bullets

Some jurisdictions have discussed enacting a law requiring serial numbers to be etched onto every bullet. Proponents of this law assert that it will improve the ability to trace bullets used in crimes. Opponents of this law assert that it is excessively expensive and will not work. North Carolina has no such law.

Microstamping

Microstamping is an experimental technology where identifying marks, serial numbers, bar codes, etc., are engraved onto the inside of a firearm's firing chamber or onto the firing pin. These identifying marks are transferred onto shell casings when the firearm is fired. Firearms will imprint the casing for each cartridge which it fires. Empty shell casings left behind at the scene of a crime recovered by police can theoretically then be traced to the particular firearm used at the crime scene. North Carolina has no law on microstamping.

Magazine Capacity Limits

Some jurisdictions have or are considering laws limiting the number of cartridges a magazine may hold for that magazine to be legally sold in that jurisdiction. These types of laws are similar to the rule in the defunct federal Assault Weapons Ban limiting magazines to 10 cartridges. North Carolina has no such law.

Assault Weapons

Some jurisdictions have laws restricting or prohibiting the sale or ownership of assault weapons. The definition of assault weapon, and the types of restrictions, vary. These types of laws are similar to the rule in the defunct federal Assault Weapons Ban. North Carolina has no law limiting assault weapons.

Ban on Handguns

Some jurisdictions have or are considering laws heavily restricting or prohibiting the sale or ownership of handguns, revolvers, and pistols. North Carolina has no such law.

Internet Gun Sales

Some jurisdictions have or are considering laws restricting or prohibiting the sale of firearms over the Internet. North Carolina has no such law.

Disassembled and Unloaded Storage Laws

Some jurisdictions have or are considering laws which require that firearms which are not in use be stored unloaded and disassembled. This can be a serious detriment to keeping a ready firearm for self-defense in the home or business, depending on how "not in use" is defined. North Carolina has no such law.

Restrictions on Reloading and Reloaders

Reloading is the hobby or sport of acquiring components (bags of bullets, boxes of primers, jugs of gunpowder, etc.) and assembling custom made cartridges. Reloaders do this for various reasons, such as cost savings, to obtain loadings not commercially available, or simply for intrinsic enjoyment of a hobby.

Some jurisdictions have or are considering laws restricting or prohibiting reloading. The usual intent is to prevent reloaders from circumventing other desired laws, such as ammunition purchase restrictions, serial numbers on bullets, etc. North Carolina has no such restrictions on reloading.

Permits to Rent Firearms

Some jurisdictions have or are considering laws which require that a permit from the local police or Sheriff be obtained before a firearm may be rented. This type of law severely limits or effectively eliminates the business of gun shops renting out firearms to customers for shooting use on firing ranges at the gun shops. North Carolina has no such law.

Regulation of the Secondary Market for Firearms Sales

The "primary market" for firearms sales is generally defined to be routine purchase/sale of a firearm from a federally licensed firearms dealer. Approximately 60% of firearms transactions occur in the primary market.

The "secondary market" for firearms sales are more informal sales, such as sales between acquaintances, sale between private parties at gun shows, and inheritances. Approximately 40% of firearms transactions occur in the secondary market.

Some jurisdictions distinguish between licensed dealers and private sellers. Some jurisdictions expressly regulate secondary market sales, sometimes in a lax manner relative to dealer transactions, sometimes relatively stringently.

Gun control advocates sometimes refer to minimal or nonexistent regulation of secondary market sales as the "gun show loophole." North Carolina does not expressly regulate secondary market sales.

Gun Shows

Gun shows are temporary public markets for the buying and selling of firearms and related materials. Gun shows are usually held in convention halls or fairgrounds. Some jurisdictions have unique laws for sales at gun shows.

North Carolina has no express statutes governing gun shows. This is especially relevant because North Carolina consistently ranks in the top ten States with the most gun shows held annually. North Carolina has a statute, NCGS 14-409.40(d), which prohibits cities or counties from regulating gun shows any differently than shows of other types of items or property. See the topic on Secondary Market Sales, above.

248

Gun Clubs

Some jurisdictions have special laws regulating the existence and operation of gun clubs, rifle and pistol clubs, etc. North Carolina has no laws expressly targeting gun clubs, except for NCGS 14-409.45, which is the Sport Shooting Range Protection Act.

Ban on Mail Order Ammunition Sales

Some jurisdictions have or are considering laws which ban or restrict mail order sales of ammunition. North Carolina has no such law.

Restrictions and Prohibition on In-Store Sales of Ammunition

Some jurisdictions have or are considering laws which restrict or prohibit in-store sales of ammunition. Examples are requiring proof of ownership of a firearm which fires the ammunition to be purchased, supply of a thumbprint when purchasing ammunition, quantity limits, punitive taxes on sales, limits on the number of rounds one person may possess, and requiring background checks as with firearms purchases.

Ammunition sale restrictions are often advanced by certain political groups in recent years as an alternative strategy to banning guns, with the belief that there will be less gun violence if the ammunition supply is restricted.

North Carolina has very few statutes on ammunition sales, and certainly nothing with the scope or intention to cause a broad decrease in gun ownership and use.

"Cop Killer" Bullet Bans

"Cop killer bullet" is not a technical phrase, but an emotional passionate phrase often used by those desiring to prohibit the sales of certain types of bullets. Qualification as a "cop killer bullet" varies from advocate to advocate. The usual definition involves consideration as to whether the bullet can penetrate typical "body armor" (i.e., bullet-proof vest) worn by law enforcement officers.

Some jurisdictions have or are considering prohibitions or restrictions on these bullets. The basic difficulty with the concept is that almost all rifle bullets will penetrate body armor. Body armor was never designed to stop rifle bullets. North Carolina has no such law.

Prohibition on "Default Proceed" Purchases

Certain federal laws require a background criminal check on firearms purchasers. The federal office producing the background search results sometimes fails to produce a response within the maximum time allowed. The federal law states that the firearm is then allowed to be sold to the purchaser under the "default proceed" procedure. In other words, the federal government has a maximum time to respond, and if it does not respond, the purchaser may go ahead and purchase the firearm. Some States prohibit default proceed purchases, which is called a "don't know, don't sell" law. North Carolina has no such law.

Ultra-Compact Firearm Sales Prohibitions

Some jurisdictions have or are considering laws which restrict or prohibit the sale of ultra-compact handguns. These very small pistols are often marketed as "pocket rockets." The restrictions on sales of ultra-compact pistols are usually based on the belief that small firearms are very likely to be used in criminal activities. North Carolina has no such law.

Ban on "Undetectable" Firearms

Some jurisdictions have or are considering laws which restrict or prohibit the sale or possession of firearms which are "undetectable." Definitions and terminology varies, but an undetectable firearm is one which cannot readily be detected by metal detectors or X-ray screening machines. The purpose of such laws is to prevent the illegal carrying of a concealed firearm through a screening checkpoint. North Carolina has no such law.

Ban on "Disguised" Firearms

Some jurisdictions have or are considering laws which restrict or prohibit the sale or possession of firearms which are "disguised" firearms. Definitions and terminology varies, but a disguised firearm is manufactured in a shape or size resembling a non-firearm item, such as a belt buckle or metal desk ornament. The purpose of such laws is to prevent possession of a firearm hidden in plain sight by its not being recognizable as a firearm. North Carolina has no such law.

Right of Employers to Impose Rules on Employees' Firearms at the Workplace

It was not an issue until recently whether or not an employer had the right to ban or restrict the carrying of firearms onto company property by employees. This became an issue in 2005 with a certain case in Oklahoma. Some jurisdictions have or are

250

considering laws which restrict or prohibit an employer from banning or restricting an employee's right to carry a firearm onto company property. Rhetoric positions this as a Second Amendment right versus a property owner's rights. North Carolina has no such laws specifically addressing this issue.

NCGS 14-415.11(c) allows landowners to post a notice invalidating use of a concealed carry permit on their premises. However, in reading the comments under NCGS 14-269, in at least some cases employees may carry concealed firearms on their employer's premises under that statute, whether or not a concealed handgun permit is held.

Surrender of Firearms After Death to Police

Some jurisdictions have or are considering laws which require the heirs or executor of a deceased person's estate to surrender to the local police of Sheriff all of the deceased person's firearms, until rightful ownership of the firearms can be determined. North Carolina has no such law.

Arsenal Licensing Rules

Some jurisdictions have or are considering laws which require licensing for arsenals. Arsenals are defined in various ways, usually as either a certain number of firearms or a certain number of rounds of ammunition, owned by one person. North Carolina has no such law.

Special Laws on Loaning Firearms

Some jurisdictions have special laws governing the loan of a firearm from the owner to another person. The usual situation is a gun owner loaning a rifle to a friend for use during hunting season, or loaning a pistol to a friend for target practice one weekend. North Carolina has no such specialized law on loaned firearms.

Prohibiting Firearms Within 1000 Feet of a School

It is a common misbelief that State law prohibits firearms within 1000 feet of a school. The origin of this belief probably sources from the federal Gun-Free School Zone Act of 1990, which was 18 USC 922(q)(1)(a). The United State Supreme Court, in U.S. v. Lopez, 514 U.S. 549 (1995), ruled that the GFSZA was unconstitutional. The basis for the ruling had nothing to do with the right to keep and bear arms, but on the power of the federal government to enact such a law. Congress re-enacted the GFSZA in 1996 with changes to make it less likely to also be ruled unconstitutional if challenged in court. Some States and lesser jurisdictions have their own version of the GFSZA. State versions of this same law may be constitutional in those States. This type of law comes with its own set of problems, not the least of which are how a citizen is supposed to know that they are within 1000 feet of a school, and whether homeowners residing within 1000 feet of a school are effectively disarmed. North Carolina's relevant statute, NCGS 14-269.2, prohibits firearms on school property and places where extracurricular school activities are taking place, but imposes no restrictions *beyond* school grounds.

Straw-Man Purchases

Straw-man purchases or straw purchases are where someone who cannot qualify to purchase a firearm, or who does not want their name connected with the purchase of a firearm, persuades an accomplice to purchase a firearm for them. The initial purchaser will then later give or sell the firearm to the end-recipient in an undocumented transfer. Straw purchases are usually a bad thing, performed for illicit purposes, such as to get a firearm into the hands of a criminal who cannot directly purchase a firearm. North Carolina has no express law on straw purchases.

Sniper Scopes

Telescopic sights are optical devices, usually tubular in shape. These sights are attached primarily to the top surface of rifles, rarely to handguns, and never to shotguns. Telescopic sights have two primary advantages. First, they allow a closer view of the target. Second, they have the optical effect of putting the cross-hairs and target into the same optical plane, which is more effective than attempting to simultaneously discern a rear iron sight, a front iron sign, and the target, all of which are in different optical planes. Telescopic sights are very common on hunting rifles, and rarely used otherwise in the civilian world.

There are many upgraded versions of the typical optical telescopic sight. Upgraded scopes may have infrared capability, a form of night vision. Some scopes have light magnification ability, another form of night vision. Some scopes have integral laser rangefinding ability.

Some jurisdictions have or are considering laws defining some or all upgraded telescopic sights as "sniper scopes," and prohibit or restrict them. The label of "sniper scope" is usually assigned to these telescopic sights by gun-control advocates to imply that these devices have no purpose other than as an aid on a sniper weapon. North Carolina has no such law.

Some jurisdictions have or are considering laws which prohibit sales of certain firearms, usually handguns, unless the firearm is on a list of firearms approved by that government jurisdiction. Firearms may not be placed on the list (and thus unavailable for purchase) due to any number of reasons or politically correct motives. North Carolina has no such law.

Urban Myths About Using Firearms in Self-Defense

There are a number of old wives tales or urban myths concerning the use of firearms in self-defense or the carry and use of concealed handguns. These myths are usually wrong. Some of these tales or myths are discussed below, to better educate the reader about North Carolina law.

The Myth: Hollow-point bullets are especially deadly, and if you use them in your firearm, your claims of self-defense will be ignored and waived.

The Law.   No statute or case prohibits the use of hollow-point bullets. No case has been found where use of hollow-point bullets even counted against an accused. No case has been found where the distinction between hollow-points and full metal jacketed bullets was even made. Nearly every self-defense publication that addresses the subject advises that hollow-point bullets be used.

The Myth: Reloaded cartridges can be especially deadly, and if you use them in your firearm, your claims of self-defense will be ignored and waived.

The Law.   Reloaded cartridges are usually assembled by a hobbyist from bulk components as an alternative to "store bought" ammunition. The reloads can be made "hotter" or more powerful than commercially available ammunition. No statute or case prohibits use of reloaded ammunition. No case has been found where use of reloads even counted against an accused. No case has been found where the distinction between reloaded and factory ammunition was even made.

The Myth: If you use a firearm with a caliber any larger than .38 Special, your claims of self-defense will be ignored and waived.

The Law.   No statute or case prohibits the use of calibers larger than .38 Special or its close equivalent, the 9mm round. No case has been found where a large caliber firearm even counted against an accused.

The Myth: If you use magnum, "+p," or "+p+" ammunition, your claims of self-defense will be ignored and waived.

The Law: Magnum, "+p," and "+p+" ammunition is loaded with a larger amount of gunpowder compared to standard ammunition. Hot ammunition has greater velocity and is more powerful and deadly. No statute or case prohibits such ammunition. No case was found where use of hot ammunition counted against an accused, or where a distinction was even made between regular and high velocity ammunition.

255

The Myth: You must shout out a warning to someone you are about to shoot, or your claims of self-defense will be ignored and waived.

The Law: There is no law or case requiring a person acting in self-defense to first shout out a warning, such as "Halt or I will shoot!" However, there is at least one case where the court took into account the person's shouted warning to substantiate their claim of self-defense, namely, State v. Gilreath, 454 S.E.2d 871 (NC App 1995). But, the court in State v. Baker, 23 S.E.2d 340 (NC 1942), pointed out that a warning is not necessary in all cases. The Baker court implied that there may be circumstances where shouting of a warning would be the best action to take, rather than abruptly opening fire, and it would be up to the jury to decide whether a prior shouted warning was reasonable and prudent under the circumstances.

The Myth: You must fire a warning shot first, before shooting to kill or wound, or your claims of self-defense will be ignored and waived.

The Law: There is no law or case requiring a person acting in self-defense to first fire a warning shot. The law generally discourages people from firing bullets into the air, due to concerns as to where those bullets would land. Many times in self-defense situations, moreover, there is no time for multiple shots. There are two cases, however, where the court took into account that the person had fired a warning shot or shots to substantiate their claim of acting in self-defense. State v. Gilreath, 454 S.E.2d 871 (NC App 1995). State v. Ataei-Kachuei, 314 S.E.2d 751 (NC App 1984), rev.den., 321 S.E.2d 146 (1984).

The Myth: If you shoot a criminal that you confront inside your house, you should drag his dead body over to an entry doorstep before you call the police.

The Law: This macabre urban myth grows from the fact that North Carolina had one set of rules for using a firearm to prevent entry into a dwelling, and another set of rules for defending oneself against an intruder already in the dwelling. The rules about preventing an intruder from entering the dwelling seemed easier to satisfy. Thus, by dragging the intruder to a doorstep, the homeowner will have an easier time proving that he acted in self-defense. While there might have been an advantage to the homeowner regarding proof of self-defense in doing this, any such advantages are outweighed by three other matters. First, that "dead" intruder might not really be dead, and the last thing a homeowner wants to do is get into close quarters with an intruder. Second, intruders often work together, and a homeowner then needs to be more concerned with securing his surroundings and summoning police, rather than diverting his attention to dragging dead bodies around. Third, artfully rearranging the situation is nothing less than the serious offenses of tampering with evidence and falsifying events. See NCGS 14-51.1 for detail.

The Myth: You must actually see a gun or knife in your assailant's hands before you can open fire, or your claims of self-defense will be ignored and waived.

The Law: There is no statute or case which requires someone acting in self-defense to first see a gun or knife in the assailant's hands before using a firearm in self-defense. The laws and cases are more flexible, instead usually focusing on the threat to the intended victim, or at least the threat as reasonably perceived by the intended victim. This myth sources from the expectation that any jury, if told that a victim was being assaulted by a criminal wielding a gun or a knife, would always find that the victim acted in justifiable self-defense in using a firearm. If the victim was attacked by a criminal who wielded anything less than a gun or knife (such as a baseball bat, a tire iron, etc.), it becomes less certain whether a jury would find that the victim was in sufficient danger to justify self-defense using a firearm.

The Myth: A firearm owner does not have to obey the concealed firearms laws if they are traveling to or from a shooting range or a gun shop.

The Law: The cases and statutes on concealed firearms give no special privileges to firearms owners traveling to or from a shooting range or gun shop. A handgun owner who placed a handgun in a zippered pouch onto the passenger seat of his automobile as he drove to the pistol range would be in violation of the concealed handgun statutes, unless he also had a concealed handgun permit and personal identification with him.

The Myth: Do not draw your firearm on an assailant unless you intend to immediately fire.

The Law: There is no statute or case on this subject. However, this "rule" is often found in various lists of rules about firearms. However, it is common for firearms carriers to display their firearm when first threatened by an assailant, and the mere sight of the firearm causes many would-be assailants to break off, retreat, and escape.

Gun Club Liability

Gun clubs face liability from two primary sources: threats not related to firearms, and threats related to firearms.

Threats Not Related to Firearms

Potential liability to gun clubs which are not related to firearms involve those matters which potentially could affect any similar business. Examples are injuries to a visitor who slipped and fell on the premises, employee injuries, or a tree located on gun club property that fell and damaged a neighbor's house. These types of threats not related to firearms are not the subject of this book.

Threats Related to Firearms

Potential liability to gun clubs which *are* related to firearms fall into two categories. The first category of threats is where someone suffered actual injury.

The second category of threats is where a complainant simply does not like firearms or gun clubs, and, although there has been no actual injury, is asserting some legal theory to hinder or eliminate the gun club.

Actual Injury Situations

A common actual injury situation, or concern for liability, is where a bullet fired from gun club premises exits the gun club boundaries, and injures someone or some thing outside gun club premises.

A similar actual injury situation is where a bullet fired on gun club premises injures someone or some thing also on gun club premises.

The most common legal theory in these cases is negligence.

In such situations, the gun club and the actual shooter (personally) can both be sued, but it may turn out that the shooter was negligent, but the gun club was not negligent.

No Actual Injury Situations

These situations usually involve an anti-gun complainant attempting to hinder or eliminate the gun club for political or philosophical reasons. The situation may be based on economic grounds where a complainant who lives near the gun club feels that his property value would increase if the gun club ceased operations.

The most common theory of attack is noise pollution. The claims are that firing firearms at the club is a nuisance to neighbors.

Another theory of attack against gun clubs is asserting damage to the environment from the lead contained in bullets fired at the gun club. This includes soil contamination, groundwater pollution, airborne lead particle pollution, and water pollution in lakes and streams.

Another theory of attack is visual pollution. This usually refers to someone complaining that the gun club's parking lots, traffic, outdoor lights, berms, shooting lane walls, etc., are visually unsightly.

Some challenges to gun clubs center on governmental zoning issues. Complainants usually allege that the club facility cannot operate under the restrictions of the local community's zoning.

An old and still viable challenge is trespass. Complainants allege that bullets, noise, smoke, odors, etc., move from the gun club premises onto their adjacent property, which is a trespass.

Gun Club Defenses to Liability

Gun clubs usually have several layers or means of defense to liability. Each gun club should assess its most likely threat sources, and plan accordingly. Some defensive techniques are as follows.

-carry good insurance
-enact documented and demonstrable safety rules
-ensure routine presence of range safety officers
-ensure members, guests, and visitors sign waivers of liability
-orient the firing range's direction of fire to the least dangerous direction
-regularly build up the firing range backstops (berms, walls, etc.)
-plant a tree line or landscaping barrier to block visual and sound migration
-build community relations with adjacent property owners
-before some bad event happens, build the gun club's image with the larger community as a caring, giving, honest organization.

Incorporation.   Another defensive technique is to incorporate the gun club. There are cases where members of unincorporated gun clubs were sued individually for

260

events occurring at the gun club, treating the gun club as a partnership of the members. The mere threat of getting to the membership personally is a powerful weapon in the hands of a claimant. Personal liability must be avoided!

Compartmentalization. Some gun clubs "compartmentalize" their operations. An example might be that the rifle range, the pistol range, and the shotgun range are all separately deeded and owed. If one entity were hit hard by litigation, compartmentalization would theoretically shield the uninvolved ranges from the range where the incident occurred. Compartmentalization would theoretically work, but as actual examples where it has been tested are sparse to nonexistent, it should not be considered a dependable primary defensive technique.

Divide Ownership From Operations. Another approach is to have one entity such as a non-profit foundation dedicated to education and sport own the shooting range land. The foundation leases the land to the gun club, which operates the rangeland and club as a tenant. Even if a tragic event in club operations (say, a negligent shooting) results in gun club bankruptcy, the land itself would theoretically not be subject to loss. This approach would likely be more successful than compartmentalization.

Build Local Support. An approach by one gun club was to identify every property owner within rifle shot of the gun club, and build a data base of addresses, etc. The gun club mailed newsletters to the owners, emphasized recruiting those neighbors as members, kept those neighbors aware of issues and situations occurring at the gun club site, and publicized the civic virtue of the gun club. This approach built support for the gun club among local neighbors through communication and education, if nothing else.

Build Police Support. It could never hurt for a gun club to build and improve its relations with the local law enforcement agencies, who might become involved during any complaints made against the gun club. Examples might be offering range time to law enforcement officers and offering training seminars tailored to law enforcement personnel.

Make the Most of Statutory Protections. Gun clubs which qualify for the statutory protections of NCGS 14-409.46 are well advised to document their proof which brings them under protection of the statute, for later use if needed. As time goes on, resurrecting historical evidence of entitlement under this statute will become ever more difficult. Such evidence may be newspaper clippings, affidavits from members, newsletters, a published history, etc.

Gun clubs which qualify for the statutory protections of NCGS 14-409.46 are well advised to ensure that they maintain their operations such that entitlement under the statute is not lost through inadvertent action or inaction. Selling or expanding range acreage, adding new shooting programs, deleting existing shooting programs, etc., could affect eligibility.

Buy Into the Statutory Protections.   A gun club which does not already have the statutory protections of NCGS 14-409.46 which desires to add an extra layer of protection might consider "buying into" that protection by purchasing all or part of an existing shooting range which *does* enjoy the protections of NCGS 14-409.46.

Deed Restrictions.   Some gun clubs try a more affirmative, but rare, approach. The clubs offer to pay surrounding landowners to sign a document recorded in the local land records consenting to the operation of the gun club. The recorded document, a deed restriction of sorts, is designed to be binding upon that landowner and all subsequent owners of that tract. Such a document is not a cure-all, but can give an added measure of protection to the gun club. This technique can be a double-edged sword, however, in that it can provoke adjacent homeowners into opposition when they might have otherwise been disposed to ignore the local gun club.

Gun Clubs Should Have a Risk Management Plan

Gun clubs should create a risk management plan. Risks should be identified, and management plan developed and implemented. The gun club should regularly review its risk exposure and management policy.

Gun Clubs Should Have a Threat Reaction Plan Ready

Gun clubs should prepare a reaction plan ready for immediate use if an unfortunate event that threatens the club occurs. The plan might include such things as immediate notification to the President, notice to the Board of Directors, action to place the affected area off-limits, designation of a spokesperson, reminding of Directors and Members to refer all questions from the media or public to the spokesperson, and to allow the spokesperson to make all comments for the club.

Index

AK-47 assault rifle..33,35
AR-15 assault rifle..33,36-39
alcoholic beverages..14,124,147,153,154
ammunition, storage of.. 67
antique firearms... 21,145
armor-piercing bullets (see "bullet, armor-piercing")
arsenal rules.. 251
assault by pointing a firearm......................................101
assault on emergency personnel................................... 105,129
assault on government officer..................................... 103,105,106
assault on handicapped person.....................................99
assault rifle..21,30,83,84,247
assault using a firearm.. 98-101,103,105,106
assault weapon (see "assault rifle")
assemblies of people...124
automatic weapon..21,35
automobile, firing into..102

ballistic coefficient (see "bullet, ballistic coefficient of")
banks (see "concealed weapons prohibited")
battered spouses, self defense using firearms.....................220
battle rifles..21,39
Beretta Model 92FS 51
blank cartridge pistols.. 143
bolt-action rifles... 43
book order form, this book...269
breechloader...53
bullet...22
bullet, armor piercing... 59
bullet, ballistic coefficient of 62
bullet energy..23,61
bullet, hollow-point...60
bullet jackets...58
bullet, magic..64
bullet, sectional density of 61
bullet shape...60
bullet size..56
bullet, softpoint..58
bullets, specialty... 59

bullet weight..57
campus police..182,184
cannelure...59
carbine rifle...40
cartridges, general..55
cartridge, handloaded..66,247
cartridge identification 55
cartridge, self defense..64
casings, shell...62
castle doctrine..113
chamber design, M-16..38
children and firearms...79,95,96,125,134-138
citizen's arrest (see "detention by citizen")
civil laws, defined...73
clips...23
common law..72,215
company police officers...182
concealed handgun permit......................................151,153
concealed handgun permit, application procedure................157
concealed handgun permit, criteria for application................155
concealed handgun permit, reciprocity between States............164
concealed handgun permit, revocation..............................160
concealed handgun permit, renewal.................................159
concealed handgun permit, temporary permit......................158
concealed weapons..79
concealed weapons prohibited.................................79,118,124
confiscation of firearms 122
Constitution, North Carolina..85
controlled substances...14,154
correctional facilities..14,105,154
corrosive ammunition...63
court case citation format, defined..................................92
criminal laws, defined...73

defective firearm design...188
defense of another person...225
defense of a home or habitation......................................80
defense of a person in a home or habitation.........................80
defense of property..229
definitions...21
detention by citizen..168
discharging a firearm into a building, car, etc......................102

domestic violence... 176
door locks, firearms dealers....................................... 207
double jeopardy... 73

effective date of this book..20
emergency, states of (see "states of emergency")
enactment of a law... 91
energy (see "bullet energy")

false imprisonment (see "felonious restraint")
felon, possession of firearm by................................... 150
felonious assault with a firearm...................................98
felonious restraint... 106,240
felony.. 73,113
firing ranges (see "shooting ranges")
5.56mm cartridge.. 34,36,37
full metal jacket... 58
funeral processions... 14,126

government property...14,126
grooves in barrel... 29
gun clubs...148,249,259
gunpowder... 68
gun shows... 248

handgun, best for self defense.................................... 51
handgun, worst for self defense................................... 51
health-care facilities.. 14,126
hollow-point bullet (see "bullet, hollow-point")
home intruder..107
How to Improve Your Chances in Court After a Shooting...... 16

increased penalty for using firearm to commit a crime........... 172
intentional torts...239

jackets on bullets.. 58
jails (see "correctional facilities")

lands in barrel... 29
lever rifle, lever action rifle................................... 45
license, concealed handgun carry (see "concealed handgun permit")
loaning firearms.. 135,140,251

M-1 carbine..41
M-4 carbine..42
M-14 rifle..36,40
M-16 rifle..36-39
M-1911A1 .45 caliber pistol..42,51
machine gun..43,144
magazines.. 25,246
mass death and destruction..83,128,151
microstamping.. 246
militia..202
minors (see "children and firearms")
misdemeanor.. 73,113
muzzleloader..53
myths about firearms and self defense..255

negligence..235
negligent entrustment.. 238
negligent storage..238
North Carolina Administrative Code..213

occupied property, firing into.. 102
orange, hunter.. 195
order form, this book.. 269
out of State firearms purchases..145
owner-posted non-concealed handgun zones.. 154

parades.. 14,126
permit, concealed handgun carry (see "concealed handgun permit")
permit, handgun purchase..77, 139-142
picket lines..14,126
pistols..47
places to shoot.. 18
preemption..74
primers.. 63
priorities between conflicting laws..74
prisons (see "correctional facilities")
products liability..187
prohibited places to carry concealed weapons (see "concealed weapons prohibited")
propellant.. 68
purchase permit for handgun from Sheriff (see "permit, handgun purchase")

Rachel's Law.. 103
rape while possessing a firearm.................................97
rate of fire.. 53
registration of firearms............................... 75,197,241
removal of serial numbers from firearms......................... 117
revolver..47
rifling in barrel..29
riots, firearms at...83,127
robbery with firearm.. 114

safe storage law (see "storage of firearms")
safety rules for firearm use.................................. 15
school zones, school grounds................... 95,122,153,198,251
security guards... 179
semiautomatic pistol...49
session laws... 20,92,211
sexual assault...97,220
shell casings.. 62,243,246
shooting ranges... 148,259
smokeless powder...69
sniper scopes...252
sources of law.. 71
states of emergency.............................83,130-134,208
statewide uniformity...................................... 146,163
StG-44 assault rifle.. 33
storage of ammunition... 67
storage of firearms....................................... 78,244
straw-man purchases...252
strict liability... 187,237
stripper clip...23
submachine gun... 27,44,144

teflon bullet... 104
temporary concealed handgun permit (see "concealed handgun permit")
theft of a firearm.. 114
Top Ten Topics... 77
torts.. 235
train robbery...117
train, shooting at.. 126
transporting firearms.....................................78,127
trespasser, shooting at.......................................230
.223 cartridge..37

twist rate... 29

uncodified local laws... 211
uniformity of firearms laws (see "statewide uniformity")
urban myths.. 255

varmint round...35-36

warnings upon sale of firearm..................................... 137
where to shoot firearms (see "places to shoot firearms")

Book Order Form
Firearms Law of North Carolina – First Edition

Complete this form, attach your check, and mail both to the publisher.

Your name: _____

Your address: _____

_____

How did you hear about this book?

_____ I saw the book
_____ I saw your website
_____ I was given this Order Form

Cost per book*: $20.00

Postage, shipping, and handling, per book: $ 4.00

Equals: total cost per book $24.00

Number of books desired: x_____

Equals: Total cost: $_____

Make your check out to: Clermont Book Publishing Company

Mail your check to: Clermont Book Publishing Company
P.O. Box 49433
Charlotte, NC 28277

* Includes sales tax. Price good to December 31, 2007. If you are entitled to buy books tax free, deduct $1.80 per book ordered and submit North Carolina Department of Revenue Form E-595E with your order.

Firearms Law of North Carolina
www.ncfirearmslaw.com